SAP® Authorization System

 **PRESS**

SAP PRESS is issued by
Bernhard Hochlehnert, SAP AG

SAP PRESS is a joint initiative of SAP and Galileo Press. The know-how offered by SAP specialists combined with the expertise of the publishing house Galileo Press offers the reader expert books in the field. SAP PRESS features first-hand information and expert advice, and provides useful skills for professional decision-making.

SAP PRESS offers a variety of books on technical and business related topics for the SAP user. For further information, please also visit our website: *www.sap-press.com.*

Rickayzen, Dart, Brennecke, Schneider
Practical Workflow for SAP
Effective Business Processes using SAP's WebFlow Engine
2002, 552 pp., hardcover, ISBN 1-59229-006-X

Werner Hertleif, Christoph Wachter
SAP Smart Forms
Creating forms quickly and easily
2003, 454 pp., hardcover, ISBN 1-59229-010-8

Helmut Stefani
Archiving Your SAP Data
2003, 334 pp., hardcover, ISBN 1-59229-008-6

Horst Keller, Joachim Jacobitz
ABAP Objects – The Official Reference
A comprehensive guide to all ABAP language elements in two volumes
2003, 1094 pp., hardcover, 2 CDs, ISBN 1-59229-011-6

Sigrid Hagemann, Liane Will
SAP R/3 System Administration
2003, approx. 450 pp., hardcover, ISBN 1-59229-014-4

Liane Will
SAP APO System Administration
Principles for effective APO System Management
2003, 240 pp., hardcover, CD, ISBN 1-59229-012-4

IBM Business Consulting Services

SAP® Authorization System

System

Design and Implementation of Authorization Concepts for SAP R/3 and SAP Enterprise Portals

 PRESS

Contents

Foreword

Because a company's business processes are largely supported by information technology (IT), the more mature these IT systems are, the greater their impact on how people work. Therefore, companies are continuously revising their established processes and their organizations, and, consequently, their IT systems. When SAP R/3 is deployed as standard software, changes to the business processes, organizations, and IT systems have to be modeled accordingly. Such changes always affect the SAP R/3 authorization concept, which at large companies reaches a complexity that cannot be developed or maintained without defined, structured procedures. At companies with several thousand SAP R/3 users and a global organization structure, this task—changes to the infrastructure of an enterprise—which can appear daunting, sometimes requires projects that take several years, during which the project team must also cultivate and demonstrate expertise in the business processes and the organizations involved, in addition to possessing a sound knowledge of the SAP technology.

In this book, we will share our experience and methodology from numerous consulting projects in order to help you get started with the SAP R/3 authorization concept through a structured framework. We will also provide you with many tips and answers to frequently asked questions by our customers, which you should find useful in revising the existing SAP R/3 authorization concepts following changes to processes, reorganizations, and release upgrades. Because, as we already noted, developments in the IT area are constantly changing, we have also devoted a chapter to the new SAP developments and SAP portals.

One brief caveat: despite the use of standard software, no two SAP R/3 installations are identical. Individual customized settings, versions, and update levels can all result in differences in the SAP R/3 authorization concept. Therefore, please note that this book is based primarily on SAP R/3 Release 4.6.

Only people who are actively involved with the SAP R/3 authorization concept can write a book of this nature. That being said, this book is the result of outstanding teamwork by our coworkers at IBM Business Consulting Services GmbH, who tirelessly submitted their contributions, in addition to their day-to-day consulting activities with our customers. We would therefore like to take this opportunity to thank everyone involved for their dedication and support, particularly the authors: Uwe Probst, Mirjana Kelderman-Matkic, Matthias Hessler, Klaus Jäck, Hendrik Hartje, Helge Hermann Fischer, Sascha-Alexander Beyer, and Gregory Guglielmetti. We would also like to thank the IBM Marketing department—especially Andrea Hoffmann, Jutta Jacobi, and Roselinde Todt—for their support.

Lastly, we want to thank Galileo Press, for their very helpful and always constructive assistance, without whom the publication of this SAP PRESS book would not have been possible. Special thanks go to Ms. Wiebke Hübner, Mr. Florian Zimniak, Ms. Michelle Kottemann, Ms. Regina Brautlacht, and Mr. Tomas Wehren.

"Gratitude is not only the greatest of virtues, but the parent of all the others."
Marcus Tullius Cicero (106—43 BCE)
Roman speaker and author

Andreas Brinkmann, Partner
andreas.brinkmann@de.ibm.com

Dr. Carsten Schinschel, Associate Partner
carsten.schinschel@de.ibm.com

IBM Business Consulting Services

Berlin and Düsseldorf
August 2003

1 Introduction

The realization that a company's information is among its most valuable asset has become widely accepted. The demand for comprehensive, effective security mechanisms has grown, along with the requirements of system administration and system monitoring in daily operations. The SAP R/3 authorization system is only one component—although a key one—that is integral to an enterprise security policy.

1.1 Notes on This Book

Because business processes and workflows (both within and between enterprises) are becoming evermore complex, it is critical to establish secure procedures for handling enterprise data and preventing its misuse. One aspect of data protection is an adequate structure for system access, particularly to ERP systems such as SAP R/3.

In this book, we'll answer your questions regarding the methodological implementation of SAP R/3 authorization concepts. Using practical experience from actual projects that we've implemented, we'll show you how to design an SAP R/3 authorization concept that supports your enterprise goals for data security. We'll pay particular attention as to how the development of an SAP R/3 authorization concept can support the cost-efficient implementation of the SAP R/3 System.

Please note, however, that this book should not be considered a complete authorization concept in and of itself; rather, it is intended to be a catalog of the aspects of the authorization concept that you have to consider. The development and implementation of an authorization concept is a customized solution for each enterprise that is characterized by the application of a specific method and several basic rules. Examples of driving factors that you should consider during the planning and implementation of an SAP R/3 authorization concept include:

▶ Fewer business risks

▶ Legal and corporate requirements for information security in SAP R/3

▶ Protection of data integrity against random or malicious manipulation or damage, or against unintended misuse

▶ Ensuring the confidentiality of internal enterprise information

► Establishing expertise that is required for an SAP R/3 implementation, but is not yet available in-house

► The cost-efficiency of administrative tasks, particularly in the authorization organization

► Ensuring that the administration of the concepts promotes ease-of-use

► Scalability of the authorization concept for planned extensions, such as acquisitions or reorganizations

This list only represents a few of the driving factors to be considered; you will find detailed descriptions of these potential influences and more in the next chapters.

1.1.1 Chapter Overview

The following overview of the chapters in this book is intended to help you find the information that you need on the SAP R/3 authorization concept both quickly and easily.

Chapter 1 outlines the book, specifically the factors that can affect the implementation of an SAP R/3 authorization concept and the consequences that may result. The special security aspects and basics of the IT infrastructure for an SAP R/3 System are also discussed.

Chapter 2, which is intended for new SAP R/3 users, introduces the technical foundation, structure, and specifics of SAP R/3 authorization management, summarizing each. In addition to defining R/3 users, authorization objects, single roles, and composite roles, this chapter also briefly explains the handling of the SAP R/3 Profile Generator.

Chapter 3 focuses on the internal control system (ICS), which is embedded in the enterprise security philosophy. This chapter emphasizes that the SAP R/3 authorization concept is only one component of the security environment within an enterprise, and must be integrated within the overall security concept.

Chapter 4 describes the procedure for designing an authorization concept, based on the initial phases of the IBM Phase Model for developing SAP R/3 development concepts. The phases include the enterprise-specific framework and the procedural steps required to design the concept. This chapter also includes many recommendations and lessons culled from recent projects that have been completed.

Chapter 5 describes the next phases of the model, using the design definitions from Chapter 4. After you analyze and define the necessary authorizations, you will read about the procedure for implementing and deploying an SAP R/3

authorization concept. The procedures are described from both the organizational (enterprise-specific) and the technical (SAP-specific) viewpoints.

Chapter 6 addresses the verifiability and comprehensibility of the implemented SAP R/3 authorization concept. You will read about the different auditing options, with the support of the SAP Audit Information System (AIS) and other available third-party products.

Chapter 7 focuses on the new SAP Enterprise Portal. It introduces you to the world of portals and shows you the difference between the portal approach and conventional authorization concepts. Special aspects and their consequences—such as the use of *Single Sign-On (SSO)* solutions—are described in more detail.

Chapter 8 focuses on planned developments in the area of SAP R/3 authorization management. Because our goal is to keep this book as current as possible, all proposed developments are discussed in this chapter.

1.1.2 Target Group

This book may be more relevant to a particular group, based on where they are with their SAP R/3 implementation at your company. We differentiate between two basic phases:

▶ Before and during an SAP R/3 implementation (project phase)

▶ After a successful SAP R/3 implementation (production operation)

Depending on which phase is currently ongoing at your company, different groups will find this book more beneficial than others at certain times during the SAP R/3 implementation, as exemplified in the following:

▶ **Project phase of an SAP R/3 implementation**

▷ *Executives and decision-makers*
who want to verify and potentially reorganize security development, deployment, and strategy at their companies. People who want to confirm that the implementation of an SAP R/3 authorization concept at their enterprise is not only an IT project.

▷ *Project managers and project team members*
who are considering new business/process-based concepts and want to utilize SAP R/3 to implement them. People who can comprehend the complexity of an SAP R/3 authorization concept and want to include it in their project planning.

> ▶ Consultants (in-house and external)
> who guide and support the implementation and the security aspects of the SAP R/3 authorization concept.

> ▶ Employees
> who will be responsible for managing user and authorization management or authorization development at their enterprise.

▶ **Production operation of the R/3 System**

> ▶ Internal auditors
> who need to verify and document the implementation of statutory guidelines and general security aspects in the production of a SAP R/3 System (see Chapter 6 for a detailed listing of existing guidelines).

> ▶ Security administrators
> who are responsible for maintaining—and possibly enhancing—an existing, successfully implemented SAP R/3 authorization concept at their enterprises.

> ▶ Employee representatives and data protection officers
> who have to evaluate and rate the security and data protection requirements at their enterprises. People who want to familiarize themselves with the interaction between all the components of a SAP R/3 system, and also with the importance of this component interaction—in the context of increasing security demands and international statutory requirements and guidelines for data protection.

You may also find this book useful during the product roll-out to estimate the effort required in the authorization area. The amount of time and resources required to analyze and develop the necessary authorizations is often underestimated.

1.1.3 The Focus of This Book

What This Book Does

This book describes the analysis, starting point, and procedure for implementing and deploying an SAP R/3 authorization concept from an organizational business perspective.

The underlying questions intrinsic to the implementation of an authorization concept are always *Why?*—What are the influencing factors?—and *When?*—When is the best implementation time and what do I have to consider during scheduling? (See the phased model in Chapter 4.) The question of *How* does not deal with technical implementation, however; rather, it summarizes the aspects that are relevant to decision-making, and practice-proven knowledge for implementing and deploying SAP R/3 authorization concepts, and renders them in a concise, informative format. Therefore, the focus is on the project-specific design and implementation of an SAP R/3 authorization concept, from which point the individual system functions are analyzed and described.

In this framework, the analysis, design, and implementation of an SAP R/3 authorization concept illustrate the conditions and procedures from countless project experiences that have to be considered, in accordance with local demands for authorizations, auditing, data protection, and other basic requirements.

What This Book Doesn't Do

This book is not intended to be a compendium or cookbook that contains all the necessary development steps for implementing an SAP R/3 authorization concept. It is not a checklist that you merely have to work through and complete.

The goal here is not to delve into the deepest regions of the SAP software, or the SAP authorization concept. You can find this information in the wide range of existing documentation and technical specifications in the SAP Online Documentation and in the book *Authorization Made Easy* (see Bibliography). The latter provides comprehensive, detailed, step-by-step instructions for using and operating the SAP R/3 Profile Generator. If you have specific technical questions, either source will provide you with the necessary information.

1.2 SAP R/3 Environment

The underlying security aspects within the SAP R/3 environment are outlined below and incorporated in the SAP infrastructure. Enhancements involving the ITS, workplace, and SAP Enterprise Portal are also introduced.

1.2.1 SAP R/3 Security Aspects

A full SAP R/3 security concept involves a multitude of different aspects. While the authorization concept is a major component, numerous other areas also have to be considered. This chapter introduces the various aspects of an SAP R/3 System, based on a typical IT infrastructure.

Starting with the traditional client/server architecture, the newer Web-based enhancements are examined in more detail in a second step. To better understand the information in this chapter, you need to be familiar with the underlying terminology. Technical security can be divided into three areas:

- ▶ Network security
- ▶ Application security
- ▶ Physical security

Network Security

The term *network security* encompasses all technology that supports the security of the *network infrastructure* and *network communication*. The *network infrastructure* consists of the physical network and all components that control communication within the network (such as routers, gateways, and firewalls). *Network communication* refers to the options for communication between two units, for example, "Can the SAP GUI running on PC A in network B communicate with application server C in network D?"

Because each type of communication within a network and the underlying infrastructure must be secured accordingly, a customized network security concept is required.

Application Security

Application security should include all security-relevant aspects within a specific application, which means when a user connects to an SAP R/3 application server with the SAP GUI, she can only perform those operations for which she is authorized, such as create material master records or display sales documents. Contrarily, application security must also define those activities that a user is *not* allowed to carry out, such as changing his own personnel master record or salary data.

Both the logon and identification for a specific application must be included in ensuring application security. Launching the SAP GUI, for example, means first logging on to the application server. The underlying operating system is itself another application, where users log on and are granted specific privileges (such as for installing software or launching an application) based on their individual user profiles. Because the SAP R/3 System manages certain kinds of information at operating-system level, the security of the R/3 System is dependent on the security of the operating system on which R/3 runs (in most cases UNIX or Windows NT). Every user who can log on at operating-system level poses an inherent risk, as this level permits unauthorized access to R/3 databases or files, as well as tampering with programs on development systems. *External commands* within the Computing Center Management System (CCMS) and in ABAP function modules can have a major impact on system security.

Therefore, an access concept must exist for each individual application—that is, for both the operating system and the applications that run on it. Accordingly, an SAP R/3 authorization concept is essentially the SAP-specific application security.

Physical Security

Physical security refers to the integrity of computers, network facilities, and data in the context of potential hazards, such as malicious intent or environmental effects (such as fire and other catastrophes). When envisioning a full SAP R/3 security concept, you must consider the physical security of the computers and the data that is most critical to sustaining ongoing operations. Such considerations are usually described as *disaster recovery planning*. Arrangements in this area include system mirroring, regular backups, and security measures for the physical protection of technical facilities—fire doors, climate control systems, window bars, and so on.

This subdivision of the different terms enables a more detailed representation of the various risks to which a far-reaching SAP infrastructure is subject. Please note that the separation between the different kinds of security that we just illustrated is only one possible representation, and that the boundaries between the three areas of technical security are not solid. In particular, network security and application security are closely linked. Depending on the underlying postulate, some security problems and technologies can be assigned to different categories.

1.2.2 IT Infrastructure

The SAP R/3 System is a completely new development and not, as the name might imply, merely an enhancement of its progenitor— the SAP R/2 System. When development of the R/3 System commenced in the mid-80s, SAP chose to implement a three-tier client/server architecture. This type of architecture can be divided into the following layers:

▶ Database layer

▶ Application layer

▶ Presentation layer

Data storage is performed in a database (*database layer*), while the processing on the application servers takes place at the *application layer*. Lastly, the SAP GUI as frontend (*presentation layer*) represents the interface to the user.

Figure 1.1 illustrates the client/server architecture of the R/3 System, and the links between the presentation and application layers, and between the application and database layers, depending on the implemented configuration hierarchy.

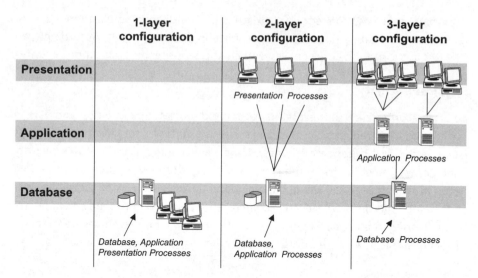

Figure 1.1 Three-Tier Client/Server Architecture

The *presentation layer* typically consists of a number of PCs with an installed SAP GUI. The SAP GUI is not a terminal emulator; it is an independent application that is responsible for the graphical display of the R/3 application data. Therefore, no particularly high demands apply to the connection between the SAP GUI PCs and the R/3 application (*access communication*). The frontend queries are processed exclusively at the two other layers.

The *application layer* consists of the application servers—servers where the core SAP R/3 applications run. If greater throughput is demanded of the R/3 application, it can be established by deploying additional servers. The *database layer* is represented exclusively by dedicated database servers running Oracle, DB2, Informix, or other database solutions.

This three-tier architecture enables you to distribute the services of the individual layers to different computers, depending on your specific requirements, which makes the SAP R/3 System extremely flexible.

1.2.3 Integration of Security Aspects and the Infrastructure

The client/server architecture that we just described is the foundation for describing various security aspects of a complex SAP R/3 landscape. The SAP R/3 authorizations must be positioned accordingly within the overall SAP security concept to be implemented, and clearly delimited with regard to access rights and restrictions.

Network Infrastructure

You first must define the overall network infrastructure. It connects the database, application, and presentation layers and is critical to system security, because it forms the "first line of defense." All unauthorized access attempts must be blocked, but without hindering the enterprise's communication needs. The design of the network infrastructure for an application such as SAP R/3, which is not isolated and is often part of an even more complex IT landscape, requires extreme care. SAP supports network security with mechanisms like the *SAProuter* and *Secure Network Communications (SNC)*:

▶ **SAProuter**

The *SAProuter* is a dedicated firewall that supports the specific SAP communication protocols for filtering and routing functions. While a conventional firewall lets through any SAP communication that comes from a specific network, the SAProuter only passes communication from authenticated users. The SAProuter therefore features a more fine-grained control of SAP R/3 communications than is possible with a generic firewall.

▶ **Secure Network Communications (SNC)**

Secure Network Communications (SNC) is a software layer that is available to every SAP R/3 component and that works together with third-party security products. SNC provides security at the application layer, for example, for communication between the SAP GUI and the application servers, or between two application servers. SNC features three levels of protection:

- ▶ The *lowest security level* only contains *authentication*, which validates the identity of the communication partners.

- ▶ The *medium security level* also supports the *integrity* of the data. Any modification to data during the communication between the parties is detected.

- ▶ The *highest security level* includes all the security checks from the underlying levels, and also protects the *confidentiality* of the data via encrypting the data during transmission.

For a detailed definition of the SAP communication links that can be protected by SNC, please refer to the corresponding SAP documentation.[1] Note that all access to settings involving network security should be restricted to administrators.

The individual layers—database layer, application layer, and presentation layer—will be described in more detail below, that is, in the context of the security aspects listed in Section 1.2.1: network security, application security, and physical security.

---

1 Such as the SAP Security Guidelines, the SAP online help, the Network Services operating concept and the IS Network Services emergency manual.

Database Layer

In most SAP R/3 installations, the database layer consists of one or more servers and storage solutions, which support data administration. These components are located in a separate network that only permits communication with the application servers. The application security of the database layer requires the server operating system, the database application itself, and any specific software products for the storage solutions. To ensure the physical security of the systems, the servers and storage solutions must be installed in specially secured server rooms that are equipped with access control systems. Moreover, no user can be allowed to access the database directly. Its complete isolation from the company network protects the database layer against unauthorized access to the sensitive data that it houses.

Application Layer

The *application layer* consists of several application servers, where the actual SAP R/3 applications run. These application servers are located either in a separate network or in the same network as the database layer. A SAProuter must control all communication with the rest of the company network. The application security of the SAP R/3 System is particularly important in this context. In addition, the operating system of the application servers has to be secured first. All relevant authorization checks take place on the servers at this layer. The SAP R/3 application checks whether a certain user is authorized to carry out a specific action. The physical security of the system is subject to the same rules as the database layer.

Presentation Layer

Standard PCs with an installed SAP GUI represent the typical architecture of the *presentation layer*. In most cases, these PCs are also part of the company intranet and are secured through access controls to the company network.

In the recent past, more and more companies have given their suppliers direct access to their enterprise SAP R/3 Systems. In this case, the firewall has to be opened to enable this access, which requires additional control mechanisms to prevent unauthorized entry into the R/3 System. The assignment of unique, fixed IP addresses uses mechanisms that identify computers in networks based on their MAC addresses before access is granted (a *MAC address* is a network address that uniquely identifies each network card).

At the application security level, the operating system represents the first control stage, as user logon may be necessary. Detailed authentication procedures use *smart cards*, or even biometric procedures, for this purpose. In turn, downloading data to local storage media can be prevented at the SAP GUI level.

The physical security of the presentation layer should also be considered in detail, even though it is as not as critical for this layer, as it is for the database and application layers. The security verification in this case is usually limited to the ID checks carried out by plant security at the entrance of an office complex.

Conclusion

This brief overview of the relevant security problems emphasizes the complexity of a traditional SAP R/3 security concept. New developments in the Web environment have contributed to not only additional functions to the SAP system, but new security aspects as well. Because, as yet, very few companies have prepared their R/3 landscape to accommodate the new Web concepts, these areas will be treated separately from the original SAP R/3 architecture. For this reason, all portal-specific observations have been grouped together in Chapter 7.

1.2.4   Further Development with the Web Architecture (ITS)

In SAP R/3 Release 3.1 and later, you can connect SAP systems directly to the Internet. SAP developed *Internet Transaction Server* (ITS) for this specific purpose. It enables the use of *Internet Application Components* (IACs), which allow users to interact with SAP R/3 via a standard Web browser. The ITS consists of two components: the *WGate* and the *AGate*.

The *WGate* is installed as an additional component on a separate Web server and is responsible for communicating with the Web browser, using an encrypted Internet protocol (HTTPS). In a second step, the WGate establishes communications with the AGate. The *AGate* uses an SAP-specific protocol that is compatible with the SNC interface discussed in the previous section. The WGate is located either in a DMZ (demilitarized zone) or in a company's intranet, depending on who uses the IACs. If the users are all in-house staff, installing a WGate on a Web server within the enterprise network will suffice. If Internet access is required, an additional WGate must be set up in a DMZ.

The AGate is usually located in the same network as the SAP R/3 application server. When an authenticated WGate connects to the AGate, the AGate establishes communications with an application server. This communication channel can also be enhanced with various security services through the SNC interface.

1.2.5 mySAP Workplace/SAP Enterprise Portal

The portal landscape features an infrastructure that enables you to integrate various heterogeneous application components, thereby creating a globally collaborative e-business solution. Figure 1.2 shows an overview of the many different application components that can be integrated.

SAP's vision is to enable people to perform their responsibilities effectively, regardless of time and space. To create this kind of workplace, it must be possible to provide convenience in the form of a system that is integrated, cohesive, business-specific, and easy-to-use. And for this vision to become a reality, a medium that fulfills all these requirements must be provided—especially because customers are most likely running applications from many different vendors (SAP, People-Soft, Baan, IBM, Lotus, and so on). Web technology provides the foundation for implementing this vision. It offers the potential of displaying different applications in a Web browser, based on specially developed views. But it is the SAP Enterprise Portal—the medium that fulfills all the requirements—that is SAP's answer to this vision of a virtual workplace.

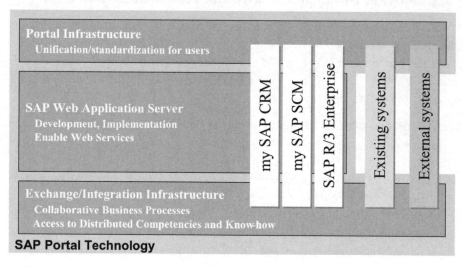

Figure 1.2 Integration of Application Components

When users can sit at an Internet café and read their company e-mail, or retrieve the latest enterprise information from the portal in a standard Web browser, this vision will have become a reality. Figure 1.3 shows an overview of the different components and applications that can be integrated in the SAP Enterprise Portal.

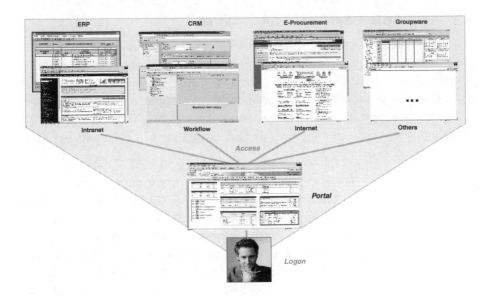

Figure 1.3 SAP Enterprise Portal Components and Applications

When integrating the SAP Portal systems in an existing IT infrastructure, and when access to an R/3 System is required, you have to ensure that the ITS (*Internet Transaction Server*) and the portal server lie in the same Internet domain and that the DNS (*Domain Name Server*) knows the names and addresses of the servers. If these prerequisites are not met, the smooth operation of a portal landscape cannot be guaranteed.

One direct benefit of the portal solution is its *Single Sign-On* (SSO) feature. This feature enables users to log on to all applications with a single user ID and password, a vast improvement over the current situation in which each user has to manage a variety of IDs and passwords for the different systems. The SSO concept is examined in more detail in Chapter 7.

This consolidation of different applications under a single *point of access* requires an extension of the traditional authorization concept. As you will learn in Chapter 7, it no longer suffices to define roles in each system (R/3 core, APO, BW, EBP, and so on). Additional, comprehensive roles have to be defined, such as the "portal roles," which contain all the roles that a user needs in the different systems. Portal roles also frequently include additional information, such as the Web sites that a user is authorized to access. Accordingly, a portal role not only contains information regarding SAP authorizations, but also information about non-SAP systems. The biggest challenge when integrating non-SAP systems in a portal landscape has been that not all applications support a role-based authorization concept (such as Web browsers).

1.3 Complex System Landscapes

This section addresses the particular problems posed by authorization concepts in large, complex SAP R/3 system landscapes. Many global corporations operate a veritable collection of SAP R/3 Systems during the development and production phases. In past years, individual installations have included more than forty SAP R/3 Systems, geographically distributed around the globe. Such scenarios have a direct influence on the development and administration of a coherent authorization system at an enterprise.

An SAP R/3 system landscape can be divided into two dimensions. The first dimension characterizes the temporal layer of the SAP R/3 implementation and is the primary factor for the subsequent maintenance of the R/3 System. It includes *sandboxes* (experimentation systems), development systems, quality assurance (QA) systems, integration test systems, and production systems (live systems). The second dimension consists of the functional SAP R/3 components—for example, an HR component, the R/3 core system (FI, CO, MM, PP, and so on), SAP Advanced Planner and Optimizer, SAP Business Information Warehouse (BW), or a separate master data repository. This amalgam of components and systems creates a two-dimensional system landscape that can reach an astounding level of complexity (see the example in Figure 1.4).

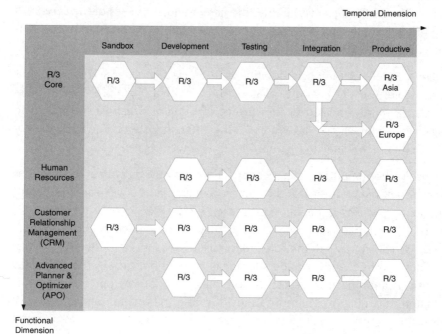

Figure 1.4 Multisystem Landscape

When implementing an authorization concept for landscapes of this type, you always have to consider the following questions:

▶ **Where will the authorizations be developed and where will they be tested?**
These questions are not as trivial as they might seem at first glance. You can develop the roles for Materials Management and Financial Accounting in the same system, for example, but not the roles for SAP CRM or SAP BW. Moreover, testing the roles requires systems with sufficient test data.

▶ **Which general method will be followed?**
SAP projects often begin at a company's headquarters (in the U.S., for example) and are then expanded to include international subsidiaries and branch offices. If the developed roles do not consider the different cultural and organizational aspects of the different countries from the start, this might result in the wrong authorization method in one of these countries. The role of the stock supervisor is a particularly illustrative example. This role would probably be "infused" with much more trust in the U.S. than in a South American subsidiary, for example. If this role was developed only from the local point of view—with far-reaching authorizations for specific release quantities (such as scrapping and other inventory adjustment postings), it probably wouldn't be applied to the South American offices on a one-to-one basis.

Different organizational structures within a company can also affect the development of an authorization concept. This fact can be illustrated by the example of a Spanish subsidiary of a German company. In this specific case, all the roles that were to be implemented in Spain were developed in advance in Germany. Because the German parent company had a much larger headcount than the Spanish subsidiary, the roles had been specialized accordingly. This degree of specialization couldn't be implemented for the smaller staff in Spain, however, because the responsibilities couldn't be divided up for individual employees. As a result, some Spanish SAP users had to be assigned more than twenty roles in order to perform their daily responsibilities—even when only a small portion of the role functionality was required. The original authorization concept, which had been developed very precisely, was the subject of much criticism.

▶ **How will the users and roles be administered?**
The administration of users and authorizations is divided among two to three roles for security reasons (see Sections 2.3.9 and 5.6.2). The concept here is to separate the authorizations for developing single and composite roles from those for assigning the developed roles. While this requirement is easy to implement in a one-system landscape, it is exponentially more difficult in a complex, global landscape.

In this case, you have to decide whether you want the user administration to be centralized for all systems, or distributed among regional user administrators—possibly by application. You also need to clarify whether it makes sense for a company to geographically separate the centralized user administrator from the local users that he or she has to administer. The employees involved have to be in constant contact, in order to keep the authorization concept coherent across the full system landscape. In contrast, a regional authorization administrator should be able to understand a user's request to change a local role within the overall concept of the enterprise authorization concept, and ensure that the person responsible grants the necessary approval.

Such considerations are just one component of the careful planning required to implement an authorization concept. Even though many enterprises consider authorization concepts to be an exaggerated expense at first glance, they often prove to be wise investments over the course of time.

1.4   Conclusion

This initial overview of SAP security issues is intended to introduce the reader to the complexities of an SAP R/3 security concept. Although the following chapters of this book deal primarily with authorization issues, we do not intend to imply that a secure authorization concept alone is enough to ensure the security of an SAP R/3 System. Imagine system security as a chain: the authorization concept is one link in this chain; in the authors' opinion, it is currently one of the weakest links at a large number of enterprises. Therefore, many companies should consider whether investing in security products that are purely technical in nature—without having a sensibly coordinated R/3 authorization concept—might not instill a false sense of security.

2   SAP R/3 Users and Authorizations

The confidentiality and integrity of enterprise data are critical aspects within an SAP system group. For this reason, an authorization concept was developed for the SAP R/3 System—in addition to other security tools—to allow you to assign extremely differentiated authorizations to users, enabling a distinctly defined user access to the SAP system.

2.1   Preliminary Remark—Security in the SAP R/3 System

The business processes that are supported by integrative aspects of the SAP R/3 System, in addition to the large quantities of data for processing, are among your most important enterprise assets and deserve special protection. SAP R/3 was developed to support the implementation of a separate user and authorization management—that is, an authorization system tailored to workflows and processes—at the application level within the system or an SAP system group.

Although SAP R/3 is transaction-based, users are not permitted to access all the data related to a given transaction, for example, without further authorizations. The detailed authorizations for doing so are based on defined and implemented organizational units within an enterprise on one hand (see Section 2.3.3 for more information), and on internal and external regulations and statutory requirements on the other hand. SAP R/3 provides powerful functions in Release 2.1. In later releases, SAP R/3 provides functions that enable you to restrict access to data and transactions at a finely detailed level. The scope of the security functions permits nearly complete access protection regarding the authorizations of individual users, that is, they can be included in some authorizations and excluded from other authorizations.

2.1.1   Risks

A poorly implemented authorization concept poses several risks, which are summarized in this section. Due to their potential effects, these risks emphasize how important the authorization concept is to the successful completion of an SAP R/3 implementation project. (For a description of risks and controls outside of the SAP R/3 authorization concept, refer to Chapter 3.)

Examples of the risks that are associated with an insufficiently developed authorization concept include:

▶ Financial losses due to human error, system error, or negligence
▶ Incorrect decisions by management due to lack of reliable decision support

▶ Industrial espionage through data theft

▶ Incorrect actions due to data manipulation

In general, the SAP R/3 authorization concept is based on a clearly defined organizational structure and the business processes that the enterprise intends to implement together with the deployment of SAP R/3. Therefore, it is important for this framework data to be available before the authorization concept is drafted. (This is not always possible, however, due to changes made at short notice).

2.1.2 Goals

The comprehensive goal of defining authorizations within an SAP R/3 project is to satisfy all internal and external enterprise requirements for information security, confidentiality, and data integrity. Therefore, the authorization concept should be designed to mitigate these risks in a cost-efficient manner and achieve the following security goals:

▶ Satisfy statutory and enterprise demands for information security in the SAP R/3 System.

▶ Protect data from random or malicious manipulation and damage.

▶ Protect data integrity against intentional manipulation and unintended misuse.

▶ Provide confidentiality of sensitive enterprise data.

2.1.3 Expense

The resources and expense required to draft a detailed SAP R/3 authorization concept are frequently underestimated. In many cases, the authorization concept is conceived much too late in the project schedule, which is often because the functions that this security tool offers are not given the attention that they deserve.

The integrative concept of the SAP R/3 System supports all business processes in their respective modules. All R/3 modules are integrated through internal connections. Because of the relational database concept of the SAP software, data is saved non-redundantly in some 43,000 tables. A typical SAP R/3 System with Release 4.6C has over 61,000 transaction codes. The associated authorization concept features over 900 different authorization objects, with which the transactions are linked for an authorization check. Customers can also create additional transactions and authorization objects in the system. Moreover, the R/3 System contains around 120,000 programs and more than 1,000 ABAP/4 reports, in addition to potential user-defined reports.

This wide range of features makes both the R/3 software and the necessary authorization concept very complex. The more finely defined an enterprise's access protection, the greater is the effort required to design the authorization concept. Moreover, all resources responsible for the implementation of the authorization concept must have the necessary qualifications in this area. The method and a procedure that has proven itself in practice are described in Chapters 4 and 5.

2.1.4 Benefits

When the defined security goals have been achieved, another major benefit of the authorization concept is its potential to reduce development costs, implementation costs, and ongoing maintenance costs.

Moreover, an enterprise that implements an authorization concept according to the method described in the following chapters will have achieved a clearly defined, standardized level of security.

2.1.5 Environment

The SAP system provides a set of standard tools for configuring users and authorizations, one that is usually sufficient for developers under most defined framework conditions. These tools are discussed in more detail in this chapter. If enterprise-specific enhancements to the standard tools are required, these enhancements can prove to be quite costly. Because of the effort required to implement and maintain these tools for configuring users and authorizations, we recommend that you only use them if necessary.

In addition to the SAP R/3 authorization concept, SAP offers other options for achieving the security objectives. Examples of these options include the adequate configuration of:

▶ Database and operating-system accesses

▶ Secure Network Communication (SNC)

▶ Secure data formats (*Secure Store and Forward*, SSF)

▶ Security in the Internet (mySAP—use of Internet technology)

▶ Single Sign-On (SSO) solutions (user authentication)

Comprehensive information on these topics is available in Chapters 1 and 7. You can also refer to the *SAP R/3 Security Guide* for detailed information.[1]

---

1 The R/3 Security Guide is available in SAPNet under *http://service.sap.com/securityguide*.

We will now explain the underlying technical components of an SAP R/3 authorization concept. The organizational implementation and the associated method are described in Chapters 4 and 5 respectively.

2.2 The SAP R/3 User

2.2.1 User Master Record

The existence of an R/3 *user master record* is a prerequisite for logging on to the SAP system. To uniquely identify an SAP R/3 user, each user must have a unique user master record, where personal data is saved and authorizations are granted by assigning composite roles. Technically, authorizations can also be assigned to users through single roles, composite profiles, and single profiles; however, the method described in this book is based exclusively on assigning composite roles to users.

When a user logs on to the SAP system, the user master record defined for that specific user is loaded and all data and privileges assigned to the user are read and saved in the user buffer. These conditions hold true for the entire duration of the user's logon in the SAP system. After a modification to the user buffer and in recent system releases, it is unnecessary for the user to log on again after the user administrator has made changes to the user master record (e.g., after adding transactions and their associated new authorization objects). A repeat logon is typically unnecessary following changes to field values for authorizations. From an administration perspective, however, we recommend a repeat logon after the change notification has been sent to the user.

The functions for maintaining user master records are located under menu path **Tools · Administration · User Maintenance · User** (or enter Transaction Code SU01). For a summary on making mass changes in transaction SU10, see Section 2.10. Administrators are generally authorized to create new user master records, either from scratch or by copying an existing user master record. The 12-character user name is the first entry prompt that you'll see when you create, change, or copy a master record. Figure 2.1 shows the initial screen for user maintenance.

The user master record consists of the user name and the assigned attributes. These attributes are displayed and maintained in tab pages as components of the user master record (see Figure 2.2):

▶ **Address data**
Use the Address data tab page to record a specific user's address data. You must enter at least the user's last name here. This information is intended to

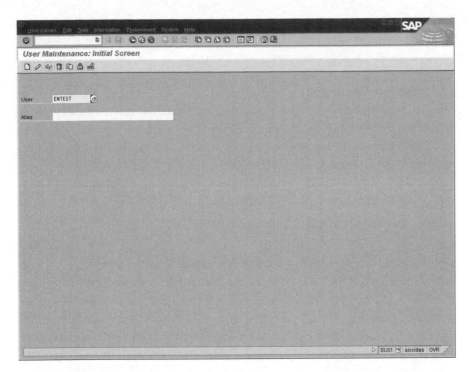

Figure 2.1 User Maintenance—Initial Screen

identify the actual employee (first name, last name, department, phone number, business address, and so on) and the 12-character user ID.

▶ **Logon data**

Use the **Logon data** (also referred to as the **basic data**) tab page to maintain user information in a user master record. In addition to the initial password (see Section 2.2.4 for more information) and the user group (see Section 2.2.2 for more information), you can optionally specify a maximum validity period for the user master record, which can be extremely effective for temporary employees, or for project team members during implementation projects.

The user administrator is prompted to assign an initial password when he or she creates a new user master record. The same value has to be entered twice for security reasons. The first time the new user logs on to the system, or when the password is reset, that user is prompted to choose a new, personal password.

▶ **User defaults**

Use the Defaults tab page to specify user defaults, such as the standard printer, type of spool control, date and decimal formats, individual start menu after logon, and logon language. This tab is optional for the administrator; users can maintain their own user defaults in Transaction SU3.

▶ **Parameters**

Use the **Parameters** tab page to set or get parameters to save default values for fields, such as the company code, plant, and sales organization for each individual user. To create a definition, you have to define the SAP field name (such as BUKRS for the company code) together with the required value (such as 0001). These entries are optional for the administrator (such values could be preassigned during the initial upload of users—if the company only uses one company code, for example), and can be maintained by the users themselves at any time using Transaction SU3.

Defining these preassigned values makes it easier for users to enter organizational units when they encounter the units again. Maintaining the parameter values can help to reduce mistakes during input.

▶ **Roles**

Use the **Roles** tab page to assign single or composite roles to the user. The necessary roles can be determined using the value Help (F4 Help). When a composite role is assigned, the single roles therein are assigned to the user automatically. Assigning a single or composite role to a user records the corresponding authorization profiles in the user profile at the same time. No explicit user comparison is needed. For a more detailed description of roles, see Section 2.3.4.

▶ **Profiles**

Use the **Profiles** tab page to assign authorization profiles to a user. You should not manually assign profiles that were created in role maintenance (Transaction Code PFCG—see Section 2.3.4). This can be prevented with a patch in Release 6.10 and later releases. In this case, the user will have the authorizations until the next user comparison in the Profile Generator, after which the authorization profiles for the roles entered in the **Roles** tab page are automatically copied to the respective user master.

▶ **Groups**

Use the Groups tab page to assign users to one or more previously defined user groups. This helps to partition the user data, which accelerates centralized user administration. This tab page was eliminated when the Global User Manager (GUM) was deactivated.

▶ **Personalization**

Use the **Personalization** tab page to allow users to preassign application parameters that include more parameters than the user parameters provided by Transaction Code SU3.

The last write access to the user master record is saved as a change document with the user ID and date of the change (**Last changed by** field).

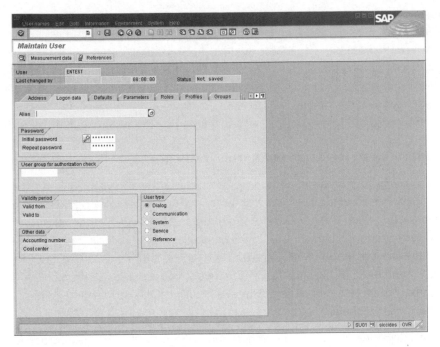

Figure 2.2 User Maintenance—Tab Pages

Due to the client concept in the SAP system, a user master record always exists only in the client (logical SAP system) where it was created. If users work in several clients, separate master records—including the corresponding authorizations—have to be created for each client, which can prove to be time-consuming. In Release 4.6 and later, administrators can use Central User Administration (CUA) to create and maintain users in a defined main system, and then distribute the users to the connected destination systems via the distribution mechanisms (see Section 2.10 for information on new features since Release 4.6). Subsidiary systems with releases between 4.5 and 6.20 can be integrated with the CUA.

In addition to creating, changing, and copying user master records, the user administrator can also lock or delete any master record (based on an approved request). This deletion should not occur immediately after the employee's separation from the company, however, because the user ID in question was used to record business activities in the SAP system. This logging serves as a primary analysis and tracing function for auditing purposes. Instead, the user administrator should simply lock the user master record after the employee's last day on the job.

User master records can be locked manually by the user administrator (e.g., for former staff, as mentioned above), or automatically by the SAP system. For example, master records are locked when a user's failed logon attempts reach the number of attempts defined in parameter `Login/fails_to_user_lock`. This systematic lock of users after a specified number of failed logon attempts can prevent passwords from being "hacked" by unauthorized third parties (such as crack programs that systematically try words from a specified dictionary). The user ID in question can either be reactivated automatically the next day (SAP default setting—see system parameter `Login/failed_user_auto_unlock` in Section 2.2.4), or configured to require manual reactivation by the system administrator.

Initial Data Load for Users and Authorizations

To avoid having to enter large numbers of user master records manually into the SAP system before going live, we recommend using a technical aid. You can accomplish this either with an ABAP program that reads the data automatically, or with an external tool for creating and managing user master records based on the SAP BAPIs (such as BAPI_USER_CREATE, BAPI_USER_GET_DETAIL, BAPI_USER_CHANGE, and BAPI_USER_DELETE). Alternatively, you can also use the SAP CATT (Computer Aided Test Tool). The advantage of using CATT is that no additional programming is required.

CATT was developed by SAP to fill transactions with mass data for test purposes. You can also use CATT to import mass data from a Microsoft Excel table to the SAP system, via the corresponding input transactions (similar to a batch input process). CATT can be used with the vast majority of existing transactions. CATT cannot be used with the new Enjoy transactions, however, or with transactions that use certain screen controls that cannot be recorded in the CATT. Accordingly, the new eCATT procedure is available in Release 6.10 and later.

A *teach-in mode* records which fields of the transaction have to be filled. This recording is comparable with a manual recording of a batch input session. Data whose parameters have to be changed by individual data records (such as the single or composite roles to be assigned) are labeled with variable names in the screens of the transaction and, when the CATT is processed, imported from the underlying Excel table. The exact function is described in the specific CATT documentation (SAP Online Documentation on *CATT, Computer Aided Test Tool*).

2.2.2 User Groups

The user groups primarily serve two purposes to coordinate and structure user maintenance, for example, by a decentralized user administration organization. We recommend defining user groups, because assigning R/3 users to different user groups enables you to restrict the activity areas and separate division assignments of those users, and therefore their potential access privileges as well.

If you define user groups ACCTG or PURCHASE, for example, you can apply them to user IDs that you define later for employees in the Accounting or Purchasing departments. You create and maintain user groups within the user maintenance transaction, with menu path **Environment · User Groups**. This entry is not required, but its use is recommended for both administrative and security reasons.

2.2.3 User Types

The *user type* attribute indicates how the user's access to the SAP system is defined. SAP distinguishes among the following user types:

▶ **Dialog**
"Typical" SAP users are defined with user type *Dialog*. During logon, the checks defined by the parameter values (expired passwords, change of initial password, and so on) take place here. Every employee should generally be defined as a dialog user.

▶ **Communication**
A user with user type *Communication* is used for dialog-free communication between systems (for RFC or CPIC services, for example, or for various applications such as ALE, workflow, Central User Administration). Because these functions usually require broader authorizations in our project experience, direct dialog logon is not possible with this user type.

▶ **System**
User IDs with user type *System* are used for dialog-free communication within a system (RFC or CPIC service and background processing). The general parameter settings do not apply here as they do for dialog users. Because authorizations are also required here in the Basis area, users with type *System* cannot log on in dialog.

▶ **Service**
A user with user type *Service* corresponds to a dialog user that is not assigned to a single person, but which instead is available to a collective group of users. *Service* users are used to grant access via an ITS service, for example.

▶ **Reference**
Like the *Service* user, the *Reference* user is a general, non-person-specific user. A *Reference*-type user cannot be used to log on to the system, however; it is used merely to assign additional roles and authorizations (with the **Roles** tab page). *Reference* users are also used for Internet users that are provided with the same roles and authorizations.

2.2.4 Password Rules

Practical experience has repeatedly shown that many employees at many companies do not take PIN codes or passwords seriously enough. Employees might "loan" each other passwords when their colleagues can't get into the system. Or, people scribble their passwords on a note that they place under the keyboard, which consequently doesn't deter anyone who might be interested in obtaining this information. Despite numerous warnings, employees also frequently choose the first names or birth dates of their own family members (which are obviously not difficult to guess) as passwords. The result—it is often impossible to determine which employee made a specific change, despite that a specific user ID was recorded in the change documents.

The SAP system supplies various effective measures and settings to support a secure password system. Despite these efforts to ensure password security, misuse cannot be prevented by system means alone. Therefore, the security officer or user administrator should communicate openly on a regular basis with the SAP users, regarding the design, selection, and care of passwords. This sensitization to the importance of protecting the security of passwords will hopefully encourage SAP users to be more careful with user IDs and passwords.

The following password rules apply to an SAP system:

▶ No check of case-sensitivity.

▶ The password must be a minimum of three characters and a maximum of eight characters long (see Table 2.1 for more information).

▶ Any character that can be entered with the keyboard (including digits and special characters) should be allowed.

▶ The password may not begin with a question mark or an exclamation point.

▶ Blanks are not allowed.

▶ The first three characters of a password must not be identical.

▶ Table USR40 defines all the illegal passwords—that is, passwords that users cannot select.

▶ The first three characters may not be part of the corresponding user ID (for example, user ID SAMPLEH would prevent all passwords that begin with three consecutive letters from that ID, such as PLE*).

▶ The strings PASS* or SAP* cannot be used at the start of the password.

▶ During the first logon to the system, each user must enter a new, personal password, which overwrites the initial password.

▶ A history prevents the reuse of the last five passwords used.

You can use the system parameters to define additional rules regarding the permitted passwords and their use. Table 2.1 shows these parameters, which you can maintain using Transaction Code RZ11 (the "Rec." column names the recommended setting, which may differ from the standard). Report RSPARAM lists the profile parameters.

Parameter	SAP	Rec.	Description
Login/fails_to_session_end	3	3	Number of failed logons that can be attempted with the same user master until the logon procedure is terminated.
Login/fails_to_user_lock	12	6	Number of failed logons that can be attempted with the same user master until that user master is blocked. At the same time, an entry is written in the system log.
Login/failed_user_auto_unlock	1	0	Controls the unblocking of users blocked by failed logon attempts. If you set the parameter to 1, user blocks due to failed logons from the previous day are generally ignored. If you set the parameter to 0, the blocks remain.
Login/min_password_lng	3	6—8	Minimum required password length.
Login/password_expiration_time	0	90	If you set the parameter to 0, users are not forced to change their passwords. Values > 0 indicate the number of days after which users have to change their logon passwords.
Rdisp/gui_auto_logout	0	3600	If no input is made in the GUI within Rdisp/gui_auto_logout seconds, the frontend is logged off automatically. If you set the parameter to 0, no automatic logoff occurs.

Table 2.1 Examples of parameters for configuring the password rules

In addition to the fixed settings in the system parameters, you can define other illegal passwords, which enables you to prevent users from entering certain frequently used, trivial passwords. Use Transaction Code SM30 with Table USR40 to enter the illegal passwords. You can use the following placeholders to define wildcard illegal passwords in Table USR40:

▶ ?—represents a single character
▶ *—represents any character string

Example: If you enter the string 123* in Table USR40, it means that passwords cannot start with the string "123". If you enter MA?, you prevent all passwords that start with "MA" and contain another character, such as "MAA", "MAB", and so on (using this placeholder reduces the number of entries required, avoiding large datasets). This ability to use placeholders to define wildcard illegal passwords enables you to prevent the use of well-known and easy-to-guess passwords, such as the abbreviation of your company or one of its products or services, by defining them as illegal passwords in Table USR40. This defining of illegal passwords applies especially to your company name, names of departments, brand names, or board members.

2.2.5   SAP R/3 Standard Users

The SAP R/3 System uses several technical users, or *standard users*, that are already present after installation. Because these users have predefined names and passwords that are well-known to third parties, these users must be protected against unauthorized access, and therefore, from misuse and data manipulation.

▶ **SAP***

SAP* is the *superuser* in the SAP R/3 System. It is the only user in the R/3 System that does not require a user master record, as it is defined in the system coding. As soon as a user master record exists for user SAP*, however, the settings in this user master record take precedence over the hard-coded user. A user master record named SAP* is created by default in all clients of the SAP system. Because the default password of this user (PASS or 06071992) is assumed to be widely known, certain preventive measures must be implemented to prevent the unauthorized use of SAP*:

▶ A user master record for user SAP* must exist in every single client of the SAP R/3 System in order to prevent the hard-coded settings from taking effect.

▶ Assign user ID SAP* to user group SUPER.

▶ Change the initial password and block user SAP* in all clients (000, 001, 066, and all other configured clients).

▶ Revoke all authorization profiles from user ID SAP.*

We recommend never using the SAP* user as superuser. Instead, you should create a new user with a specifically defined name that is given comprehensive authorizations (profile SAP_ALL) and that can be used by the user administrators in an emergency.

▶ **DDIC**

The DDIC user possesses special authorizations for installation, software logistics, and the ABAP/4 Dictionary. These authorizations are hard-coded in the system. Accordingly, you should not add any other authorization profiles to the DDIC user, as it already has all the authorizations that it requires for its particular tasks.

The DDIC user is present in clients 000 and 001 after system installation (the initial password is 19920607). Be sure to change the initial password.

▶ **SAPCPIC**

SAPCPIC cannot be used to log on in dialog, but it does permit several programs and function modules to be called in the SAP system. It is only required by the EarlyWatch service to collect performance data, launch external background programs, and retrieve values for the Computing Center Management System (CCMS).

In addition to changing the standard password, *admin* (in clients 000 and 001), you might also consider blocking this user as a protective measure. Before you decide whether to implement this measure, be sure to read the disadvantages of both options in SAP Note number 29276 in the SAP Service Marketplace.

▶ **EarlyWatch**

This user is defined by default in client 066 with password *support* and is used by the *EarlyWatch* service. It is only used for the Performance Monitor. To protect this user ID against unauthorized access, change the initial password in client 066.

The rules and regulations for password assignment are defined in detail in Section 2.2.4.

2.2.6 Relevant SAP Tables for User Master Records

The comprehensive data and their interactions involving the user master record are saved in various tables within the SAP system. Table 2.2 lists the tables that are relevant to user master data.

Table	Description
USGRP	User groups
USGRPT	Text table for USGRP (user groups)
USH02	Change history for logon data
USR01	User master (runtime data)

Table 2.2 Tables for user master records

Table	Description
USR02	Logon data
USR03	Address data: users
USR04	User master: authorizations
USR05	User master: parameter ID
USR10	User master: authorization profiles
USR11	User master: texts for profiles (USR10)
USR12	User master: authorization values
USR15	External user name
USR20	Date of last reorganization in user master
USR40	Table of illegal passwords
UST04	User masters
UST10C	User master: composite profiles
UST10S	User master: single profiles
UST12	User master: authorizations
USRBF2	User content for fast RFC logon

Table 2.2 Tables for user master records (Cont.)

2.3 The SAP R/3 Authorization Concept

Generally, you should grant authorizations for accessing data in the SAP R/3 System according to the principle "as loose as possible and as restrictive as necessary". Unauthorized parties must not be allowed to access critical data. In adhering to that principle, you must distinguish the critical data from the non-critical data, and determine whether detailed restrictions are compatible with your enterprise goals, or if they will unnecessarily complicate your staff's day-to-day activities. Even when non-critical data is involved, restricting access to an employee's specific area of responsibility may be appropriate to prevent the inadvertent—and incorrect—modification of data.

Background and Approach

Developing an SAP authorization concept is by no means a strictly technical job that is the sole responsibility of Basis support; much of the work has to be performed by the user departments and the project team members. All active transactions have to be assigned to the subsequent roles individually, based on the user department requirements and the underlying security strategy; you also have to check whether access within each individual transaction has to be restricted to specific authorization levels. Lastly, because the SAP system currently features over 61,000 transactions, do not underestimate the effort required to develop an authorization concept.

The complex structure of the authorization system has often been criticized. The numerous individual authorization scenarios and representation of them in the system can become extremely complex. Authorization concepts and their structures are usually much less restrictive at small and medium-sized enterprises, for example, when only one company code and one plant have been modeled in the system. Defining authorizations at the transaction level is often sufficient in such cases. At larger companies, however, especially global corporations, restrictions at transaction level are not sufficient; a much finer, more detailed approach is required.

The restrictions have to be based on specific values in the organizational levels, such as *company codes*, *plants*, *sales organizations*, and so on. An authorization concept should always be tailored to a specific company and its requirements. Use of the SAP standard roles is not recommended under any circumstances. The SAP Profile Generator, which is available in Release 3.0F and later, supports both the procedure for defining concepts, which enables you to define extremely complex authorization relationships down to a detailed level, and much simpler developments.

Chapters 4 and 5 describe a procedure that satisfies all the requirements described here.

2.3.1 Profile Generator

The introduction of the *Profile Generator* has greatly improved the integration of the object-oriented concept with the transaction-oriented concept (see Section 2.12 for more information). The Profile Generator is fairly simple to use (when compared to previous solutions) and easy (for employees) to learn.

Tables USOBT and USOBX (or the customer settings in tables USOBT_C and USOBX_C) control the behavior of the Profile Generator when generating the authorization profiles for the respective single roles.

Method

Prior to the introduction of the Profile Generator, authorizations were assigned using single profiles and composite profiles. When activity groups were introduced, however, authorizations were not initially accompanied by composite activity groups (see Section 2.12) that grouped together and structured the single activity groups. Each single activity group (now "single role") was supposed to contain a clearly defined set of transactions. Therefore, those companies that wanted to define an authorization concept had three basic options:

▶ Defining large single roles that contain all the relevant transactions for a work center. These single roles became unreasonably large and increasingly person-specific instead of function-specific, which made changes to them difficult. The administrator could no longer use modular components.

▶ Defining small single roles that corresponded to one task. The result was that users had to be assigned many single roles, which meant an increased assignment effort for the user administrator.

▶ Some companies implemented an interim solution as a workaround. The single roles were created at the task level, and the resulting single profiles were grouped together into composite profiles; these composite profiles were assigned to the users instead of the composite roles.

With the introduction of composite roles, it became clear that the third solution was optimal for most companies, because the composite profiles could be converted to composite roles.

2.3.2 Transactions, Authorization Objects, and Authorizations

Even before the introduction of the Profile Generator—and of course afterwards—the SAP R/3 authorization concept was based on transactions and authorization objects, that is, on the relationship between these two entities. To improve your comprehension of these and other terms, we have included the following technical definitions:

▶ **Transaction**
A transaction corresponds to a function call in the SAP system. The transaction starts the corresponding program, for example, Transaction Code FB50 (G/L account posting) starts program SAPMF05A.

Release 4.6 contains more than 61,000 transactions. This doubling of transactions compared to prior releases resulted from reports and Customizing activities being assigned new, separate transaction codes in order to simplify the assignment of these functions. Reports no longer have to be protected only via the program name, authorization group, or customer-specific transaction code; now, they can also be protected by a clearly defined transaction code. Moreover, the technical name of a transaction can be up to 30 characters long in more recent releases, compared to the 4 characters previously allowed. Two report transactions from HR are excellent examples of these "new" transaction codes:

▶ S_PH9_46000216—Reporting of service anniversaries in HR management

▶ S_PH9_46000225—Reporting of powers of attorney in HR management

User authorizations for starting transactions are granted through authorization object S_TCODE (some modules require an additional authorization object, such as P_TCODE in Human Resources Management and I_TCODE in Service Management).

The SAP system typically enables you to control access to individual transactions flexibly.

▶ You can block all access (locking the transaction in Transaction Code SM01, for example, for module areas that have not been released yet or for especially critical functions).

▶ You can release them only for specific users by assigning the corresponding roles (or profiles), through the authorization concept.

▶ You can secure them through additional, customer-specific checks (by programming additional authorization objects or changing the system configuration).

▶ You can secure them through the authorization checks contained in the coding (standard).

You will have to choose one of these options, based on your specific enterprise requirements, when you define your project-specific authorization concept.

▶ **Authorization objects**
Authorization objects protect access to a functional area or data area in the SAP system. The existence of an authorization object in the user buffer can be checked at various places in the system. The check can be performed both at the start of a transaction as well as anywhere within the program flow. Different objects can protect the same area together, and a single object can also protect several different areas. Some 900 authorization objects exist in Release 4.6, divided into some 40 object classes by functional area, such as Financial Accounting or Human Resources Management (you can call a list of object classes in Transaction Code SU21). Authorization object "S_TCODE—Check of Transaction Code at Transaction Start" is contained in object class "AAAB—Cross-Application Authorization Objects."

Each individual authorization object can contain between one and ten authorization fields, which have to be filled with specific single values or value ranges. Therefore, an authorization object is somewhat like a variable or a template with several fields, which can be filled with different values.

The possible fields of an authorization object are defined in the AUTH* tables and structures.

► **Authorizations**

You can define any number of instances for a given authorization object. First, you must define an additional *value set object*, the set of permissible values for the fields of the corresponding authorization object, which is also referred to simply as an *authorization*. Therefore, an *authorization* is an expression of an authorization object in which all fields are filled with specific field values, in accordance with the authorization concept. The individual authorizations can be displayed in Transaction Code SU03, in line with their classification by object class and authorization object.

The *authorization check* is always based on an AND combination, which means the checks of all fields contained in an authorization object have to be successful in order for the authorization check to pass.

An example from Financial Accounting illustrates the relationship between the aforementioned three terms: Table 2.3 lists the authorization objects that can be checked within Transaction FB50—G/L account posting.

Object	Field
F_BKPF_BUK	Company code (BUKRS)
	Activity (ACTVT)
F_BKPF_BUP	Authorization group (for posting periods) (BEGRU)
F_BKPF_GSB	Business area (GSBER)
	Activity
F_BKPF_KOA	Account type (customers, vendors, assets, G/L accounts, material) (KOART)
	Activity (ACTVT)
S_TCODE	Transaction (TCD)

Table 2.3 Authorization Objects and Fields for Transaction FB50

Specific field values are entered in the authorizations for each of the defined fields in the authorization object. These values determine the access privileges within the transaction, for example, for a single company code, a business area, or an account type. You can also set field ACTVT to choose between write and read-only access. Possible values of the individual fields in an authorization are listed in Table 2.4.

As the following table shows, many different authorizations are possible, depending on the number of company codes and business areas, as well as the degree of detail required in the authorization concept.

Field	Possible values
Company code	Dependent on Customizing settings, i.e., 0001
Authorization group	* (according to Customizing/master data entry)
Business area	Dependent on Customizing settings, i.e., 01
Account type	D, K, A, S, M
Transaction	FB50
Activity	01—Create 02—Change 03—Display

Table 2.4 Possible values of the authorization fields for Transaction Code FB50

Figure 2.3 illustrates a sample flow of the individual authorization checks that can take place in Transaction Code FB50. Of course, the check of individual authorizations that occur during the course of a transaction always depends on which functions a user selects within the transaction (that is, which menu items or buttons are selected). Tables USOBT and USOBX contain the authorization objects that are required in the typical course of each transaction.

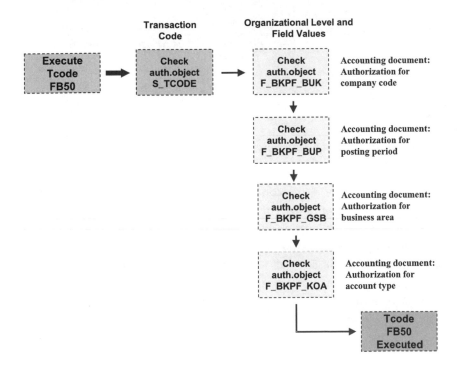

Figure 2.3 Transaction Code FB50—Authorization Check

2.3.3 Enterprise Structure and Organizational Levels

The organizational levels available in the standard SAP system enable you to model your entire enterprise structure, with all its enterprise areas. You then model your customer-specific enterprise structure as organizational levels and areas in Customizing. Transaction SUPO lets you display and maintain all organizational levels that are relevant for the Profile Generator (see Section 5.2.5 for more information). Transaction SUPO should not be used in Release 4.5 and in later releases. From this release onward, various reports are available for displaying and modifying organizational levels (see SAP Note number 323817 for more details).

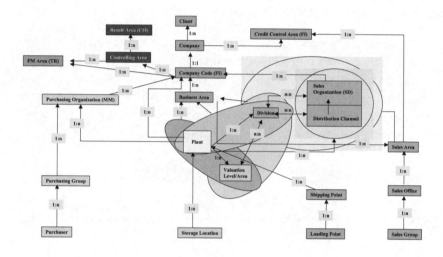

Figure 2.4 Examples of different organizational levels and their intermodular relationship (FI, CO, TR, MM, and SD)

With few exceptions (such as the company code), the organizational levels that are subjected to the authorization check vary by module. Most of the organizational levels have functional relationships, as shown in Figure 2.4 (refer to the SAP documentation for more information): it shows an overview of the relevant organizational levels in the Sales and Distribution, Materials Management, and Financial Accounting modules. You can clearly see the module-specific hierarchical relationships between the organizational levels. You will also note the exceptional role that the company code (field BUKRS) plays.

Chapters 4 and 5 describe a procedure for properly configuring the authorizations within the organizational and field values. This aspect is very important, because of its immediate impact on the number of authorizations needed, and on the overall effort required for the project.

2.3.4 Roles

In the SAP R/3 environment, the entire security and authorization concept is based on function-specific units called *roles* (roles were called *activity groups* in Release 4.6B and earlier). Roles perform a key function, as they control not only authorization assignments, but also the appearance of the user interface—via the role-specific user menus.

A *role* contains some transactions that the corresponding user requires to perform his or her daily and periodic activities. You use the Profile Generator to transfer these transactions to a role (in the role menu). The Profile Generator proposes the appropriate authorization objects and field values for these transactions in accordance with the entries in tables USOBT_C and USOBX_C.

At the technical level, we differentiate between *single roles* and *composite roles* within the SAP system:

▶ **Single roles**
A single role contains a certain number of transactions and the corresponding authorizations, depending on the degree of detail and methodology of the chosen authorization concept. The size of a single role can vary; however, large single roles have been proven difficult to handle in practice. When the method introduced in Chapters 4 and 5 is used, a single role contains the semantically related transactions of a subitem within the SAP menu tree.

Table USOBT contains the authorization objects and field values for each transaction that the Profile Generator proposes for a role containing this transaction (see example Table 2.3 in the case of Transaction Code FB50). For a role to function properly, all field values of the authorization must be filled correctly and completely. Finally, the Profile Generator creates the appropriate single profile for the role during the generation process. For details of the process for creating roles, see Chapter 5.

The single role serves as a type of "container" that permits the Profile Generator to collect transactions and generate the corresponding authorization profiles from them.

▶ **Composite roles**
To better structure the developed roles, you can group single roles together to form composite roles. A composite role represents a work center and its corre-

sponding tasks and areas of responsibility, and always consists of at least one single role in the method described in the next chapters of this book. When combining single roles into composite roles, you should always keep the *functional separation* (*dual control principle*) in mind—that is, a composite role should not contain combinations of single roles that have to be performed by different employees due to the nature of their functions (see Section 4.1.4).

Using composite roles also simplifies user administration, because you only have to enter the blanket composite role in the user master record, and not in all the single roles.

Role Design

Developing and defining the single roles and composite roles requires an integrated collaboration between the individuals both on the project team and in the user departments at your company. When determining the functions, it is imperative that you model the organizational structure that will apply when you go live. This is the single most important step in an implementation project.

Both units should have a similar granularity (level of detail for the units to be protected) and meaning (understanding of the user departments), system-wide and in all modules. You should implement organizational separation wherever necessary. Experience shows that only assign roles that are absolutely necessary should be defined. In particular, it is essential that the dual control principle is followed (internal control system (ICS)—see Chapter 3 and Section 4.1.4).

Chapters 4 and 5 describe a detailed, best-practice procedure for designing and creating single and composite roles.

Please note that the renaming of "activity groups" as "roles" resulted in misunderstandings of the meanings of these terms at many companies, because the term "role" is often already in use. When working on your project, please be mindful of the possibility of this misunderstanding.

Inheritance Function

Starting in Release 4.6, you can also use the *inheritance function* to design roles, which means that the new roles inherit functions and characteristics from a different role (the *template role*)—(see Figure 2.5 for more information). Some features of the inheritance function were already contained in Release 4.5; however, this release is still missing several important functions that would enable the practical use of the inheritance function at an acceptable effort. Therefore, practical considerations preclude the use of the inheritance function in releases earlier than Release 4.6.

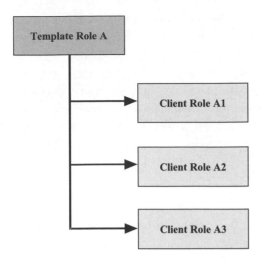

Figure 2.5 Template roles

The inheritance function enables you to define a template role, which can pass on its included transactions and their menu structure, as well as specific field values, to all derived roles. Subsequent changes only have to be implemented in the template role, and are then copied automatically to all the roles that are derived from the template role (see Section 4.3.5 for more information).

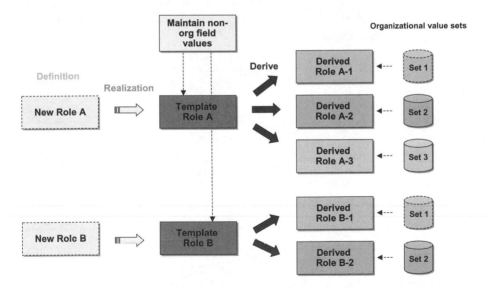

Figure 2.6 Inheritance functionality

The inheritance function lets you define roles that all contain the same functions (that is, the same transactions), but with different characteristic values for organizational levels such as the company code, controlling area, purchasing organization, plant, and so on. Different possible combinations of these organization levels that are based on a logical outline are called an "organizational value set." These template roles then form the basis for inheritance, as shown in Figure 2.6 (also see Section 4.3.5 for more information). All other roles can be entered in the system as single roles, in the conventional manner that we just described.

2.3.5 Authorization Profiles

Once the single role has been created in the system, the Profile Generator in the SAP system automatically generates the corresponding *authorization profile*, based on defined naming conventions, when you generate the corresponding authorization profile. Developers previously had to perform this step manually, prior to the availability of the Profile Generator (see Section 5.3.7).

Each user can be assigned a single profile in his or her user master record in addition to a role. Any maintenance of a generated profile must be performed through the role, however. To create a clear, well-structured authorization concept, we recommend assigning roles and composite roles exclusively, and only assigning single roles in exceptional cases (see Chapter 4). The authorization profiles contain the authorizations that are defined by an authorization object and the corresponding fields and values.

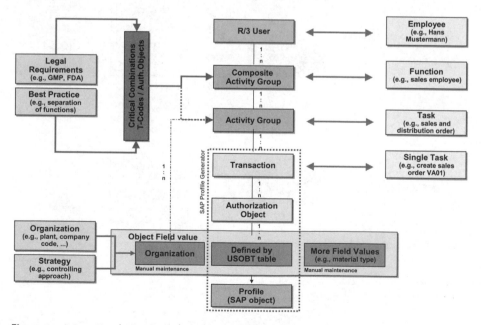

Figure 2.7 Interaction between technical and organizational components

Because the authorization checks in the system still take place using the authorizations contained in the profile (and not those authorizations from the role), you have to create and generate the profile—even though it is of no further use to the authorization concept.

Figure 2.7 shows the relationships between the technical, SAP-oriented view of an authorization system and the organizational view. All terms are portrayed based on how they interact with one another.

2.3.6 Technical Procedure—SAP Profile Generator

The next section briefly describes the process flow and possible options. For a detailed explanation and additional information, refer to *Authorization Made Easy* (see Bibliography).

Single Roles

You start the Profile Generator with menu path **Tools · Administration · User Maintenance · Roles** (or Transaction Code PFCG). The initial screen (see Figure 2.8) shows the first steps in defining and creating roles with the Profile Generator.

When you enter the technical name of the single role and the short and long descriptive texts (we recommend following defined naming conventions for the short text), you first create the corresponding role menu for the role. The following three methods are available, among others:

▶ **Selection from the SAP standard menu**
The developer is given the full standard menu, from which he or she can select the transactions that are to be included in the role.

▶ **Selection from an SAP area menu**
To reduce the number of transactions offered for selection, you can select transactions from predefined sections of the SAP standard menu.

▶ **Selection from role-based menus**
You can select an existing role menu to display an even smaller selection of functions. Only those transactions that are contained in the role menu of the underlying role are offered for selection.

Transactions and reports can also be inserted simply by entering the name of the transaction or report in the role menu. You can also add Internet and intranet links directly, in addition to the SAP transactions (see Figure 2.9).

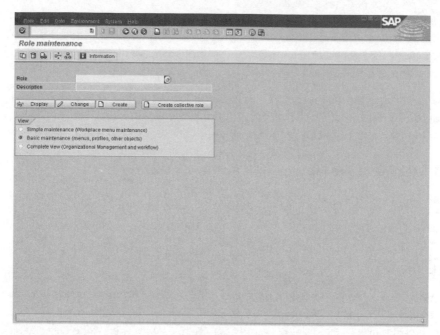

Figure 2.8 Profile Generator—Initial screen

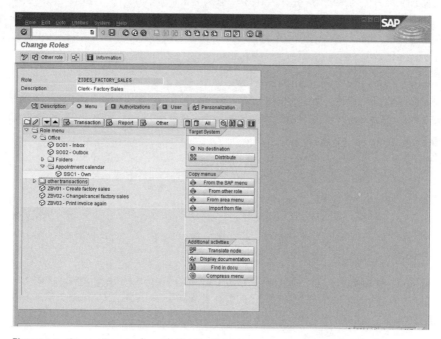

Figure 2.9 Generating a role with the Profile Generator

After you define a role, the Profile Generator can read all the authorizations required for that role. The authorizations required to execute a transaction are saved for information purposes in tables USOBT (or USOBT_C) and USOBX (or USOBX_C) and are retrieved during role creation.

The field values/value ranges for the role are then maintained for these authorizations in a second step, along with the organizational units of the respective enterprise. The Profile Generator sets several fields in accordance with the table entries; the authorization developer can then modify and overwrite these fields in line with your company's specific needs (see Section 5.2.1 for more information). The displayed traffic lights indicate the maintenance status of the authorizations—that is, whether all relevant fields have been filled with values (see Figure 2.10 and the SAP Online Documentation *Role Maintenance: Elements of the Hierarchy Display*).

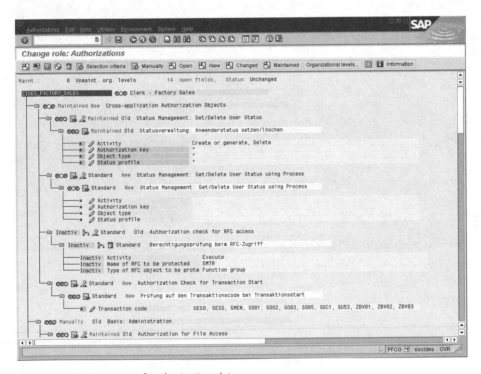

Figure 2.10 Maintenance of authorization data

The display of the authorization data is divided into the object class, the authorization object, and the contained authorization fields. Changes to and the maintenance status of the authorizations are displayed in the *status text* (for more information, see the SAP Online Documentation *Role Maintenance: Elements of the*

Hierarchy Display). The meanings of the traffic lights and the relevant status display are described in detail in Section 5.2.1.

To ensure that the role functions properly, all open fields have to be maintained manually, so that all the displayed traffic lights are green. Do not generate the authorization profile until this point. The generated role can then be assigned to the user, either in the User tab page (see Figure 2.11), or in the user master record in Transaction Code SU01.

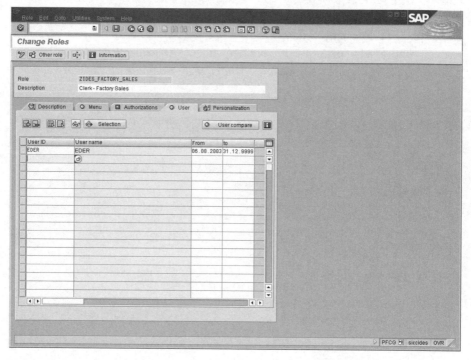

Figure 2.11 Assigning roles to users

Composite Roles

A *composite role* consists of one or more single roles. Because both the role menus (transactions) and the authorization profiles are copied from the single roles, transactions or authorization objects cannot be edited individually when creating composite roles.

You have to set the **Composite Role** field in the initial screen for role creation (Transaction Code PFCG). After you assign the name (see Section 2.3.7 for more information) and maintain the short/long text description, you group the single roles together and insert them into the composite role (see Figure 2.12).

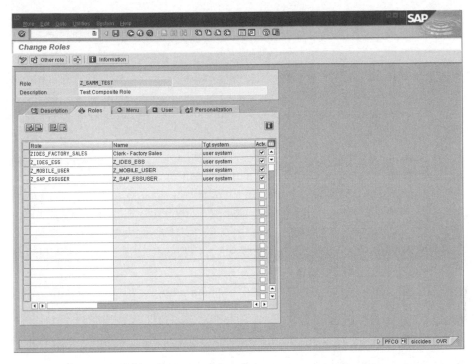

Figure 2.12 Assignment of single to composite roles

In the next step, you can import the individual role menus from the inserted single roles to the role menu of the composite role, and adjust them if necessary. You must pay attention to several technical settings during this process, which are described in more detail in Section 5.2.4.

Assign the composite roles to users as shown in Figure 2.11. To ensure that all authorization-relevant data is recorded automatically in the user master record, you must end every assignment with the user comparison, which should be scheduled to run daily as a batch job (see Section 5.4 for more information).

2.3.7 Naming Conventions

During the implementation of the SAP R/3 System, you must define separate names for all SAP elements (user-defined roles, composite roles, tables, ABAP/4 reports, and so on) of the authorization concept that your enterprise develops. To achieve a clear and concise logical structure of the authorization concept and subsequent administration, it is critical that you follow precise naming rules. SAP has defined naming conventions for all SAP elements, which are also adhered to in all new system releases; however, the available authorizations and roles in the SAP namespace can change after a release upgrade or update. Therefore, you should always create your own, customer-specific authorizations and roles; otherwise, you'll have to check and adjust each and every authorization and role after every system change (such as a release upgrade).

To distinguish the SAP names from the customer-specific names for SAP authorizations, do not use an underscore "_" as the second character of the SAP element's name. And, of course, customer-specific roles should never begin with "SAP_".

These naming conventions, and hence, the role names, are extremely important for two reasons: to separate the SAP namespace from the customer namespace; and, to enable the restrictive, area-based assignment of authorizations. The methods described in this book assume certain requirements of the naming conventions. These requirements ensure that the authorization concept can be administered easily and efficiently. The details of the naming conventions are described in Chapter 4.

The naming conventions must satisfy the following requirements and criteria:

▶ Uniqueness of the name
▶ Comprehensibility (the content of the role should be apparent from its code)
▶ All aspects that pertain to decentralized maintenance and administration of the roles should be adhered to.
▶ The customer namespace must start with Y or Z
▶ Do not use hyphens or underscores as the second character
▶ The first letter and separator of single roles should be different than those letters (or separators) used for composite roles
▶ Inclusion in major organizational levels (such as the company code in accounting or the plant in Materials Management)
▶ Brief code for the areas of responsibility (such as customer master data, material master data)

> **Examples** of the preceding requirements for naming conventions are listed in detail in Section 4.3.6.

2.3.8   Relevant SAP Tables for Authorizations and Roles

The relevant SAP tables for roles and authorizations are listed in Table 2.5. Like the tables for the user master data, these tables contain the corresponding data and the relationships between the individual units.

Table	Description
AGR_1016	Name of profile for activity group
AGR_1250	Authorization data for activity group
AGR_1251	Authorization data for activity group
AGR_1252	Organizational levels for authorizations
AGR_PROF	Profile name for activity group
AGR_SELECT	Assignment of activity groups to transaction codes
AGR_TCDTXT	Assignment of activity groups to transaction codes
AGR_TCODES	Assignment of activity groups to transaction codes
AGR_USERS	Assignment of activity groups to users
TOBJ	Objects
TOBJC	Classification of authorization objects
TOBJT	Texts for objects (for TOBJ)
TSTC	SAP transaction codes
TSTCA	Values for transaction code authorizations
TSTCP	Parameters for transactions
TSTCT	Transaction texts
USH04	Change history: authorizations
USH10	Change history: authorization profiles
USH12	Change history: authorization values
USKRIA	Critical combinations of authorizations for transaction codes
SUKRI	Security-critical combinations of transactions
USOBT	Relation transaction > authorization object
USOBT_C	Relation transaction > authorization object (customer)
USOBT_CD	Change history for field values
USOBX	Check table for table USOBT
USOBX_C	Check table for table USOBT_C
USORG	Organizational levels for Profile Generator
USPRO	Authorization profiles
USR07	Object and values of the last failed authorization check

Table 2.5 Tables for authorizations and roles

Table	Description
USR08	Table for entries in the user menus
USR09	Entries for the user menus (work areas)
USR13	Short texts for the authorizations

Table 2.5 Tables for authorizations and roles (Cont.)

2.3.9 Separation of Responsibilities in Administration

The maintenance of authorizations and their assignments to users, along with the associated administrative tasks, should be organized flexibly through a clear separation of responsibility between user administration and authorization administration.

Clear separation between user administration, authorization development, and authorization generation is a key prerequisite for apportioning the individual administrative tasks (see Section 5.6.2 for more information). The user administrator, for example, is responsible for creating a user master record and assigning the appropriate roles. Accordingly, you should assign responsibility for maintaining and generating the roles to someone else. By separating the responsibilities for user administration and authorization administration, you meet the requirements for both functional separation and system security.

However, many smaller companies cannot achieve this level of separation of responsibilities, because only one or two employees must manage all the various tasks. In exceptional cases, one person can perform both user administration and authorization administration. In this case, however, authorization development should be kept separate from the other areas, that is, the user administration responsibilities.

Authorizations for SAP User Administration

Table 2.6 lists an overview of the technical authorization objects that are relevant for separating responsibility for user and administration authorization. Appendix A lists the fields and potential field values for each authorization object in detail.

Object	Description
S_USER_GRP	User master maintenance: user groups
S_USER_AUT	User master maintenance: authorizations
S_USER_PRO	User master maintenance: authorization profile

Table 2.6 Authorization objects for user and authorization maintenance

Object	Description
S_USER_OBJ	Authorization system: global deactivation of authorization objects
S_USER_SYS	User master maintenance: system for Central User Administration
S_USER_VAL	Authorization system: field values in activity groups
S_USER_TCD	Authorization system: transactions in activity groups
S_USER_WWW	User master maintenance: Internet users
S_USER_AGR	Authorization system: check for activity groups

Table 2.6 Authorization objects for user and authorization maintenance (Cont.)

2.4 Default System Settings

To configure system-wide settings in SAP, you must maintain the profile parameters in the Computing Center Management System (CCMS—menu path **Tools · Administration · Computing Center Management System · Configuration · Profile Maintenance** or Transaction Code RZ11).

Transaction RZ10 provides structured documentation on the various profile parameters. You use these system profile parameters to define the runtime environment in terms of resources (such as main memory, buffers), services (number of work processes, for example), and the location itself (names, and so on). These parameters are saved in *profile files*.

Different profile files exist for different areas of validity. When you start the R/3 instance, the values of the profile parameters are retrieved as shown in Figure 2.13 (see also the SAP Online Documentation).[2] Several of these parameters, which are relevant for user and authorization management, are described below.

Most of the relevant parameters begin with "auth" or "login" and are therefore easy to spot in the profile. Many parameters have special variables that can be used for processing information or passing it on to a calling program. Because a detailed description of these parameters would exceed the scope of this book, please refer to the SAP Online Documentation for more information.

The specific parameters used for password rules were described in Section 2.2.4. The parameters in Table 2.7 refer to the authorization environment in general.

---

2 SAP Online Documentation: Computing Center Management System—Configuration—Profiles

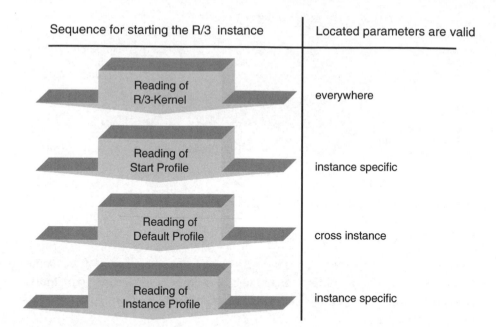

Sequence for starting the R/3 instance	Located parameters are valid
Reading of R/3-Kernel	everywhere
Reading of Start Profile	instance specific
Reading of Default Profile	cross instance
Reading of Instance Profile	instance specific

Figure 2.13 Instances and System Parameters

Parameter	SAP	Rec.	Description
Login/system_client	000		The production client is entered here.
Login/no_automatic_ user_sapstar	0	1	This parameter prevents logons with SAP* and the initial password PASS after the user master record for SAP* has been deleted.
Auth/no_check_in_ some_cases	Y (since 4.6)	Y	Transaction SU24 enables you to deactivate any authorization checks. The checks are only deactivated, however, when the parameter is set to Y. Required to use the Profile Generator.
Auth/rfc_authority_ check	1	1	Authorization check for RFC
Login/disable_multi_ gui_login	0	1	If this parameter is set, the system will block multiple R/3 dialog logons (in the same client and under the same user ID).
Login/multi_login_ users	, ,	ID	This list contains the R/3 logon names (without clients) of users who are authorized to have several concurrent logons in the system. Separate the user names by commas; blanks between the user names are not supported (for example: developer, hotline).

Table 2.7 System profile parameters (selection)

2.4.1 Instances and Profile Parameters

The set of all processes of an application server that can be started and stopped together and configured by a shared profile is called an *instance*. You can configure and maintain different profile parameters—for background processing, user and authorization values, and password rules—in an instance profile. When you have made changes to a profile, always use the available check, in order to omit the possibility of fundamental inconsistencies. The logical consistency of the profiles is checked—that is, whether the parameters contain the proper values from the specified value range, for example. New and changed parameters do not take effect until the active instance is shut down and restarted.

In addition to Transaction Code RZ10, you can display a full overview of the configured parameters in Transaction Code TU02 or report RSPARAM (call in Transaction Code SA38), as shown in Figure 2.14.

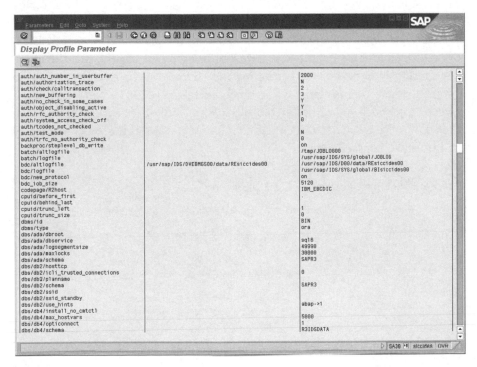

Figure 2.14 Report RSPARAM (excerpt)

Both the handling of and access to the profile files pose a severe risk, and are of primary importance to system security. Incorrect settings can cause significant drops in performance, among other things. Therefore, you should exercise a policy of restrictive access to profile files and only assign authorization to a selected group of users in the Basis administration. Moreover, as already described, you should always use the SAP user interface to maintain the profile parameters; otherwise, you won't have any versioning control. Then, you have to import the modified contents to the databases.

2.4.2 Transferring the SAP Proposals to the Customer Tables

The relationship between each SAP transaction and the corresponding authorization objects are defined in tables USOBT and USOBX. These tables contain the initial values for check indicators for the authorization objects of each transaction that are defined in the standard system. Before these default values can be customized for specific customers, you have to use Transaction Code SU25 (upgrade tool for the Profile Generator) to copy these default values to the customer-specific tables USOBX_C and USOBT_C (see Figure 2.15).

You can then use Transaction Code SU24 to maintain the default values for the check indicators that you just copied. For a detailed description, see Section 5.2.2 or the book *Authorization Made Easy*. You can set the tables to the check indicators described in Table 2.8. In this context, it is important to note that the check of a specific authorization object during the course of a transaction cannot be enforced simply by maintaining the object in tables USOBT_C and USOBX_C. Instead, the check indicators in table USOBX_C only define how the system responds to the authorization checks that are contained in the ABAP coding of the respective transaction.

Check indicator	Long text	Explanation
U	Not Maintained	No indicator has been set. The check is always performed. The object is not proposed in the Profile Generator.
N	No Check	The check is not active. The object is not proposed in the Profile Generator.
C	Check	The check is always performed. The object is not proposed in the Profile Generator.
CM	Check/Maintain	The check is always performed. The object is proposed for maintenance in the Profile Generator.

Table 2.8 Check indicators

You can display and change these assignments in Transaction Code SU24 (Transaction Code FB50 is shown as an example in Figure 2.16).

Two options are available for preventing the authorization check, both of which are described as follows:

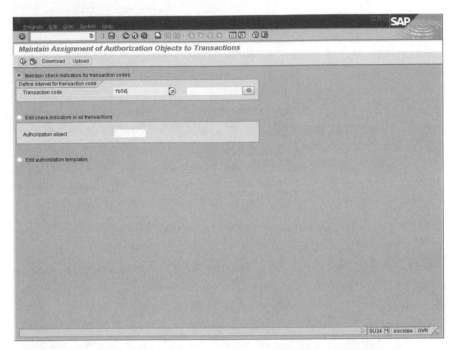

Figure 2.15 Assignment of Authorization Objects to Transaction Codes—Initial Screen

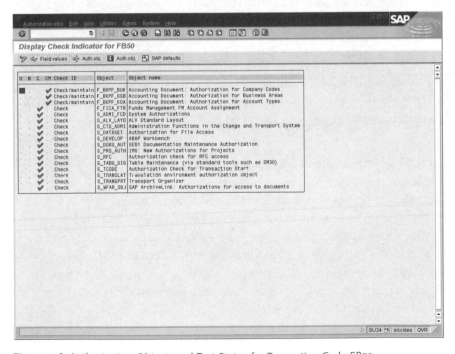

Figure 2.16 Authorization Objects and Test Status for Transaction Code FB50

- ▶ In the first option, you deactivate the authorization check globally, which deactivates the authorization check for an authorization object throughout the entire system. Use the Transaction Code AUTH_SWITCH_OBJECTS to perform this operation.

- ▶ In the second option, you define for each transaction whether you want to run the authorization check defined in the transaction. If not, you simply select the corresponding transactions and then set their check indicators to "N". You can also use the *Maintain check indicators for transaction codes* option in the initial screen of Transaction Code SU24 to change the check indicators of each individual transaction. All the authorization objects that are checked for the selected transaction are listed with their respective check indicators.

The following example illustrates each of these options.

Example: The optional authorization object F_KNA1_BED (account authorization) exists in the "Accounting" object class, with fields "Authorization group" and "Activity," to protect customer master records at account level. This authorization object enables you to divide the customers into authorization groups and then assign the responsibility for maintaining customers in a particular authorization group to a specific accounts receivable clerk. If you do not require protection at this level (that is, if each of your accounts receivable clerks is authorized to maintain all of your customers), you can exclude this authorization object from the authorization check using one of the options previously described.

If you want to run an authorization check of the *authorization group* to maintain customer master records, but not to display them, you should deactivate the authorization check for the display transaction in SU24.

If your company has created its own transactions or authorization objects that use authorization checks, you will have to add them to tables USOBT_C and USOBX_C manually with Transaction Code SU24 and set the appropriate check indicator. Generally, you should never manually add authorizations in the Profile Generator—only in exceptional cases. Instead, you should always use Transaction Code SU24 to add the corresponding authorizations to table USOBT_C. Although the initial maintenance requires more effort, in the long run, it will make it easier to create additional roles for similar cases, improving ease-of-maintenance, transparency, and uniformity of the live system.

2.5 Authorization Checks in the SAP Applications

As described in Section 2.3.2, the authorization concept classifies authorization objects in module-specific authorization classes. Transaction SU03 displays a list of all authorization objects, summarized by authorization class (see Figure 2.17).

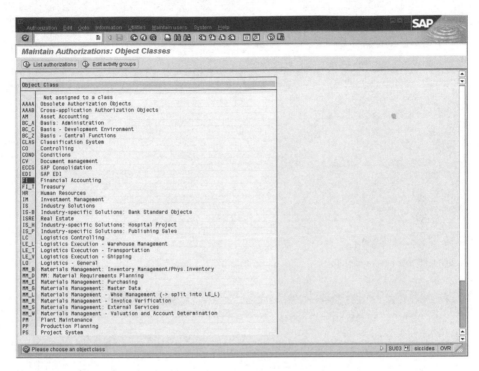

Figure 2.17 Object Classes

Select a class and press the **Documentation** button to display documentation for an authorization object contained in that class (see Figure 2.18). The fields and technical names of the authorization objects that are displayed when you press the **Display fields** button (Figure 2.19), along with any displayed field values, are the relevant terms for the authorization check performed in the system.

Each transaction starts a corresponding program and the name of that program is stored (maintain with Transaction Code SE93). For Transaction Code S_BCE_ 68001400, for example (users by complex search criteria), the corresponding program is RSUSR002. For the previous example of Transaction Code FB50, the corresponding program is SAPMF05A.

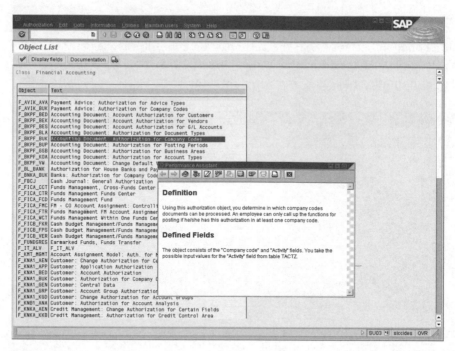

Figure 2.18 Authorization Objects—Documentation

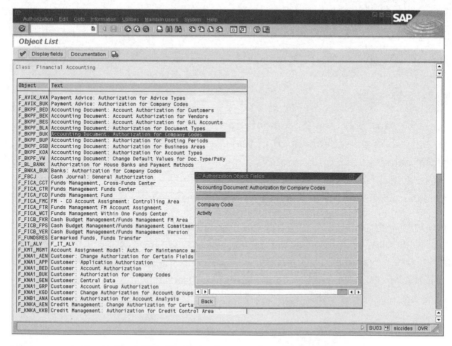

Figure 2.19 Authorization Fields for Authorization Object F_BKPF_BUK

One way of finding authorization checks in the program code is to search the source text of the ABAP program for the string "AUTHORITY" in the ABAP Editor (Transaction Code SE38). This search displays all the authorization checks within the respective program. Figure 2.20 shows the check of authorization object F_BKPF_GSB for the FI business area, with the corresponding fields, within the source text of program SAPMF05A.

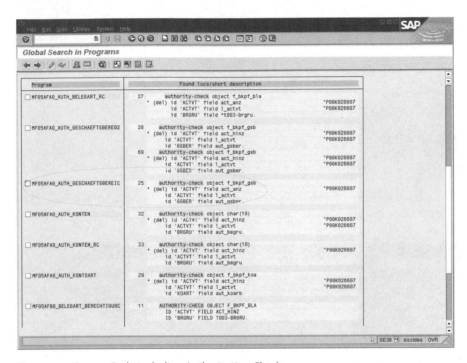

Figure 2.20 Source Code including Authorization Check

After the AUTHORITY-CHECK statement, the return value of system field SY-SUBRC indicates whether access in general and the tested type of access specifically are permitted. If the field is set to a value other than zero, access is denied. Figure 2.21 illustrates this situation for authorization object F_BKPF_GSB.

Example: The functionality of the AUTHORITY-CHECK was already shown above based on authorization object F_BKPF_GSB (accounting document: authorization for business areas). The documentation provides the following help for the object:

▶ **Definition**
Use this authorization object to define which business areas can be used to process, display, and evaluate document items.

▶ **Defined fields**
The object consists of the fields "Business area" and "Activity."

▶ **Business area**
Determine which business areas are allowed to perform the defined activities.

▶ **Activity**
Determine which activities are allowed. The following values are possible:

- ▶ 01—Add or create
- ▶ 02—Change
- ▶ 03—Display
- ▶ 08—Display change documents
- ▶ 77—Park
- ▶ *—All activities

As the previous description shows, the field IDs for the business area, GSBER, and the activity, ACTVT, are saved in the program coding (as illustrated in Figure 2.21).

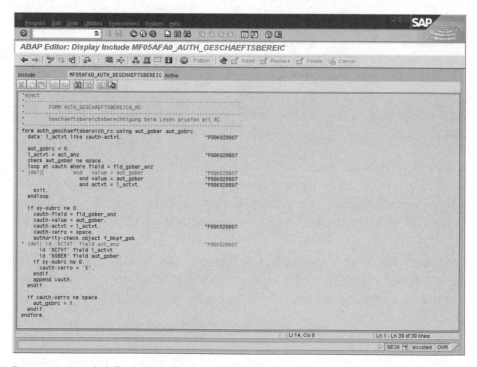

Figure 2.21 Detailed Illustration of an AUTHORITY-CHECK

If parameters do not have to be checked, the key word DUMMY is used instead of the required field value (such as ACTVT). If the AUTHORITY-CHECK is passed (that is, the return value SY-SUBRC = 0), the data that belongs to this business area can be processed. If not, a message that is defined in the program coding (MESSAGE E305 . . .) is output.

The ABAP AUTHORITY-CHECK command explicitly checks whether the user has the necessary authorization (for Transaction Code FB50 in this case). In the process, all the fields for the authorization are checked (value USA01 for field BUKRS, for example, or a wildcard value (*), which would grant access to all existing company codes).

You have to differentiate between two cases for the authorization check:

▶ **At the start of a transaction**
Authorization object S_TCODE and another, optional authorization object for each transaction (you maintain this object with Transaction Code SE93) are checked directly at the beginning of the transaction.

▶ **Authorization check in program flow**
In the course of ABAP programs, authorization checks are performed whenever the ABAP AUTHORITY-CHECK command appears and the authorization check has not been deactivated using one of the methods described. The program response to a failed authorization check is at the programmer's discretion. Usually, a message is output and the program cancelled. Another possible response to a failed authorization check is to deactivate or hide icons, function buttons, or data fields.

Authorization checks can generally be added anywhere within a program, by inserting the AUTHORITY-CHECK command at the appropriate position. We recommend the exclusive use of Transaction Code SU24 to maintain the object for the corresponding transactions in tables USOBT_C and USOBX_C.

In some cases, none of the available authorization objects meets your demands. In this case, you can create new authorization objects. Choose menu path **Tools ·** **Workbench · Development · Other tools · Authorization Objects · Objects** (**· Fields**), or call Transaction Code SU20 and SU21 directly. First select an object class for the new object and then create the object in accordance with the valid naming conventions. Figure 2.22 shows the required information.

You can select the fields for the new authorization object from the selection list of existing fields. You can also use Transaction Code SU20 to create new, additional fields. As the selection in Figure 2.23 shows, each field is displayed with a list of the authorization objects that have been assigned to it.

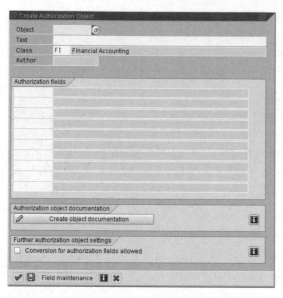

Figure 2.22 Authorization Objects Input Screen

Again, you should only define new authorization objects and fields in exceptional cases.

Create Authorization Object

Object ⟨⟩
Text
Class   FI   Financial Accounting
Author

Authorization fields

Authorization object documentation
✎ Create object documentation

Further authorization object settings
☐ Conversion for authorization fields allowed

✓ 💾 Field maintenance ℹ ✖

Figure 2.23 Additional Fields Input Screen

2.6   Protecting Tables

The underlying component of the relational data model is the storage of all data in tables (relations). A *table* is a two-dimensional matrix that consists of columns and identically structured lines that represent relations within the database system.

The SAP system uses tables to store both application data (master and transaction data) and system data (Customizing values). Tables are divided into client-specific and client-independent tables. Tables are usually accessed through application or Customizing transactions (SE11, SE16, SM31, OBA5, and so on). To control access, tables are grouped together in authorization groups, for which the explicit authorizations have to be assigned. In the standard SAP system, however, most of the tables aren't assigned to an authorization group (authorization group &NC& is assumed explicitly). To protect these tables, you can change the assignment from this pseudo-authorization group to a standard or customer authorization group. Because changing table assignments is a modification to the SAP standard itself, we recommend that you only modify those tables where the risk (i.e., that incorrect changes can result in inconsistent data or an unwanted system response for Customizing tables) is very high.

In general, we recommend that you never maintain tables directly in the production system. However, if you do have to maintain tables in a production system (in exceptional cases), ensure that you generate the appropriate table maintenance dialog. Access to the table must be controlled through authorization groups. The authorization groups for authorization object S_TABU_DIS are maintained in table TBRG; the assignment of existing tables in the SAP system to the defined authorization groups is defined in table TDDAT. You can also use Transaction Code SE54 to access this assignment. If necessary, you can also use authorization object S_TABU_CLI for cross-client table maintenance, in addition to authorization object S_TABU_DIS.

SAP R/3 Release 4.6 features a new authorization object, S_TABU_LIN, which enables you to grant authorization for specific lines of a table. You can use this object to restrict access to certain data ranges and work areas within the table, for example, to specific plants, or company codes.

You have to define adequate naming conventions for the necessary authorization groups in table maintenance, in order to ensure that the authorizations have a clear structure. Names of authorization groups are limited to four characters in length.

You no longer have to define authorization groups for programs, because programs and reports are accessed by calling transactions from area menus in Release

4.6 and later (as described in Section 2.10). Accordingly, you should no longer assign Transaction Code SA38 for end users. Authorization groups for table maintenance, in contrast, are still required.

In addition to configuring authorization groups to protect tables, you should also activate logging for all posting/reporting-relevant tables to ensure that all changes to such tables are recorded. All reporting-relevant tables must be configured for logging and archiving in line with local statutory requirements. Two parameters are available in the SAP system for setting the logging flag:

▶ In the system parameters (instance profile, evaluate with RSPARAM; see Section 2.4.1 for details), you can set parameter `rec/client` to define the clients in which logging is generally active. However, you can only check the logging for the application server where you are currently logged on. For performance reasons, we recommend that you only set the `rec/client` parameter for the production clients of an SAP system.

▶ You also have to set the logging flag for all tables that are relevant for accounting. You configure this in Transaction Code SE16 for table DD09L. Table 2.9 only lists a few of the tables with required logging from the FI, MM, and Basis modules.

Module	Table	Description
BC	T000	Clients
BC	TSTC	Transaction code management
BC	TBRG	Authorization groups for tables
BC	TDDAT	Authorization groups analyzable by table
BC	TACTZ	Valid activities for each authorization object
BC	TADIR	Development objects with reference to original system (WBOT)
BC	TSYST	Directory of available systems (WBOT)
BC	TASYS	Description of transport routes (WBOT)
FI	T001*	Company code
FI	T003*	Document types
FI	T004*	Charts of accounts
FI	T007*	Tax codes
FI	T008*	Blocking reasons for automated payment transactions

Table 2.9 Tables with required logging (selection)

Module	Table	Description
FI	T011*	Balance sheet/P&L structure
FI	T012*	House banks
FI	T030	Table of standard accounts
FI	T030*	Account determination
FI	T033*	Payment transactions
MM	T001K	Valuation area
MM	T001L	Storage locations
MM	T003	Document types
MM	T024E	Purchasing organization
MM	T025	Valuation classes
MM	T030D	Account determination for exchange rate differences for open items

Table 2.9 Tables with required logging (selection) (Cont.)

Logging and history tracing will only be activated for the tables that are transported from the development system to the live system (via the Correction and Transport System) when SAP system parameter **r3transoptions** has been set correctly in parameter file **tpparam** (this is the **tp** program at operating-system level). The settings for the transport system are defined in parameter file **tpparam** and are typically located in directory **\usr\sap\trans\bin** at operating-system level. To guarantee that Customizing changes imported to the live system are logged, you have to set parameter **r3transoptions** to the production client or to ALL.

You should evaluate the table change logs and history of changes regularly (using reports RSTBPROT and RSTBHIST, respectively).

According to statutory regulations and expert opinions, the person responsible for accounting is required to document the system settings (Customizing) and program changes that affect the accounting processes. Therefore, it must be possible for third parties to audit program changes and Customizing settings throughout the statutory retention period.

2.7 Protecting Reports

2.7.1 ABAP/4 Programs

The development of ABAP/4, a language for business application programming, began in the early 80s and has continued ever since. The name *ABAP* is an acronym for *Advanced Business Application Programming*. *ABAP/4* has all the features of a true fourth-generation programming language, especially its manageability, its functionality, and its versatility.

A program written in ABAP/4 is referred to as an ABAP program or, colloquially, simply as ABAP. An ABAP/4 program can be classified further depending on how its results are generated.

ABAP programs that generate a list or analysis are traditionally called "reports." This class of programs is primarily used to create lists and analyses, most of which are quite extensive. In addition, an extended form of reporting can include an interactive user dialog, in which the user can control the process flow of the report through direct input and the function keys provided.

2.7.2 Protecting Programs

In the past, access to SAP programs was protected by authorization groups. These authorization groups are part of the program attributes. Because this method resulted in various risks and problems (creating authorization groups, maintaining the authorizations, call via Transaction Code SA38), access to reports was restricted through *report trees* in releases up to Release 4.5:

▶ Using authorization groups in the program attributes associated with accessing Transaction Code SA38

▶ Using report trees; access protection is provided through the respective report tree transaction

In Release 4.6 and later, the extended area menu functionality has completely replaced the previous report trees. The SAP system only permits the display of report trees or their conversion to area menus. The other report tree functions are no longer supported (e.g., display only). In addition, the conversion of report trees to area menus gives each report its own transaction code through which it can be protected.

You define which roles will be authorized to execute which ABAP programs and reports during the project phase. You then have to structure the new area menus accordingly, based on this information. The individual project teams (department teams) are responsible for having their custom reports included in the right locations in the new area menus (a sample area menu is shown in Figure 2.24).

You can use Transaction Code RTTREE_MIGRATION to convert existing report trees from older SAP versions to the new area menu function, which reduces the amount of manual migration effort required. The existing roles that previously enabled access to the report trees have to be modified after the report trees are migrated. Because each report has its own transaction code in the new area menu in Release 4.6 and later, the roles that are affected have to be extended with the appropriate S_TCODE authorizations for the corresponding reports. Any authorization groups that were used to launch the reports in the previous roles should then be deleted. Because of the great risk that unprotected reports could cause severe damage to system integrity and thereby permit unauthorized access to sensitive data, the importance of a uniformly implemented authorization concept is critical.

2.7.3   Using Customer-Developed Transactions

Customer-developed transactions are dealt with in a similar manner to customer-developed ABAP programs and reports. Here, as well, you should integrate these objects (i.e., transactions, programs, and reports) in the area menus, in order to provide users with a uniform access method (specifically, the user menu). This uniform implementation of an authorization concept will also ensure uniform authorization processes. In all other aspects, the information described in the previous section on reports also applies to customer transactions.

Figure 2.24 Inserting customer transactions and nodes into a new area menu

2.8 Basis Security

In addition to the reporting and tables areas, a significant number of other authorizations exists in the Basis environment, whose critical importance demands special attention within any SAP R/3 authorization concept. You should restrict these Basis authorizations to a small, select group of users, and not grant them to functional users in the user departments. Unfortunately, no general recommendations can be made on restricting or granting authorizations for these transactions or authorizations, as the requirements depend on the structure and security needs of each specific enterprise. The following information is intended as a guide to help you examine the underlying processes during the creation of an authorization concept; however, it is by no means complete.

2.8.1 Preliminary Remark

Because of their inherent importance to data integrity, you must pay particular attention to the areas requiring protection and their basic protection recommendations. Certain transactions and objects in the Basis area should not be assigned to users, or, if assigned, done so only under tight restrictions. Nonetheless, certain authorizations from this area also have to be granted to non-Basis users, for example, to enable batch processing and printing. You have to restrict these authorizations accordingly and integrate them in the respective functions. Because we already covered in detail the aspects of reporting and table security in Sections 2.6 and 2.7, respectively, they are not repeated here.

2.8.2 Affected Basis Authorizations

This section introduces several transactions and the respective underlying authorization objects for each area.

Transaction Management—SM01/Custom Transactions—SE93

Authorization for blocking and unblocking transaction codes should only be granted to a select group of users. This also applies to the creation of customer-developed transactions. If your company defines its own transactions, you have to equip them with the following authorization checks:

▶ Authorization check when the transaction is started (entry in table TSTCA through Transaction Code SE93)

▶ Further authorization check, if necessary, through an AUTHORITY-CHECK statement in the program coding

System Change Option—SCC4

We recommend that you set the System Change option of live systems to "No Changes." Only system administrators should be authorized to activate and deactivate this function. The System Change option for the individual objects (programs, screen masks, menus, tables, and structures) must be defined manually within each R/3 System. This option applies to objects that customers have developed or enhanced by themselves, as well as the objects provided by SAP.

Background Processing—SM36

Under the default settings, every user is authorized to schedule reports for background processing, but not release them. An authorization for authorization object S_BTCH_JOB is required to release such jobs (activity RELE). Activity PROT is required to enable the log display. The authorizations for other operations such as delete, change, or move should only be assigned to the batch administrator. The "Job Group" field in object S_BTCH_JOB is not used in Release 4.6C and should always be set to "*".

Only the batch administrator should be granted authorizations for object S_BTCH_ADM (manage background processing and control access to jobs in all clients of a system—including the release of other users' jobs) in production systems.

You can use object S_BTCH_NAM (schedule jobs under a different user ID) to grant authorization to start batch jobs under a different user ID. The corresponding user name must be entered in one of the authorization fields. You should never grant this authorization with user name "*" in a live system, as this would allow the user to start batch jobs under any user ID, providing unauthorized access to all the authorizations that these user IDs possess.

This object is useful, however, to develop a department-specific concept for batch processing. If you define a batch user called FI_BATCH and give all users in your Accounting department the authorization to start batch jobs under this ID, this will ensure that department-specific batch jobs can only be started and processed by employees in that department.

Batch Input—SM35

Batch input sessions are processed in Transaction Code SM35, which requires an authorization for object S_BDC_MONI. You can restrict the privileges to certain sessions by entering the respective session name, or a name range (all sessions from Financial Accounting, for example). Of course, the specified naming conventions must be followed exactly for creating the sessions (through an interface to an external program, for example). You can also define which actions are permitted (delete, release, process, block, and so on) for the corresponding sessions.

The person who creates a session can specify the user ID whose privileges will be used to process the session later. As a result, anyone who is authorized to process batch input sessions should have the session processed by a different user. In this case, the specified user ID must have authorization for the transactions used to process the session. This alternate user ID is only required for background processing, however. If the creator of the session processes it in dialog, that user must have all the necessary authorizations in his or her master record.

Transport System and Workbench

Do not make any changes directly in the production system, in accordance with the system landscape. All changes must be implemented in the development system, and only transferred to the production system after testing in the quality assurance system. Therefore, it's critical that the Transport Management System (TMS) is designed adequately. The authorizations for transports, especially authorization and release, should be granted restrictively. The Correction and Transport System and the ABAP Workbench contain the following transactions:

▶ **Transaction SE09**
Maintain transport requests for Repository objects and cross-client Customizing

▶ **Transaction SE10**
Maintain transport requests for client-specific Customizing and maintain transport requests for Repository objects and cross-client Customizing

▶ **Transaction SE01**
Only for special transports

▶ **Transaction STMS**
Execute and approve transports; configure the transport landscape

▶ **Transaction SE03**
A collection of various utilities in the Correction and Transport System

▶ **Transaction SE11**
Maintain the ABAP/4 Dictionary

▶ **Transaction SE06**
Set up the Workbench Organizer

Authorization object S_TRANSPRT controls access to the Workbench Organizer, Customizing Organizer, and Transport Organizer. You can define the activity (such as 01 to create) for each request type (TASK for a task, for example, or CUST for a Customizing request). The TMS also uses authorization object S_CTS_ADMI. You can use it to enable various activities within the TMS (such as TABL configuration, IMPA/IMPS import, QTEA/TADM QA approval).

Computing Center Management System—SRZL

Object S_RZL_ADM generally protects the Computing Center Management System (CCMS). Depending on the activity, values can be maintained (value 01 — only assign to system administrators, as it enables major intervention in system control and system response) or only displayed (value 03). The same authorization object is used to protect the system profile parameters (see above, Transaction Codes RZ10 and RZ11). You can use authorization object S_ADMI_FCD to define additional activities within the CCMS.

Lock Management—SM12

Only the system administrators are allowed to delete their own and other users' locks in Transaction Code SM12 (field value ALL or DLFU for deleting other users' locks in object S_ENQUE, field value S_ENQ_ACT). Every user is authorized to display his or her own locks.

Update Tasks—SM13

Transaction SM13 is used to analyze the update process and handle update records. Authorization object S_ADMI_FCD protects this transaction. The **System Administration Function** field must be set to UADM. To prevent users from interfering with the update mechanism, ensure that only the system administrators are authorized to execute the update process.

Spool—SPAD/SP01

No standard user should be authorized to administer the configured printers (Transaction Code SPAD). Each employee should only be authorized to view his or her own output (Transaction Code SP02), at least in the production system. You can use system authorization S_ADMI_FCD to define the administration authorizations for the spool system and the TemSe database (value SP01 or SP0R for the **System Administration** field in S_ADMI_FCD); however, these administration authorizations only apply when the objects are not protected by other authorization fields. Spool requests that have authorization protection can be subjected to an authorization check with object S_SPO_ACT.

Logical Commands—SM49/SM69

Logical commands are defined and maintained in Transaction Code SM69 (object S_RZL_ADM, activity 01), and are executed in Transaction Code SM49 (same object and also S_LOG_COM). All activities—that is, definition and execution—should be restricted to a system administrator. Transaction SM69 is protected by authorization object S_RZL_ADM with activity 01. See Chapter 1 for information about the underlying security requirements at operating-system level.

Changes to Check Indicators in the Profile Generator—SU24

You should only grant restrictive access to Transaction Codes SU24 and AUTH_SWITCH_OBJECTS, as authorization checks can be deactivated here. See Sections 2.4.2 and 5.2.2 for detailed descriptions of these procedures. Execution requires object S_DEVELOP and object type SUSO.

Queries (Object S_QUERY)—SQ*

For each specific area, you have to develop a concept that documents the functional areas, the user groups, and the assignment of user groups to functional areas. In production and QA systems, you have to ensure functional separation between the developers/users of a query and the administrator responsible for configuring functional areas and user groups. The users should only be authorized to execute queries.

Customizing—Objects S_PRO_AUTH/S_IMG_ACTV

Customizing (Transaction Code SPRO) must generally only be permitted in the development system. In all other systems, Customizing must be locked. Some settings can be displayed with SO70.

All table changes made through Customizing (see Section 2.6 for more information) must be recorded in transport requests and transferred to the downstream systems (quality assurance, production) through the Correction and Transport System (see above).

User and Authorization Administration

Transactions and authorizations in this area must only be granted to administrators. For a detailed overview and information regarding the separation of responsibilities and functions, see the administration concept (Section 5.6.2).

Troubleshooting

This area includes transactions that are used for error localization, correction, and monitoring. These transaction codes are not typically used in functional authorizations.

- ▶ SM19—Configuration of security audit
- ▶ SM20—Security audit log evaluation
- ▶ SM21—Online evaluation of system log
- ▶ ST01—System trace
- ▶ STAT—Analyze users
- ▶ SU56—User buffers
- ▶ SM04—Overview of logged on users per instance
- ▶ AL08—Overview of logged on users in all instances

RFC Connections and ALE

Both of these areas should be defined in a separate project. In general, the following transactions (as well as all other transactions in this area) should be restricted to the corresponding administrators:

- ▶ SM59—RFC destinations (display and maintain)
- ▶ SMT1/SMT2—Trusted systems (display and maintain)
- ▶ SALE—Display ALE Customizing
- ▶ BALE—Area menu for administration
- ▶ BALM—ALE master data

2.9   HR Security

The Human Resources (HR module) area provides various other options for restricting access authorization, in addition to the options previously described. These additional options are required because the HR area contains critical personal data, which requires additional protection that cannot be provided by the standard functions used by the other modules—that is, a degree of protection that the logistics modules do not have to meet. Still, the relationships between transactions, authorization objects, and fields in tables USOBT* described above also apply in this area.

Note the following additional options. The standard protection options, such as reporting, HR clusters, and HR transaction codes, are not described in detail here.

If the organization of your Personnel department permits it, the additional options can be excluded from your specific implementation.

2.9.1 Authorization Objects—Authorization Main Switch

Like the other SAP modules, the Human Resources application in the SAP standard has a fixed number of authorization objects. The measures available in authorization object class "Human Resources" are often insufficient for implementing all the required security, however. In contrast to the other object classes, you can activate additional checks for the HR environment in Customizing. Set the *authorization main switch* in Transaction Code OOAC and notice that this function does not enable you to add just any authorization checks; instead, SAP provides a standard set of objects that can be activated (see Figure 2.25).

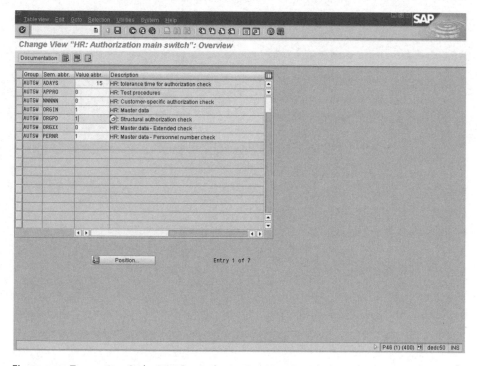

Figure 2.25 Transaction Code OOAC—Authorization Main Switch

Activating the authorization objects contained in the authorization main switch modifies the underlying entries for the Profile Generator, which means that the authorization check is added to the corresponding transactions automatically, and the Profile Generator utilizes the additional authorization objects during role creation. Transaction OOAC updates both table T77S0 for the authorization main switch[3] and all associated tables in the authorization environment (tables USOBT*).

The authorization main switch enables you to control the checks for the following authorization objects in the standard SAP system

▶ **P_ADAYS — Tolerance interval for the authorization check**
Use this authorization object when an employee is transferred, and you have to control the number of days that that employee can still access the data he or she created, even though that employee is now assigned to a different organization with different authorizations.[4]

Default setting: 15

▶ **P_APPRO — Test procedures**
Use this authorization object when it is active to add infotype 130 — test procedures. Before you can add the test procedures, however, you first have to define and save the underlying test procedures in the Implementation Guide.

Default setting: 0 (no check)

▶ **P_NNNNN — Customer authorization object**
Use this authorization object for a customer-specific authorization check in Human Resources. Configure the appropriate definitions for the relationship between transaction and authorization object (such as P_ORGIN, P_ORGXX, or P_PERNR) with Transaction Code SU24, both to fill the Profile Generator and to activate the authorization check.

Default setting: 0 (no check)

▶ **P_ORGIN — Master data**
Use this authorization object to restrict access to personnel master data. Because this is the SAP standard (i.e., because this object is the default for SAP), no further details are described here.

Default setting: 1 (check)

▶ **P_ORGPD — Structural authorizations**
Within Organizational Management, you can use structural authorizations to restrict access to employee data (see below).

Default setting: 0 (no check)

▶ **P_ORGXX — Master data: extended check**
If the protection for personnel master data in object P_ORGIN is not sufficient,

---

3 For information on the incorrect standard delivery of this table in Release 4.6B, including correction instructions, see SAP Note number 317722.
4 When you adjust this variable, you also have to change variable ALMOST_HIGH_DATE. This value equals the value of HIGH_DATE minus ADAYS, which is always 99991231. For more information, see SAP Note number 148495.

use this authorization object to select more criteria for an additional check (see below).

Default setting: 0 (no check)

▶ **P_PERNR—Master data: personnel number check**
If you activate this check, use this authorization object to restrict access to personnel master data, limiting access to only the employee's respective personnel number (see below).

Default setting: 0 (no check)

In releases prior to 4.6, you used program MPPAUTSW to activate the authorization main switch, instead of Transaction Code OOAC. In Release 4.6 and later, the activation is implemented directly in the program coding. The program does not, however, permit you to change the authorization objects P_ADAYS and P_APPRO, which don't even exist in some earlier releases.

2.9.2 Personnel Number Check

Authorization object P_PERNR enables a check of the employee's personnel number (and *only* that personnel number). In releases prior to 4.6, you also had to maintain table T513a (using maintenance view V_T513a), in addition to the activation in program MPPAUTSW (set P_PERNR to 1). This table saved each employee together with the respective personnel number used for the authorization check.[5] You also have to maintain the assignment in the personnel master with infotype 0105, subtype 0001.[6]

In Release 4.6 and later, this relationship is represented exclusively in infotype 0105, subtype 0001. It is required for the check and must be maintained accordingly. Table T513a is no longer used for the authorization check (whether or not the table will be deleted in future releases is an open issue). Report RPU46AXT513A is available for migrating table T513a to infotype 0105; report RPU46AXT513A_REPAIR is available to fix errors.[7]

If the personnel number-specific check is activated, it takes precedence over the checks from master data objects P_ORGIN and P_ORGXX, as well as the information regarding the access path from Organizational Management.

---

5 If your release does not offer additional protection in standard with P_PERNR, follow the instructions in SAP Note number 124949 to install it. For more information, see SAP Note number 130035.

6 For information on reports that compare the entries in table T513a with the assignments in the personnel master in each release, see SAP Note number 127225.

7 See SAP Note number 207516. SAP Note number 353861 describes the required modifications when upgrading to Release 4.6C due to the automatic delivery of table T77S0 if the plan version is not set to 01.

You can edit the following fields within authorization object P_PERNR:

▶ **AUTHC—Authorization level**
This field defines the actions (read, write, write blocked, and so on) that a user can perform on the underlying data.

▶ **P_SIGN—Interpretation of an assigned personnel number**
In this field, you can set the personnel number to E for "excluded authorizations for the assigned personnel number," and I for "including authorizations for the assigned personnel number. The full authorization (*) is not supported here (also applies to the addition of two authorization objects for infotype/subtype combinations with the interpretation E and I). Contrary to this official information, it was possible to implement the full authorization in some tests—that is, the entry "*" passed the authorization check.

▶ **INFTY—Authorization for infotypes**
In this field, you can list the HR infotypes for which the user is to have full access or none at all. The number ranges for infotypes have the following structure:

  ▶ Infotypes 0000-0999 are for personnel master data and (possibly) applicant data

  ▶ Infotypes 1000-1999 are for Organizational Management

  ▶ Infotypes 2000-2999 are for time data

  ▶ Infotypes 4000-4999 are for applicant data

  ▶ Infotypes 9000-9999 are available as the customer namespace

▶ **SUBTY—Subtype**
In this field, you can specify the corresponding subtypes as substructures for the infotypes.

2.9.3   Additional Master Data Check

You can use the standard check of authorization object P_ORGIN to include additional protection criteria with object P_ORGXX. You can also substitute P_ORGIN completely with P_ORGXX, instead of using them in a complementary manner. (In order to do this, you have to enter "0" to deactivate P_ORGIN in the authorization main switch.) The individual fields of additional master data check P_ORGXX have the following structure:

▶ Information about the administrator of the person to be processed (infotype: organizational assignment)

  ▶ SACHA—Payroll administrator

  ▶ SACHZ—Time recording administrator

- ▶ SACHP—Personnel master data administrator
- ▶ SUBMOD— Administrator group (characteristic PINCH)
  Organizational area of personnel or applicant management
▶ Information about the data that can be accessed
  - ▶ INFTY—Infotype
  - ▶ SUBTY—Subtype
▶ Information about the active authorizations for the data (read, write, and so on).
  - ▶ AUTHC—Authorization level

System processing of this object corresponds to that of authorization object P_ORGIN.

2.9.4 Structural Authorizations

If the Organizational Management component is installed in HR, the link to Human Resources Management can also be used to define structural authorizations. The employee/personnel data to be protected is defined with object type P. Two processes for configuring this function are available in the Implementation Guide (you also have to set the value for ORGPD to 1 in the authorization main switch, as described above) (see Figure 2.26):

▶ **Maintain structural profiles**
In this step, you define the authorizations that can be assigned (this can also be performed with Transaction Code OOSP).

▶ **Assign structural authorizations**
In this step, you assign the profiles that you maintained in the first step to the respective users.

Structural authorizations can contain the following information:

▶ **Object type**
The *object type* determines which objects are defined for the corresponding structural authorization. Figure 2.27 shows the input screen for defining structural authorizations.

You have to enter an appropriate object ID for each object type (such as the ID of an organizational unit).

▶ **Plan version**
You can select an existing plan version from the drop-down box.

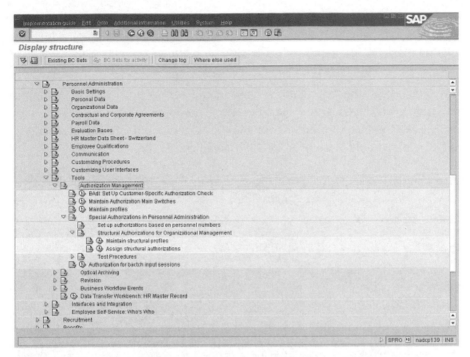

Figure 2.26 IMG—Structural Authorizations Setup

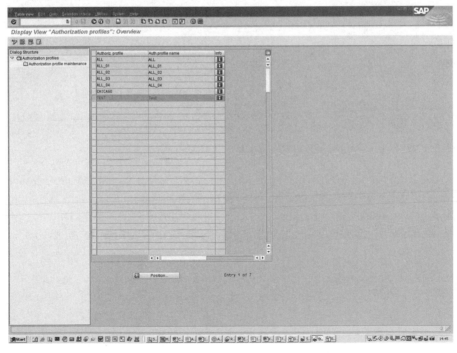

Figure 2.27 Authorization Profiles for Structural Authorizations

You can also use authorizations to restrict evaluation paths (selectable), status vectors (to be defined), display depth (to be defined), periods (selectable), and function modules (to be defined). The structural authorizations contain the individual entries in the relevant fields.

Now, you assign the generated profiles to the users—possibly with temporal restrictions, which you define in a table entry. The following example shows user ID CHICAGO with authorization profile CHICAGO without any date restrictions, that is, released until December 31, 9999 (see Figure 2.28).

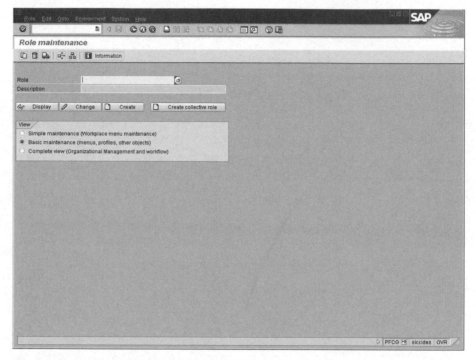

Figure 2.28 Assignment of Users to Structural Authorizations

To save the assignments permanently in the system, run report RHBAUS00. While this report can be started manually, we recommend scheduling it as an overnight batch job (see SAP Note number 21933). Permanent saving is especially recommended for users with the all-encompassing structural authorizations, that is, large profiles.

The SAP Service Marketplace contains several relevant notes on structural authorizations, which also include any necessary corrections. The following notes are of particular interest:

▶ **SAP Note number 50076**

HR-OM [Human Resources/Organizational Management]: Structural authorization—no authorization

▶ **SAP Note number 339367**
Access of personnel number with default position

▶ **SAP Note number 363083**
Maintenance of the switch AUTH_SW P_ORGPD

▶ **SAP Note number 339378**
Structural authorization check in PA30 is incorrect

Now, unwanted side effects can result from the use of structural authorizations in combination with the master data authorization object P_ORGIN. If different substructures and separate authorizations are used for infotypes, inheritance can take place between the substructures. In future, this will be corrected by a new authorization object, P_ORGCON. This object, whose structure is identical to that of P_ORGIN, contains an additional field with a reference to the underlying substructure.

2.9.5 More Authorization Checks That You Can Activate

You can make entries in table T77S0 to activate additional authorization checks in HR.

▶ **Personnel Development—PPPM**
If you set integration switches PLOGI QUALI and PLOGI APPRA (for qualifications and appraisals) to 1 for Personnel Development, this activates additional checks against infotypes 0024 (qualification) and 0025 (appraisals). These values have to be used in authorization object P_ORGIN for Personnel Development (see SAP Note number 440559).

▶ **Employee Self Service—ESS (216036)**
To enable use of the Employee Self Service (ESS), you have to set P_PERNR to 1 in the authorization main switch (field PSIGN must be set to I). Infotype 0105, subtype 0001, which is described above, is also required for each user. Be sure to investigate the potential side effects with active authorizations in the personnel area (such as PA30—see SAP Note number 216036).

▶ **Shift planning (PLOG)**
The standard access protection provided by authorization object PLOG (shift planning) can be supplemented and refined by adding structural authorizations (see SAP Note number 496993 for a detailed description of the available options).

2.9.6 Conclusion

Developing authorizations for the HR environment, as you can deduce from the complexity of this task, is no easy feat. You first have to examine the necessary protection levels and their potential implementation in the SAP system before you can decide which additional tools you need to activate and use. The more complex the defined authorizations are, the more difficult it is to analyze the authorization errors that occur. "Often it is not enough for SAP to simulate the problem to find the cause."[8]

An additional factor of complexity arises when you use the HR module and other Financials or Logistics modules in the same system and client. Because HR authorization objects and HR infotypes are required for several logistics activities (such as viewing the partner role in an SD order, as well as several matchcode analyses), you have to pay particular attention to the potential interaction with active authorizations in the HR area (such as entering trips, hours/overtime worked, on-call duty, and leave in CATS). Non-critical display authorizations for infotypes (such as address data) may be passed on through active HR transactions, which will result in unintended display authorizations.

The assignment of HR authorization objects and transactions should be restricted exclusively to functions or roles within the Personnel department. Comprehensive testing of the authorizations here is extremely important—even more so than in other areas.

2.10   New Features in Release 4.6

With the advent of Release 4.6, comes a wide assortment of changes to the authorization environment, which are described below (refer to the SAP Online Documentation for more information):

▶ **Flexible design of user menus**
Starting in Release 4.6C, the transactions, reports, and internet/intranet links used in a role can be combined to form a specific user menu—thereby enabling each user to select from a menu structure that contains the specific functions that he or she is authorized to use.

The term *activity group* has been replaced with *role* in Release 4.6C and later. The abstract term *activity group* was replaced by the role concept in light of the increasing relevance of the Internet and the mySAP philosophy.

▶ **Composite roles**
You can combine several single roles to form a composite role. Whenever possible, however, you should use single roles as modules in different composite roles. This will help you to achieve a high level of reusability, which also will improve ease-of-maintenance for the authorization structures.

---

8   SAP Note number 138706, P. 1

▶ **Distribution of roles**

Roles that have been created and defined in one (source) system can be distributed to other (target) systems, provided the target systems are also running Release 4.6C or later.

▶ **Importing roles**

You can import defined roles from the component system to the Workplace server via RFC. You can also import roles to the workplace from earlier releases (down to Release 3.1H), provided the corresponding plug-in has been installed.

▶ **Linking roles with the Knowledge Warehouse**

In the *Change Roles* screen, you can choose menu path **Utilities · Info Object · Assignment** to link a role with a document from the Knowledge Warehouse.

▶ **Role comparison**

In Release 4.6C and later, you can use this transaction to compare roles—even across systems—and modify them directly from within the comparison screen.

▶ **Mass generation of derived roles**

You can derive roles from existing roles within the role maintenance transaction. The role menus are then copied to the derived roles. If you also want to copy the authorization data, you can initiate mass generation of the derived roles in authorization maintenance for the original role. The data for these organizational levels is only transferred during the initial modification of the authorization data from the derived roles. If the data for organizational levels is maintained in the derived role itself, this information is not overwritten after subsequent adjustments.

▶ **Central User Administration**

In Release 4.6 and later, SAP supports the configuration of a central user administration, in which you maintain users for all the systems. Subsidiary systems with releases between 4.5 and 6.20 can be integrated with the Central User Administration (CUA). This method increases clarity, reduces errors, and shortens the time required to administer SAP systems. Now, however, the use of the CUA in the SAP system is still associated with increased technical effort and increased risks during installation.

Starting in Release 4.6A, the *Global User Manager* (see Section 2.11.2 for more information) provides an overview of all existing users, users groups, the individual systems in the SAP system group, and the roles in detail—based on the CUA. You can use the Drag&Drop technology to make changes, which take effect after they are distributed to the relevant systems.

▶ **Simplified configuration of the ALE system landscape**
Starting in Release 4.6C, you can use Transaction Code SCUA to configure simple system landscapes. For more information, refer to the SAP Online Documentation.

▶ **Area menus**
In Release 4.6 and later, the new area menus to call reports are used instead of the report trees or Transaction Code SA38 (see Section 2.7). The maintenance transaction for area menus (SE43) was developed for this purpose. You use this transaction to integrate the reports in a menu structure. The reports are then accessed through area menus or the transaction codes assigned to each report in the area menu transaction (SE43).

▶ **Mass changes**
You can perform mass changes to logon data, parameters, roles, and profiles for a selected group of users with Transaction Code SU10.

▶ **Alias names for users**
When you create a new user, you can assign an *alias name* in addition to the 12-place user ID. This 40-place user name is also used to identify a dialog user in the Internet.

▶ **Reference user**
You can assign a reference user to each user by assigning the corresponding roles. The reference user is primarily responsible for granting identical authorizations to groups of Internet users.

For more information on these new features, refer to the SAP Online Documentation.

2.11 Central User Administration and Global User Manager

2.11.1 Central User Administration

If you use SAP system groups—that is, multiple SAP systems (APO, BW, CRM, etc.) with multiple clients in which the same user master records have to be created and maintained—SAP provides the Central User Administration function (CUA) to maintain user master data and assign authorizations to the user master records. Under Central User Management, you maintain the users in a single, centralized SAP system. The user information and authorization information are automatically distributed to the connected child systems.

In particular, CUA administration includes the following activities:

▶ Defining and configuring the CUA

▶ Linking the clients with the logical systems

▶ Configuring and maintaining the ALE distribution model and the partner agreements in the main system and child systems

▶ Entering and maintaining the ALE distribution model to be used for the CUA

▶ Defining the fields that have to be maintained centrally and locally

▶ Maintaining and copying the user master records from new SAP systems that are connected with the main system

▶ Monitoring and troubleshooting in the event of distribution problems

Because SAP systems usually store and process extremely sensitive enterprise data, you must exercise extreme care when configuring user master records and granting access privileges. The administration concept has to consider the enterprise's specific security needs, including all internal and external formalities. Use of the CUA offers the following benefits:

▶ The user master records and role assignment (Transaction Code SCUG) are maintained uniformly in a main system and then distributed to the defined, integrated destination systems through the ALE interface.

▶ User data is maintained uniformly.

▶ You can define which fields are maintained centrally, which fields are maintained locally (Transaction Code SCUM), and which fields can be maintained by the users.

▶ You have a clear picture of existing users and their assigned roles for monitoring and review activities.

If you elect to use the CUA, note the following aspects, as the functionality here is limited at several junctures:

▶ If you use the CUA, the comparative evaluations that are possible under local user administration—especially the change history—are not available (see SAP Note number 492589). However, you can use table logging of tables USL04 and USLA04 for this purpose.

▶ During the distribution to the connected target systems (Transaction Code SCUA), an incorrect authorization check is performed for authorization object S_USER_SYS.

▶ When you delete roles in the main system (using the role assignment functionality), they are not removed from the user master record, which causes problems during the distribution to the target systems (see SAP Note number 333441 for more information).

▶ When locally defined fields (such as printer parameters) are changed in the target systems, the changes are distributed back to the main system (see SAP Note number 493715 for more information).

▶ If the reference user is used in the main system, the authorization check is missing.

▶ An incorrect authorization check takes place during role assignment.

▶ Delta distribution of user master data from the main system to the target systems causes problems if errors are present. In this case, the administrator will have to analyze and check the distribution logs (Transaction Code SCUL) in detail in order to correct the errors.

2.11.2 Global User Manager

The *Global User Manager* is another tool that simplifies the administration of users under CUA. To use the Global User Manager, you define the different grouping categories:

▶ User groups at the user level
▶ System types at the system level

If you use the Global User Manager, any fields in the user master data that are not defined (or not defined completely) will be deleted during distribution to the target systems

According to SAP, the Global User Manager function should not be used until further notice, as its use can result in data loss and inconsistencies without any prior indication or warning.

Therefore, you should deactivate the Global User Manager (Transaction Code SUUM and the corresponding report RSUSR500) by blocking it, as it is not reliable. For more information on how to deactivate the Global User Manager, refer to SAP Note number 433941.

2.12 History of SAP Technologies in the Authorization Area

2.12.1 Background

If you work with different releases, and therefore, use different authorization concepts, you will also use different tools ("traditional" authorizations and profiles, the Profile Generator, HR organizational units, and so on). Therefore, when changes are made to existing profiles/activity groups, the authorization administrator has to know the history of the authorizations being used and make decisions on a case-by-case basis. Moreover, other differences—such as changes to naming conventions—can cause minor annoyances that lead to enhanced error susceptibility, increased maintenance requirements, and reduced transparency. Of course, these factors also make it more difficult to train new users, and add any extensions to the authorization concept.

When different releases are used concurrently, another technical problem that arises is that roles, activity groups, and profiles can merge to grant additional, unintended access authorizations. The "traditional" procedure often activates many additional transactions, as the use of object S_TCODE is not mandatory. Fortunately, technical options are currently available to avoid this situation. When new profiles and single roles are merged with "traditional" profiles, the less restrictive concept overwrites the more restrictive concept; then, transactions that are supposed to remain closed in the "new" concept are opened.

Both organizational and technical aspects have to be considered. Decisions regarding the separation of responsibilities and organizational units from earlier concepts will affect the current concept. The settings in new authorization concepts can also affect the previous concepts.

If your previous concepts did not implement an organizational separation at division level for order processing, for example, you may want to do so when you adopt the "new" concept. However, the * authorizations from earlier concepts would destroy the divisional settings of any "new" concept that they are merged with, and therefore, the new settings would have no effect.

Regardless of these aspects, we recommend that you always use the most current SAP authorization concept technology whenever possible to pave the way for using current and new features in the future. To restate what we hope is already understood from the previous arguments, we highly advise against the parallel use of different authorization concepts.

2.12.2 Object-Oriented Concept

The strict *object-oriented concept* does not support the restriction of individual transaction codes. Access to the various SAP functions is protected using authorization objects, which are queried within the program codes of the respective transactions.

The advantage of this method is that it integrates function-based, data-based access protection (enabling you to split access to SD documents, for example, and restrict access to orders by division, sales organization, and so on).

The major disadvantage of a strictly object-oriented method is that it is nearly impossible to ascertain who has access to which transactions. As such, no transparency is provided. Accordingly, only limited dialog with third parties (users, project team members) is possible.

2.12.3 Object-Oriented Concept with S_TCODE

The *object-oriented concept with S_TCODE* supports restrictions at transaction code level, in addition to the "traditional" concept described above. While authorization objects still protect access to the SAP functions, the transaction code is also queried. The advantage of S_TCODE integration is its increased transparency: you can ascertain which users are authorized to use which transactions at any time.

This method always suffered from one direct disadvantage, however: because SAP did not initially clearly define the relationship between a transaction and an authorization concept, it was difficult to create an object-oriented concept that utilized the S_TCODE functionality. The authorization administrator was dependent on authorization traces and trial-and-error tests. Consequently, what ensued was that many customers initially chose not to use the transaction code in the authorization check. This omission of the transaction code is apparent throughout the assignment of full authorizations for object S_TCODE, or the use of intervals (for example, access to Transaction Codes V*).

2.12.4 Migration and Migration Tools

Various methods are available for migrating existing authorizations.

▶ **Hybrid method**
The hybrid method is a two-pronged procedure. The existing authorizations are retained in their conventional (object-oriented) state, while the Profile Generator is used only to create the new roles. While this method saves time, it poses significant risks and disadvantages. New authorization objects have to be added manually to the existing authorizations and profiles (around 250 additional new authorization objects between Releases 3.0F and 4.6). What results is the need for an increased, time-consuming testing of the changed authorizations and profiles.

▶ **Use of SAP migration tools**
SAP offers support for the automatic conversion of the object-oriented authorization structure in the Profile Generator, using Transaction Code SU25. The detailed steps involved in this process are described in Section 5.2.2. Please note that the effort required for migration is highly dependent on the distance between the source and target releases, as well as on the number of roles or activity groups to be migrated.

▶ **New setup in the Profile Generator**
You revise the existing authorization concept and generate it again using the Profile Generator. This is an extremely time-consuming process, as you have to define, implement, and test each role. Because of its uniform results, however, this method is clearly the preferred one.

2.13 Summary and Conclusion

A configured access protection system and the assignment of individual authorizations must primarily meet the following requirements:

▶ Confidential data must be protected against unauthorized access.

▶ Data must be protected against unauthorized, unintentional alteration or deletion.

▶ The procedure must be clear and enable you to determine who has which authorizations in the system and at what times.

▶ The access protection system that is to be configured must enable you to model the areas of responsibility for business functions, keeping in mind the principle of functional separation. In this context, a proper access protection system supports the establishment of an internal control system (ICS) (see Chapter 3). The access protection system comprises all rules involving system access, user administration, and the authorization concept.

The implemented *system access protection* must guarantee that only authorized individuals with a user ID can gain access to the SAP R/3 System.

The defined *user administration*, the procedure for creating users and assigning authorizations, must support the external propriety of the authorization concept. User administration must be organized, ordered, and traceable, as well as sufficiently monitored as described in Section 5.6.2.

The implemented *authorization concept* must enable you to restrict a user's privileges to the specific activities and system access required, based on his or her position and areas of responsibility in the enterprise (minimal authorization principle).

2.13.1 System Access Protection

The system access protection regulates

▶ Security at operating-system level
▶ Security at database level
▶ Security in the network
▶ Basic settings in the SAP R/3 System regarding the logon procedure

In an initial step, access to the SAP system is protected by several parameters that control the logon. To ensure that the logon procedure provides effective protection, it is imperative that you set the system parameters to appropriate values such as those values listed in Table 2.8 of Section 2.4.

2.13.2 User Administration

Users in the SAP system should only be configured based on written requests submitted to the appropriate user administration (change management as described in Section 5.6.3).

The written request to configure a user and assign authorizations must be approved by both the new user's departmental superior and by all data owners whose data will become accessible as a result of the new authorizations. The request should be based on a standardized form and must contain at least the following information:

▶ The employee's name, department, and area(s) of responsibility
▶ Time frame for granting the authorizations
▶ Technical description of the scope of activities in the SAP system (role description) and representation of the required authorizations
▶ Approval by the employee's superior
▶ Approval by the involved data owners
▶ Inspection and approval flags by internal auditing

On a regular basis, the user administrator should ensure that the newly configured users immediately change their initial passwords, and block the users who don't change their passwords from using the SAP system. In addition to the application and approval procedure for configuring users and assigning rules for new users, you also have to install procedures that ensure that changes to the employee structure and changes to individual employees' areas of responsibility are reflected in the authorization concept in real time.

2.13.3 Authorization Concept

Application-Independent Area

The application-independent area of an SAP system can be divided into the areas of *user administration* (see Section 2.13.2), *system administration*, and *application development*. These areas must be strictly separated by the designed and implemented authorization concept. In addition, the authorization concept also has to guarantee the functional separation between the application-specific and application-independent areas. In general, the authorization concept should give individual users only those authorizations that they require to carry out their responsibilities and functions in the SAP system. Therefore, do not assign standard roles or grant far-reaching system privileges in the application-independent area of an SAP system.

Application Development

Application development should only be granted authorizations from object class "Basis development environment." In particular, the authorization concept must implement a clear separation from general system administration. Authorizations for application development should only be granted in development and test environments; a general display role can be configured for the production system. Granting development authorizations (such as those based on authorization objects S_DEVELOP or S_TRANSPRT) in a production system is a major breach of any in-place internal control system (ICS).

System Administration

The critical security tasks performed by the system administration are far-reaching and always carry with them a certain amount of risk. From the perspective of a functional ICS, system administrators should never have authorizations from the user administration or application development areas. Therefore, you should configure an emergency user ID with the global authorization profile (SAP_ALL) in the production system. The name of this emergency user ID must be confidential (for example, by giving the user ID to one individual and the password to another, both of whom keep this information locked up in their office safes). Any time that the emergency user ID is used, it must be specified in writing (with the dual control principle always kept in mind), in clear organizational instructions, and it must be logged without exception.

Application-Specific Area

In the application-specific area, the authorization concept must reflect the ICS implemented in the responsibility-oriented and process-oriented organization. In general, however, you should ensure that the following requirements are met in all applications:

▶ The creation/maintenance of master data should be organizationally separate from the entry of transaction data (dual control principle).

▶ Authorization to maintain cross-client tables must be eliminated in the application-specific area.

▶ Authorization to maintain client-specific tables must be modified to reflect the user's specific areas of responsibility, through the configuration of authorization groups (see Section 2.7 for more details).

▶ Changes to Customizing settings in the production system must be restricted to exceptional cases (such as changes to the currency table, posting periods, and so on).

▶ Appropriately delimited authorizations (or the use of workflows to automate processes) must support a multilevel release procedure within the process structure.

In general, a user's authorizations should always reflect that user's specific responsibilities in all application-specific areas.

2.13.4 Documentation of the Access Protection System

User Administration

All user administration procedures, including the request and approval procedures and all checks to ensure that changes are included in the authorization concept, should be documented in clearly written instructions for the organization. You should document the design, frequency, and sequence of all monitoring measures, as well as their execution. All requests for configuring users, along with all change notifications, should also be documented and traceable as modifications to the authorization concept.

Authorization Concept

The documentation of the authorization concept must contain at least the following components:

▶ The organizational structure of the user departments, including SAP Basis administration

- The user's task description (job description and a technical description of the roles)
- An overview of users and the user IDs they have been assigned
- A technical description of the configured roles and composite roles, for synchronization with the areas of responsibility and main activities of the users (the users' assigned roles and authorization profiles)

2.13.5 Retention Periods

In general, documentation on user administration, the authorization concept, and any changes must be retained for a legally defined retention period, within the framework of a process documentation for the entire system.

2.14 Important SAP Notes in the Authorization Area

The most important SAP Notes involving the SAP R/3 authorization system and security (in addition to those already mentioned above) are listed in Appendix B. This list was current as of October 2002, and is based on the information from the book *Authorization Made Easy* and the SAP documentation; however, the list is by no means complete.

3   Embedding in the Internal Control System

The SAP authorization concept is only one component of an overall internal control system (ICS). Not all the required control mechanisms can be modeled using the standard SAP tools. Therefore, logical inter- action with other control types is required and must be defined accordingly.

"An internal control system encompasses the principles, procedures, and measures (rules) that enterprise management implements in order to realize their decisions at an enterprise."[1]

This definition of an internal control system within an enterprise shows that it is composed of different subareas, of which the SAP authorization concept is only one module—albeit a very important one.

"The ICS generally refers to the entirety of all coordinated and connected controls, measures, and regulations."[2]

You first have to define the objectives of the controls—in other words, specify the entrepreneurial foundation.

Each enterprise has to establish a custom control environment that is designed to mitigate the specific risks of its underlying business processes. Controls that do not lessen a specific risk (or a negligible one), and only exist for their own sake, are of limited use. To identify these risks, you have to consider the factors that will affect risk such as legal requirements and enterprise guidelines. The risk analysis that you conduct then enables you to derive the necessary controls. Here, you can also define which control tool (authorization concept or organizational meas- ures, for example) you want to use to model the defined controls.

Then, based on the need for a control system, you can describe the procedure for developing an ICS as shown in Figure 3.1. The following sections explain this fig- ure and provide an overview of the general structure. In this analysis, special

---

1   IDW EPS 260, P. 2 (IDW stands for "Informationsdienst Wissenschaft", the Science Informa- tion Service which publishes press releases from research institues and universities in Ger- many, Austria and Switzerland. For more information, go to *http://www.idw-online.de*; EPS stands for "Entwurf Prüfungsstandard" which means "Draft Auditing Standards". EPS 260 deals with "The Internal Controlling System in Connection with the Final Audit".)
2   Grundsätze ordnungsgemäßer DV-gestützter Buchführungssysteme (GoBS), AWV-Schrift 09546, P. 12 (Generally Accepted Principles of Computer-assisted Accounting Systems (GAP- CAS), available in English at *http://www.awv-net.de/schriften/Schr9.html*)

emphasis is placed on the anchoring of the SAP R/3 authorization concept within the internal control system.

Phase 1	**Definition of company objectives and risk strategy**
Phase 2	**Risk analysis based on defined risk levels (Business Process, Business Units, etc.) and external requirements**
Phase 3	**Identification of possible controls – Definition of the control environment**
Phase 4	**Mapping of risks and controls – Setup of an ICS**
Phase 5	**Monitoring and auditing of ICS efficiency**

Figure 3.1 Internal Control System—Setup Phases

3.1 Necessity of an Internal Control System

The benefits of an Internal Control System (ICS) are clear. Because modern information and communication technologies are used almost exclusively, many activities that were previously conducted manually have been replaced, and many enterprise-external processes have become the responsibility of the enterprise.

"New communication technologies such as the Internet will connect accounting systems beyond the enterprise boundaries..."[3]

The new information and data-processing systems make a sensibly designed ICS necessary in order to guarantee the integrity of the information.

Such controls are not limited to the conventional enterprise processes, but also include the processes for transmitting and processing the relevant data. The objectives of operating an ICS can be summarized as follows (individual objectives may vary by enterprise):

▶ Ensuring the effectiveness and operational excellence of business activities (including the protection of assets and prevention and discovery of financial impairments) [4]

---

3 Heese, P. 3
4 IDW EPS 260, P. 3

- ▶ Ensuring the integrity of internal and external data, processes, and systems that exist and are utilized at an enterprise (such as accounting rules, organizational regulations)
  - ▶ Ensuring correct data transmission inside and outside the enterprise (interfaces)
  - ▶ Minimizing input and processing errors
  - ▶ Ensuring uninterrupted operational availability
- ▶ Minimizing potential penalties and sanctions through compliance with legal requirements

These aspects are the most important features of an ICS. Additional objectives may arise based on each enterprise's specific requirements.

Any ICS is only as strong as the weakest link in the chain, however. Accordingly, any of the following factors can result in the temporary ineffectiveness of the ICS, or necessitate that adjustments be made to the defined requirements.

- ▶ Individual errors by staff (misuse, maintenance, technicians)
- ▶ Unforeseen events (infrastructure defects, natural disasters)
- ▶ Intentional criminal intent (fraud, manipulation, theft, hacking)
- ▶ Organizational defects (external staff, networks)
- ▶ Changed framework conditions or incorrect risk estimations

While an ICS can consider these influencing factors, they can still never be completely discounted.

Within the enterprise, management must approve a target for developing a suitable risk environment and therefore, for the design of an ICS. These targets specify the "actual steering and control of risks by the enterprise's user departments or functional areas,"[5] which means they define the areas of responsibility for the enterprise within the definition of an ICS. The result of these targets, and therefore, the risk environment, can be referred to as the risk strategy of the enterprise.

From its inception, this risk strategy can define basic decisions such as limits or risks that have to be controlled at all costs. In addition, the optimal degree of protection must be defined (which is generally higher for a bank or insurance company than for a manufacturer). Another determining factor is the *criticality* of the processed data.

---

5 PwC Deutsche Revision Aktiengesellschaft Wirtschaftsprüfungsgesellschaft (Publisher), P. 8 (PwC Deutsche Revision Aktiengesellschaft is the German branch of PriceWaterhouseCoopers)

3.1.1 Determining the Risk Environment

"Risk is a measure of the hazard posed by a threat. Risk consists of two components: the probability that an event will occur and the amount of damage that event has the potential to cause."[6]

After you define the targets and the organization for creating the ICS, the next step is to analyze the enterprise-specific risk environment. The first task here is to determine all corresponding factors that can influence the level of risk in an environment. In this analysis, you should investigate whether the following factors are relevant for your enterprise and if so, what their effects are:

▶ **Enterprise**
The most important influencing factor is the specific enterprise itself. The foundation is far-reaching and encompasses the required security level (target ICS), enterprise size, industry, degree of internationality of activities, legal form, complexity of the organizational plan and structure (especially regarding corporations), process depth, technology structure, personnel policies, growth, and so forth. You have to consider all enterprise-specific details, such as the use of shared service centers or the outsourcing of software and hardware support. Your primary goal is to identify and analyze risks—risks that threaten your existence, or risks that are material to your wealth, your finances, and your profit situation—by business unit/area, business process, or project.

▶ **Statutory regulations**
Statutory regulations and guidelines can vary widely depending on the location of the enterprise or its subsidiaries (and the locally valid laws), the industry, and the business activities conducted. Most countries have specific regulations, whose variety precludes a detailed description here. The following, internationally valid regulations are listed below as examples.

▶ *IAS—International Accounting Standards*
Accounting standards

▶ *US-GAAP*
Accounting standards

▶ *"Safe Harbor" principles*
Private American companies are permitted to exchange data with the EU if they voluntarily submit to a control concept (principle of efficient self-control through self-certification).

Several countries have recently passed risk management laws to reduce the risk of corporate collapse (such as Enron, WorldCom). Examples include the "Sar-

---

6 IT Management—Issue 03/99, P. 49

banes-Oxley Act of 2002"[7] in the U.S. and the Corporate Governance Code ("KonTraG") passed on May 1, 1998 in Germany. In addition to strengthening corporate governance, these regulations aim to implement risk-monitoring systems.

In addition, country-specific, industry-specific, or enterprise-specific rules such as the following may also apply:

▶ FDA (Food & Drug Administration)

▶ Requirements associated with GMP (good manufacturing practice)

▶ *GoBS, the German equivalent of GAAP (ICS/4 GoBS* - German framework for electronic data processing accounting systems)
  Describes an ICS as a "component of process documentation" within the framework of memory-based accounting. "The ICS applies (...) that the definition of organizational control mechanisms (...) defines the propriety of an accounting."[8]

▶ National Security Agency (NSA)—U.S.
  American government agency for monitoring enterprise communication

▶ EU directive (Directive 95/46/EG)—Europe
  Directive from the European Parliament and the Council of October 24, 1995 on the protection of private individuals in the processing of personal data and on free data traffic

▶ **Internal guidelines**
All existing enterprise requirements also have to be considered, and examined as to the extent to which they are still valid. Control processes that have already been implemented can always be replaced by new, more efficient tools.

▶ Signatory rules by value limit or approval requirements (can be modeled efficiently through the SAP authorization concept)

▶ Organized labor guidelines (controls may not result in overt employee monitoring)

▶ Requirements stemming from local privacy/data protection laws (administration of personal data—guidelines, laws and regulations for dealing with personal data differ from country to country)

---

7 U.S. Congress, Sarbanes-Oxley Act of 2002, Pub. L. 107-204, 116 Stat. 745 (2002)—*http://financialservices.house.gov/media/pdf/H3763CR_HSE.PDF*
8 Grundsätze ordnungsgemäßer DV-gestützter Buchführungssysteme (GoBS), AWV-Schrift 09546, P. 2 (Generally Accepted Principles of Computer-assisted Accounting Systems (GAP-CAS), available in English at *http://www.awv-net.de/schriften/Schr9.html*)

- Quality assurance requirements and organizational and technical security guidelines

- Process instructions such as those for change management, administration, and operating

▶ **Internal auditing**

Internal auditing requirements must be included in the definition of the ICS from its inception. You can integrate existing audit guidelines or audit plans in the system from the beginning. The same applies to audit reports, including any defined weak-point analyses, and to directives. A strong internal auditing department can lend excellent support to the development of an efficient, effective ICS.

▶ **External auditing**

In addition to internal auditors, external auditors should also be involved in development. In most cases, the external auditors supply audit handbooks, reports, or recommendations, which have to be considered from the start. Information on other country-specific requirements that go beyond US-GAAP or IAS, which the external auditors can integrate in the benchmarking process, can be another important aspect.

▶ **Implementation of new systems/processes/guidelines**

In most cases, the developed ICS is not static, but rather adjusted dynamically based on changes to the influencing factors mentioned above. Ideally, the enterprise should establish a change management process together with the internal and external auditors. At some companies, the internal auditors are the catalyst for maintaining and verifying the ICS. This is because risk-based methods for future checks can be developed based on the defined risks, and specifically focused on the critical processes for the enterprise.[9]

Results from monitoring or checks (see Chapter 6) can also be a trigger for future adjustments.

▶ **Macroeconomic risks and market risks**

Enterprises are also exposed to other market risks, in addition to these control aspects. Because the focus for the ICS is on the technical side, however, these additional risks are merely listed below and not explained in any detail:

- Business cycle, recession, globalization, and structural shifts

- Interest risks, exchange risks, and currency risks

- Exercise risk, distribution risk, and price risk

- Resource risks (staff qualification, age structure)

---

9 Information Systems Control, Volume 1/2001, P. 28

- Liability risks and legal risks (product and environmental liability, legal violations)
- Tax risks (changes to fiscal laws, legal remedies)
- Installation risks (incorrect dimensioning, capital expenditures)
- Financial risks (liquidity and capital procurement)
- Technological risks (research and development, production technology)

3.1.2 Identifying the Risk Source (Processes, Areas, and so on)

To develop the risk environment further, the defined units are classified for risk assignment with regard to the risks that actually exist (business processes, business fields/areas, projects). Because business processes are generally used as the risk level in this procedure, the information below is based solely on this level. The identification process is similar even if other units are used.[10]

You can also extract defined subareas from the business processes and examine them as separate areas, as an additional aspect. Such areas could represent the securing of interfaces and data transmissions, an existing ALE concept, or job and batch control at an enterprise.

3.1.3 Risk Analysis

Enterprise processes that are not adequately secured can mean a potential loss of data, inventories, and assets; these processes can also invoke sanctions. Therefore, nearly every business process poses an inherent risk, which is to be secured by the ICS. The respective risk usually depends directly on the degree of criticality of the underlying process. Business processes that are deemed less critical (such as reporting from a certain division) can be given much lower priority within the ICS.

Examples of processes that affect the data integrity within the enterprise or system include:

- Postings without document (a receipt), making it difficult if not impossible to reconcile the general ledger with subsidiary ledgers.
- Inventory differences that are posted at the warehouse without further controls; missing stocks in any amount are not pursued further.
- Uncoordinated changes to bills of material or solutions that result in different prices per plant or article, or in inventory differences.

---

10 See Heese, P. 6, for an example breakdown by risk field.

Risks are assigned to a business process according to specific criteria. Risk can be assigned by risk category and risk level: *risk categories* define the type of underlying risk, while *risk levels* describe their degree of criticality.

Risk Categories

Business risks are process-specific and can be identified through a risk analysis of the business processes.

Business risks can be divided into the following risk categories:

▶ **Regulatory risk**
Possible violation of or conflicts with underlying laws or country-specific regulations that may result in fines, contractual penalties, legal proceedings, or contingent liabilities.

▶ **Financial risk**
Refers to mistakes that can result in a financial loss for the enterprise. Example for a risk in the purchasing business cycle: vendor invoices are paid without a recorded goods receipt (goods missing).

▶ **Operational risk**
Risks associated with incorrectly or insufficiently performed business process (duplicate entry, incorrect entry, untimely entry of data that can result in delays in delivery, production, or similar processes).

Risks Levels—Consequential Losses of an Event

The risks identified within a risk category can be further rated in levels with regard to their impact on the enterprise. We recommend defining only a small number of levels. Typically, three levels are used; however, this can vary depending on the particular enterprise.

▶ **High risk**
Applications and tasks requiring extremely high protection. The expected damage amount is extraordinarily high (natural disaster).

Examples of high risks include system breakdowns, incorrect balance sheet or financial data, loss of assets or inventories, and the disclosure of personal data. Identifying these high risks enables you to specify, for example, that the controls aimed at high risks are conducted prior to execution of the business processes, and not only after their results are known.

▶ **Median risk**
Applications and tasks requiring median protection. The expected damage amount is noticeable for the enterprise.

Examples of median risks include incorrect orders, delivery delays, or false container labels.

▶ **Low risk**
Low risks are posed by all business processes that do not entail critical workflows or results for the enterprise. The expected damage amount is negligible. Low risk is typically covered by the basic protection implemented at an enterprise, and usually has little or no impact on the financial results.

Likelihood of Occurrence

In addition to the risk levels that we enumerated, you also have to assess the likelihood with which a defined risk will occur.

You can distinguish between different levels of risk as follows:

▶ Occurrence is most likely

▶ Occurrence is likely

▶ Occurrence is unlikely (nearly negligible)

Determining likelihood of occurrence of risk enables you to define which specification of the control each risk classification demands for each business process at a specific enterprise. Therefore, a low risk with a high likelihood of occurrence might be assigned a control that is atypical yet adequate for the low risk level, while a high risk with an infinitely small likelihood of occurrence might be deemed as tolerable and defined without assignment to a control (risk index "likelihood × amount of loss"[11]).

Risk Valuation

The objective of *risk valuation* is to identify all major risks, which are given priority in their examination and the assignment of appropriate controls. Overall, there is an inverse relationship between the potential amount of loss and the likelihood of occurrence—that is, the higher the likelihood, the lower the expected loss. This is due partially to proven statistical trends,[12] although it can be expected that potentially higher losses will be monitored particularly before they have a chance to occur.

You can now design a matrix to define and document which processes have to be linked with which type of control and mode of action (see Figure 3.2).

---

11 IT Management—Issue 03/99, P. 50
12 IT Management—Issue 03/99, P. 50

Amount of Loss/Risk

	High	Medium	Low
Most likely	Very strong	Strong	Individual case decision
Likely	Very strong	Strong	Individual case decision
Unlikely	Individual case decision	Individual case decision	None

(Row label: Risk Likelihood; bottom label: Development of Adequate Controls)

Figure 3.2 Risk/Control Matrix

3.2   Transformation into the Control Environment

The risk environment is identified in the first two phases—that is, the classified risks and the risks with their respective values—and then are implemented in an efficient, effective control environment. An *effective control* is a "specific measure for dealing with risks that have already materialized or measures for risk prevention and risk minimization".[13]

> "Controls are performed by monitoring instances that are integrated in the workflow and are responsible for both the result of the monitored process and the result of the monitoring process itself. Controls are intended to reduce the probability that errors will occur in the workflows and discover existing errors (for example, manual target/actual comparisons or programmed validation checks in the software)."[14]

3.2.1   Structure of the Control Environment

The structure of the control environment and the design of the controls depend on various influencing factors. The determining factor here is the enterprise decision as to which degree of security is required (see above), which was made during the prior risk analysis phase. How and which ICS method you employ varies widely within the framework of control and risk structure that is required by the

---

13 PwC Deutsche Revision Aktiengesellschaft Wirtschaftsprüfungsgesellschaft (Publisher), P. 8
14 IDW EPS 260, P. 3

enterprise. When this structure is implemented in ICS, the following factors help to determine the framework:

▶ **Degree of criticality of the process—risk**
As described above, risks are assigned by level, where each level defines a certain degree of control requirements. Therefore, considering the likelihood of occurrence, business processes are classified based on their degree of criticality for the enterprise; at the same time, the adequate control for the risk is also determined.

▶ **Type of required control method**
The control method describes the time the control takes place (see section 3.2.4 for more information). The implemented control will have to take effect either before or after the transaction or process is complete, depending on the underlying risk.

▶ **Type of requested control category**
The instantiation of the control can vary widely. A control can be automatic (such as SAP R/3 authorization checks within the system), or manual (such as the review of a periodic report).

▶ **Potential implementation of the control**
Not every control that was identified as the correct measure for a risk can actually be implemented. Not implementing a control can be due to technical restrictions (check data is not available in the system), or organizational reasons (the review has to take place at night between two processing runs). In this case, compensatory controls have to be identified.

▶ **Expense of implementation**
How much a control will cost is another critical aspect that must be considered. One specific measure (control) for a risk could involve the complete recording of all data modifications during a time period, for example, with many users actively logged onto the system during this period. The resulting expense (several gigabytes of storage space and the need for a nearly infinite amount of time to adequately inspect the compiled information) makes this control very impractical.

3.2.2 Requirements of a Control Environment

The total set of implemented and defined controls in the future ICS should meet the following requirements:

▶ **Correctness**
The entered data must be correct. Examples include input and processing checks, such as validation checks during data input, sequential number assign-

ment to prevent duplicates, and system-supported check sums and control totals.

▶ **Confidentiality**

Data and communication tools must be protected from unauthorized accesses. This requirement applies especially to personal and sensitive data, as well as to secure transmission of same. This aspect is especially important in the HR area (see Section 2.9 for special HR functions within the SAP R/3 authorization concept).

▶ **Integrity**

There must be proof that the data has not been manipulated subsequently. One possible control for this objective is to prevent changes to information calculated by the system, such as calculated totals or estimates. If manual changes are possible, untraceable variances will result.

▶ **Authentication**

Clear proof of the user's identity must exist. Users must be authenticated as soon as they log on to the system. In addition, it must be possible to trace who has changed data—both inside and outside the system—and to check whether the person in question was authorized to do so (approvals, emergencies, and so on).

▶ **Validity**

The data must be valid at the time it is entered. In most cases, verifying the validity of the data can be achieved through validation checks like those defined for the correctness of data above (for example, blocking the entry of invalid days or months in a date).

▶ **Completeness**

Transactions must be entered completely. In most cases, security mechanisms within the application have to ensure that any and all incomplete processes can be identified—and in the best case, corrected or reset—in case of program termination or system failure.

▶ **Non-repudiation**

A user must not be allowed to subsequently deny that he or she accessed the corresponding resources or data. The best way to achieve this requirement is by logging all data changes. As a result, any implemented adjustments or changes can be completely traced.

▶ **Timeliness**

The data must be allocated to the correct period. This timeliness can be achieved by closing posting periods, for example, to prevent the posting of incorrect assignments.

▶ **Authorization**

Controls must exist that dictate what an identified user is permitted to do. Meeting this goal is the primary objective of the SAP R/3 authorization concept. When the roles and functions within an enterprise are adequately designed, users will only be assigned the tasks within the system required in which they can perform their duties. This authorization also includes further restrictions involving the separation of critical processes (*dual control principle*) and the definition of generally unwanted functions (see Chapters 4 and 5 for a detailed description).

▶ **Availability**

There must be unrestricted, unencumbered access to resources and data. An operating concept is required to ensure that the systems are available to the enterprise's staff at any time (that is, even outside of "normal" working hours"). The same applies to peak periods such as month-end and year-end closings, along with other periods of increased activity.

▶ **Reproducibility**

It must be possible to reproduce past business transactions (such as postings) and the procedures used to execute them, within the framework of an analysis. You can usually achieve this objective by analyzing the change documents.

▶ **Immutability**

It must not be possible to subsequently change data stored in the system. Special attention must be paid to users who possess a wide range of authorizations (such as the SAP_ALL profile or comprehensive Basis roles) that allow the deletion of data.

▶ **Recoverability**

Any data that is lost must be recoverable. In most cases, this data recovery requires the existence of adequate backup preparations, such as regular tape backups, mirrored hard drives, or entire duplicate systems. Controls of this type are usually covered completely by a disaster recovery concept. Effective controls in this area are of vital importance for most enterprises due to the massive costs that a catastrophic loss of data would incur, despite their almost negligible likelihood of occurrence—not least because most enterprises cannot continue operations through a longer-than-24-hour IT breakdown.

▶ **Verifiability**

When you define controls, you have to ensure that their compliance and effectiveness can be verified and proven (see Chapter 6). Otherwise, you won't be able to identify necessary adjustments to the implemented measures.

A single control cannot satisfy all requirements at the same time. Accordingly, you have to sensibly combine different types of controls in order to develop the control environment. An integrated coordination between the manual and automatic controls is highly recommended.

Not least, the costs and effort associated with implementing the control also have to be considered. Therefore, it is entirely possible for the authorization concept to achieve goals that are not actually listed as requirements for a control environment (such as timeliness or integrity). The cost issue is discussed separately in Section 3.3.2.

3.2.3 Control Categories

Different types of controls can be used to satisfy requirements. The expression *control category* refers to the way the control works. We differentiate between the following primary control categories:

▶ **Automatic controls**
Controls firmly anchored in the SAP system, irrespective of how the system is configured. Examples of automatic controls include standardized checks that cannot be modified, as well as the logging of system errors.

▶ **Configurable controls**
The settings and values that are defined in Customizing. Different status values can be specified for an input field: required entry field, optional field, display field, or hidden field.

▶ **Functional separation—application security**
Corresponds to the basic demands of the *dual control principle* (no single user may hold control over an entire process flow). Examples include the adequate separation of master data maintenance by view, or the distribution of purchase order processing, vendor processing, and goods receipts postings to different users or roles. The majority of issues in this area are covered by the SAP authorization concept. During the function/role definition, the activities/functions requiring separation are defined, developed, and documented for subsequent administration.

▶ **Access protection—application security**
The restriction of user privileges based on defined roles and functions at the enterprise (see Chapters 4 and 5 as the linchpin of this book). This control category also involves limiting access to certain critical transactions in the Basis area (such as table maintenance, system administration, and batch runs) and the applications (such as releases and approvals).

This section is the central element of the SAP authorization concept. As described in Chapter 2, many options are available for defining this protection in detail and adapting it to your specific enterprise organization.

- **Reporting controls**

  Those controls that support active monitoring and verification at an enterprise, using reports and analyses to implement adequate measures in response to any discovered improprieties. SAP provides various reports and analysis options for these purposes. You can also use the ABAP functionality or SAP Query to develop specific reports to satisfy virtually any requirement.

- **Guidelines**

  The internal company requirements, such as management guidelines, travel, or requisition directives, letters from the company board.

- **Instructions**

  Are located outside the SAP system. They conclude the procedure, for example, the authoring, monitoring, approval, and verification of the documentation to be written.

3.2.4 Control Types

Efficient controls in the ICS should always be selected appropriately for the verified potential business risks. The control objective is to minimize or avoid the identified risks and protect the enterprise against damage and loss. Each of the control categories defined above can be differentiated by its control objective. We differentiate between two types of controls: *preventive* and *detective controls*.

- **Preventive controls**

  These controls are implemented to prevent or avoid faults from occurring—before the process has started. These controls can also be implemented via concepts for system configuration, security, and authorization.

- **Detective controls**

  These controls are implemented to discover existing errors within a review process. They often include activities such as the analysis of reports or verification of system logs and change documents.

Figure 3.3 illustrates the sequence of the two control types. Both control types are integral to the integrity of the business processes. When both preventive and detective controls are available, the respective underlying risk and process determines which of the controls is most appropriate.

In some cases, a somewhat downstream detective control is preferred to a preventive control, due to process-related (e.g., effort required) or transaction-related (e.g., result not available yet) reasons. Accordingly, you have to make pragmatic, sustainable decisions for each individual business risk. Over and above the previous factors, the cost/benefit ratio plays a major role, just as it would in any other entrepreneurial decision.

Business Process

Start of risk-related activity

End of risk-related activity

Preventive controls

Detective controls

Figure 3.3 Scheduling Preventive / Detective Controls

3.3 Identifying the Implementation

Once the existing risks have been defined, you have to select the most suitable controls from the available set, based on the criteria defined for each risk.

A comprehensive ICS concept includes the minimization, the avoidance, and the controlling of all identified and valuated risks. Most of the influencing factors that we already described will require more organizational than technical controls within the risk management system. We have not included a detailed description of the structure of a risk management system at this point. For more information, see the appropriate references.

The next section describes how the SAP R/3 authorization concept can help you to limit identified risks.

3.3.1 SAP R/3 Authorization Concept

The SAP R/3 authorization concept boasts a wide range of features for modeling controls within an ICS. As already mentioned, the SAP R/3 authorization concept primarily supports the control categories *functional separation* and *access protection* in the area of application security.

When you begin to develop your concept, you have to make decisions regarding the required level of protection (see Chapter 4 for more details). In most cases, these basic decisions already include some of the identified risks. Examples of these *framework conditions* are:

▶ General locking of critical transactions or (sub-)processes for business users

▶ Defining organizational levels to be protected (modeling organizational separations, such as legal units, within the enterprise)

▶ Identifying specific responsibilities that must be restricted to a limited number of users (applies to both Basis and application responsibilities)

    ▶ System/user administrators

    ▶ Operating concept, including support

    ▶ Payment authorizations

    ▶ Master data for customers, vendor, G/L accounts, or materials

▶ The identification of functions and responsibilities within the enterprise that have to be kept separate at all times (*dual control principle*)

In addition, once the risk analysis is complete, you have to define which risks you want the authorization concept to include, based on the following examples:

▶ **Identified risk: cross-company code postings**
You can minimize this risk by specifying that authorizations (roles or composite roles in this case) are restricted to the company code. In a second step, you then have to ensure organizationally (system administration) that no user receives single/composite roles for more than one company code, which would circumvent the control within the authorization concept.

▶ **Identified risk: full control over the vendor payment run**
SAP enables you to restrict activities for the payment run, such as editing parameters, starting and displaying the payment run, generating and processing the proposal (field values for authorization objects F_REGU_BUK and F_REGU_KOA for Transaction Code F110). Again, in a second step, you have to ensure organizationally that the separation is not only satisfied within the single and composite roles, but also with a user master.

▶ **Identified risk: unauthorized approval of purchase orders or requisition notes**
You can restrict requisition notes and purchase orders by release group within the SAP authorization concept. You have to define them first in Customizing, however, by modeling the release strategy accordingly. Protection solely through transactions and authorizations is not possible.

► **Identified risk: material-scrapping transaction unprotected**

You have to block a type of movement in order to minimize this risk. Only specially authorized users are then allowed to scrap materials.

3.3.2 Implementation—Constraints

SAP offers a wide range of options for implementing access restrictions (see Chapter 2 for a technical description). Implementing access restrictions is subject to some constraints, however: not every required or targeted protection can be implemented within the system.

Technical Constraints

Within the standard SAP modules, you can only protect the organizational and technical fields that are covered by SAP authorization objects. In the Purchasing module (MM-PUR), for example, you can implement protection for the following units:

► Company code

► Purchasing organization

► Plant

► Purchasing group

► Segment

Purchasing departments can be organized differently, and therefore have different authorizations—such as a merchandising department split into several subdepartments. These subdepartments can, in turn, be further divided by different or varied products. These organizational units cannot be used as a decision/authorization criterion for requirements, reports, or purchase orders, however; they each exist merely as a reporting criterion in the Purchasing area.

Therefore, we highly recommend that you consider the technical restrictions of the SAP authorization concept when you are still in the design phase of your implementation project, in order to develop security processes that can be modeled in the standard SAP system.

Budgetary Restrictions

Often, financial concerns determine how much and what type of authorization protection an enterprise can implement (i.e., authorization protection is possible, but will be expensive to develop and administer). Examples of enterprises that are often faced with such budgetary constraints include master data maintenance, Profit Center Accounting, and restriction to individual cost centers.

If the authorizations had to be restricted to a single cost center, profit center, or view of a material master, the result would be a huge number of single and composite roles. This will both increase the effort required for the development and test phase and, due to the large number of defined variants, also increase the costs of administrating users and authorizations (see Chapter 5).

You have to consider this trade-off every time you define a control for the corresponding risk. You can do so, for example, by moving the required protection up by one organizational or field value level (to cost center groups instead of individual cost centers, profit center name ranges instead of individual profit centers, and so on).

3.3.3 Compensatory Controls

If a required protection cannot (or should not) be modeled through the SAP authorization concept, you can minimize the risk through *compensatory controls*.

Compensatory controls can include organizational rules (procedures, guidelines, and directives), and the threat of sanctions for noncompliance. Another option is running periodic reports as a detective control to discover incorrect actions. Compensatory controls generally reduce costs, because a detailed definition of the authorization concept can prove to be too expensive, regardless of how effective.

3.3.4 Classifying the Authorization Controls

As already described, the SAP R/3 authorization concept is based on the control categories *functional separation* and *access protection*. In general, restrictions within the roles and composite roles are preventive controls, as each user's authorizations are restricted to prevent errors. In contrast, compensatory controls are usually detective controls that do not take effect until after data entry, if the user is generally authorized to execute the transaction or process in question.

3.3.5 Documenting the Controls

You have to document the controls that you implement through the SAP R/3 authorization concept, in order to trace enhancements to and adjustments of the control concept. In addition, this documentation is an important tool for the authorization administrator, because functional separations are defined within single roles, composite roles, and user master records. The administrator thus has a tool that indicates critical combinations for assigning composite roles to user master records. No fixed rules for documentation have been defined.

3.4　Monitoring and Auditing the ICS

The effectiveness of the implemented ICS can only be verified through a combination of ongoing monitoring and periodic checks of the identified risks and controls. New information (or even the occurrence of a risk) can make it necessary to change a risk classification or choose a different control for a risk.

See Chapter 6 for information on the technical inspection of SAP R/3 authorization concepts and related areas. This section briefly describes the potential organizational measures available to support adequate ICS monitoring.

3.4.1　Internal Audits

A strong internal auditing department can be the driving force behind a well functioning ICS. Ultimately, an increased frequency of internal audits will strengthen the department's position at a given enterprise and its connection with the business processes. For example, audit methods or audit schedules can be planned and executed with a specific focus on the identified risks. This method will help you concentrate on your critical enterprise processes.

The control method of the ICS is based on the materiality and complexity of the respective processes and systems. For ERP systems such as SAP R/3, "the process-oriented check (...) is essential for such systems."[15]

Accordingly, an internal auditing department that is familiar with the enterprise processes can adapt and improve the control environment on an as-needed basis, depending on the audit results. Next, the internal auditing department can develop check programs or software tools that improve and enhance the ICS with every check.

3.4.2　External Auditors

Periodically—possibly as part of your annual audit—the effectiveness of the ICS should be checked by an external auditor, which can be specified in the audit schedule for the internal audit. This type of exchange helps your enterprise integrate *benchmark analyses* and *best practices*. Please note that the different auditing firms follow different methods.

3.4.3　Enterprise Awareness

Enterprise management must emphasize the necessity of controls among all staff, to prevent these controls from being perceived as entirely negative and monitory. If guidelines and organizational instructions are followed and exemplified throughout the company and their necessity recognized, draconian penalties for transgressions can be avoided.

---

15 Heese, P. 13

4 Procedure Model for Designing an Authorization Concept

Based on the experience of successful projects and the continuous development of the respective project approach, a phased model for establishing an authorization concept in a conventional SAP R/3 System was developed. This chapter describes the individual steps of this phased model, the parties involved, the decisions that were considered, and the results that emerged from designing such a concept.

4.1 The IBM Phased Model

4.1.1 Overview

Based on its years of experience with various consulting projects, *IBM Business Consulting Services* (formerly PwC Consulting) has developed a uniform, structured procedure model for the design, definition, and implementation of a role-based SAP R/3 authorization concept. This method was already used with the previous, object-oriented approach and has been adjusted to incorporate the latest technical (Profile Generator) and organizational (new protection options) possibilities. The elements, which have proven their worth in numerous projects, have been retained.

An important component of this procedure, one that is critical to the success of the project, is the earliest possible involvement of employees from all areas of the customer's company. This involvement at the inception of a project emphasizes the importance of the "authorization concept" for all participants when a project is first implemented. It also enables the required resources to be informed early on about the responsibilities they face, to prepare accordingly, and to have the freedom to work on the project. A clear management commitment within the company is of particular importance. Moreover, the individual employees and structures for the subsequent knowledge transfer should be defined, in order to ensure a smooth transition to the line organization and corresponding support departments.

The IBM Phased Model covers the entire life cycle of an SAP authorization concept and is divided into twelve separate phases (see Figure 4.1).

While some phases can be worked in parallel, other phases are critical prerequisites of later phases and therefore must precede them. The individual phases are introduced briefly in the next section. A detailed description of individual aspects follows in the subsections.

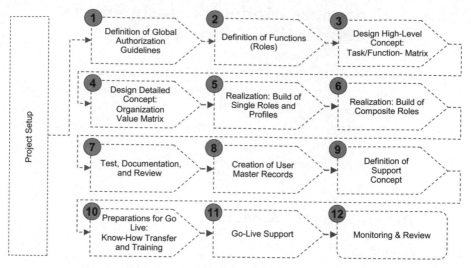

Figure 4.1 The IBM Business Consulting Services Phased Model

4.1.2 Project Preparation and Framework Conditions

To enable an economically appropriate process that considers both the special needs of the enterprise and external guidelines and statutory regulations, the requirements of the authorization concept are first specified as *framework conditions*.

The foundation is formed by an analysis of the system/technical and business environment. Do not underestimate the importance of this area, which requires resources from different departments. By now, you should already have recorded all existing internal and external guidelines that can affect the authorization concept, and its design. You can also begin to outline the structure and depth of detail that you want to implement. Important parts of the framework conditions include definitions of naming conventions for the new objects, as well as the basic technical requirements of the design and implementation of the authorization concept—for example, the use of new tools or technologies in an SAP environment. The necessary processes and task areas for the later user/authorization administrators are also defined in this phase, as they typically differ from the previously implemented processes. The primary decision is whether these administrative tasks are better suited to a centralized or a decentralized structure at the enterprise. Before the project begins, this issue must be resolved.

A major result of this step is a list of proposals for the areas in which a separation of responsibilities is advisable, as well as other measures for fulfilling the control requirements within SAP R/3. Ensuring auditability is a critical factor in all these basic decisions. Please note that while consultants can support these definitions through best practices, the necessary degree of control has to be defined by the respective enterprise itself (see Chapter 3).

The defined framework conditions have to be approved by the decision-makers at the enterprise and create the foundation for further project work.

It should be mentioned, however, that the framework conditions are always subject to change or revision over the course of a project, due to changes in external factors or technical and administrative restrictions that were unclear at the start of the authorization project. Of course, if the framework conditions change subsequently, the components of the authorization concept that have already been implemented will have to be checked for compliance with the new conditions. For a detailed structure of the framework conditions, see Section 4.3.2.

4.1.3 Definition of Functions (Roles) at an Enterprise

In this phase, the necessary functions (roles[1]) within the organization are analyzed and described, based on interviews and workshops with experts from the respective user departments or on existing materials (available process documentation or job descriptions can be used). In particular, you have to ensure that a sufficient separation of responsibilities among the individual functions exists. You must consider the control requirements defined in the framework conditions. Understandably, the interviews and workshops are held by area, for example, one workshop each for accounting, controlling, purchasing, warehousing, production, and sales. You must ensure that not too many contact persons or persons responsible for each area are named; this will avoid having too many workshops, not to mention the associated coordination effort.

Please pay special attention to defining functions independently of individual users. The objective of the phased model described here is a role-based authorization concept, not a user-based one, which means that users have to be collected into groups, to the extent possible, based on the tasks they perform in the SAP system. The functions (composite roles), and therefore the access privileges in the SAP system, are always defined for the whole group, not for individuals. This way of defining functions by group is essential, because user-based authorizations are unnecessarily expensive to develop and subsequently to maintain, and therefore become an expense that cannot be justified.

To get an overview of the number of functions that are required compared to the number of SAP users in the respective area, it helps to create a quantity structure first. Generally, a reasonable ratio defined functions to users should be chosen. In

---

1 Please note the difference between the various enterprise definitions of the role and the technical SAP definition.

the extreme, this ratio could even be 1:1, which means one role would exist for nearly every user. This case only represents an exception, however, and should only be implemented in divisions with very few employees whose areas of activity are strictly separated. In most cases, however, several users will execute a given function, which means the number of defined functions is much smaller than the number of users in the SAP system.

The result of this phase is a list and rough business description of all required functions in the SAP system, which are recorded in a function matrix. Now, you should document the defined separation of responsibility and control requirements—such as combinations of functions that must never be assigned to the same user.

4.1.4 Rough Design—Creating a Task/Function Matrix

Functions

In this step, the SAP transactions required to carry out an activity are identified and documented as a rough concept for each function defined within the function matrix.

Of course, this rough concept has to be developed in close cooperation with the individual business areas at the enterprise. In addition to experts from the individual user departments, we also recommend involving SAP module experts, to ensure that both the business and technical SAP perspectives are included in the authorization concept design. The module experts are responsible for balancing the options within a specific area of the SAP system. When decisions have to be made regarding details in the design of the authorization concept, the SAP module experts can provide information such as which settings and restrictions are feasible. These design details always have to be considered in the big picture of overall Customizing as well. It also helps you to judge whether it might be preferable to use other options in SAP software, such as *substitution*[2] or *validation*[3], to achieve a specific *control requirement*.

---

2 *Substitution* in SAP R/3 is a procedure for replacing values during entry. In this process, the values can be compared with a user-defined *Boolean expression* (prerequisite) and corrected automatically in case of error (for example, "always replace document type X with document type Y, because document X is currently blocked").

3 *Validation* is the verification of values and value combinations during entry into the SAP system. The input values are compared with a prerequisite, similar to the substitution process, but then checked also against a *check statement*. If this statement is also correct, the value is updated. If the check statement is false, the system issues a user-defined message. The update does not take place in all circumstances. Therefore, validations let you catch obvious incorrect entries that can be defined in rules (possibly even combined with authorizations).

An extremely helpful approach to drawing up the rough concept is to not define restrictions (during the workshop) all the way down to the transaction level, but instead to the *task level*, which is required to arrange the roles and can be seen as a module area (within SAP). The advantage of restricting tasks to the respective module areas (such as Materials Management → Purchasing) is that only authorization objects from this area will be required for these tasks; you can therefore avoid a duplication of objects due to combinations of authorization objects from other areas.

Tasks

Within the IBM Phased Model, a *task* is a grouping of transactions that is logical from a business perspective and based on the standard SAP menu tree. In the later implementation, the functions are implemented as composite roles and the tasks contained therein as single roles. When you define the tasks, you should keep in mind the need for maximum reusability of the individual tasks in different functions. This will reduce the number of single roles that have to be created in the system, improving both the clarity and maintainability of the authorization concept.

Generally, the functions in this phase should be defined as completely as possible—that is, they should contain cross-division and cross-module transactions as well as special functions. Your objective is for the role to contain all the authorizations required to perform a task, which means the user can perform all the required tasks in the SAP system with this role, without needing any others. Therefore, in the ideal case, a user will only require one role in line with his or her position in the enterprise organization.

This is usually harder in practice, however. Conforming to the restrictions and requirements defined in the framework may require the separation of certain functions, transactions, or authorization objects (to fulfill the *dual control principle,* for example). Also, it is often better to partition the function and assign the users multiple roles for the performance of their duties. You can define a separate role containing general, non-critical Basis functions such as printer authorizations or SAPoffice and assign it to every user in addition to his or her functional roles, for example, or define special, critical authorization functions separately.

Summarization in a Matrix

You will now take the function matrix that you defined in the previous phase and expand it to form a task/function matrix. The matrix documents all the functions with their corresponding transactions at task level. The task/function matrix is the second determining element of the authorization concept, after the framework conditions. The matrix is used to define the roles in the System in the subsequent implementation phases (see Chapter 5).

The task/function matrix is the main tool for defining roles. You use it to collect all the information required to define the roles. This matrix also functions as documentation of the implementation and the foundation for any subsequent changes to the roles. It is an especially helpful tool for troubleshooting, as it helps you to quickly check whether a design error is the reason why a user can't access a transaction, or whether that transaction was intentionally excluded from the role.

Figure 4.2 shows an excerpt of an example task/function matrix. The left-hand column of the matrix contains the standard SAP menu tree. The nodes of the menu tree can be expanded down to a certain level (e.g., the fourth level), or all the way down to the transaction level. Any lower levels should not be deleted, however, as they are useful for information purposes and for identifying potentially critical authorizations within the defined task area.

The top line of the matrix contains the defined roles that correspond to the composite roles. These roles can be grouped together logically by SAP module, or by subteams in the SAP project.

SAP 4.6C Standard Menu 1st 2nd 3rd 4th level	Task	S_TCD	Finance & Controlling	AR/AP Master Data Administrator	Risk Manager	Accounts Payable	Accounts Payable Associate	Accounts Payable Specialist	Accounts Payable Viewer	Accounts Receivable	Accounts Receivable Associate	Accounts Receivable Specialist	Accounts Receivable Viewer	General Ledger	General Ledger Associate	GL Accounts Administrator
				ok	ok		ok	ok	ok		ok	ok	ok		ok	ok
Logistics																
Accounting																
Financial Accounting																
General Ledger	FI:GL						V01				V01				V02	V08
Document Entry							V01				V01				V02	
Document							V01				V01				V02	
Account							DIS				DIS				ALL	
Master Records							DIS				DIS				DIS	ALL
Periodic Processing																
Reporting															ALL	
Information System							DIS				DIS				ALL	
Environment															ALL	
Accounts Receivable	FI:AR			V03	V06		D01				V01	V02	D03		D01	
Document entry											V01					
Document							DIS				V01	V01	DIS		DIS	
Account							DIS				ALL		DIS		DIS	
Master records				ALL			DIS				DIS	DIS			DIS	
Credit management					ALL		DIS				DIS	DIS				
Periodic processing																
Reporting							DIS				D01		D01		DIS	
Withholding Tax												ALL				
Information system											DIS		DIS			
Environment											DIS	ALL				
Accounts Payable	FI:AP			V01			V02	V03	D01		D01				D01	
Document entry							V01									
Document							V02		DIS		DIS				DIS	
Account							ALL	DIS	DIS		DIS				DIS	
Master records				ALL			DIS	DIS	DIS		DIS				DIS	
Periodic processing																
Reporting							D01		D01		D01				D01	

Figure 4.2 Excerpt from a Task/Function Matrix

The intersections of the matrix indicate which menu nodes or transactions should be included in the task. Groups of nodes (highlighted boxes with versioning at the third menu level in the previous figure) are the single roles to be created in the R/3 System from a technical standpoint. From the start of the project, you should not only indicate which menu nodes and transactions will be used, but also the instantiations of the authorizations in the single role. You can use the following entries for this purpose in the matrix:

▶ **Entry ALL**
The role in this column has unrestricted access to the transaction in the corresponding line, or all transactions of the menu tree node named in this line.

▶ **Entry DIS**
The role is only authorized to display the data within the corresponding transaction(s), to the extent possible. Transactions that cannot be limited to display only are not included in the role.

▶ **Entries V01 to Vxx and D01 to Dxx, etc.**
In addition to unrestricted access and display-only access, other variants sometimes also make sense, and are numbered consecutively. Be sure to record a description of the corresponding variant (Vxx for variant; Dxx for display variant) in the comment field of the matrix. A variant can contain authorizations to display and change data records, for example, but not to delete or create new records. In most cases, variants have to be created for particularly critical authorizations, such as for approval, release, and payment functions.

The authorization developer must have the necessary knowledge to implement these three variants. Therefore, we do not recommend development by temporary staff or trainees without instructions from qualified supervisors.

Various automatic and semi-automatic tools are available for displaying the SAP menu tree in an Excel table, expanded either completely or down to a certain level. You can use a table of this type as the foundation for creating your matrix.

Of course, the task/function matrix only has to include those parts of the menu tree that are actually used in roles. If an SAP module or application is not used, you can omit the corresponding section of the menu, which can help you to reduce the complexity of the matrix.

Once the design phase is complete, you should submit the entire matrix to the user departments again for coordination. You have to pay special attention to cross-module and cross-area authorizations here. In general, such authorizations should be granted based on data and function ownership, and only with the permission of the area whose data ownership is being affected. This is easier to achieve in relatively encapsulated areas such as accounting, than in enterprise areas that don't have a singular character—such as several independent sales divisions that have the same function but different processes. In this case, detailed coordination is required among the participating areas. Please note that a generally accepted function/data owner must be identified for all issues.

The conclusion of this step is a major milestone in the overall project. Accordingly, a formal, written acceptance of the deliverables is required of the persons responsible from the involved user departments and areas.

4.1.5 Detailed Design Concept—Creating an Organization/Value Matrix

To adapt the generic task and function definition in the rough concept to the organizational requirements of the enterprise, the organizational and value-based constraints requiring protection are defined for each individual role. The goal here is to protect sensitive data and enable each role to access the specific data required to execute its task area—the objective being to develop the authorization concept in an economical manner, while creating roles that meet the enterprise's security needs.

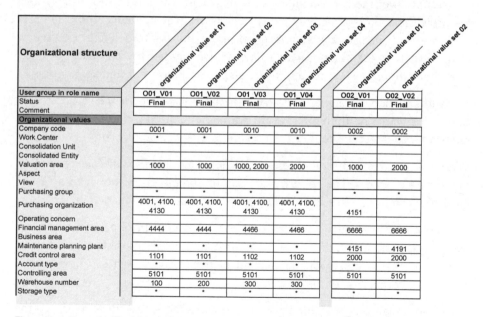

Organizational structure	organizational value set 01	organizational value set 02	organizational value set 03	organizational value set 04	organizational value set 01	organizational value set 02
User group in role name	O01_V01	O01_V02	O01_V03	O01_V04	O02_V01	O02_V02
Status	Final	Final	Final	Final	Final	Final
Comment						
Organizational values						
Company code	0001	0001	0010	0010	0002	0002
Work Center	*	*	*	*	*	*
Consolidation Unit						
Consolidated Entity						
Valuation area	1000	1000	1000, 2000	2000	1000	2000
Aspect						
View						
Purchasing group	*	*	*	*	*	*
Purchasing organization	4001, 4100, 4130	4001, 4100, 4130	4001, 4100, 4130	4001, 4100, 4130	4151	
Operating concern						
Financial management area	4444	4444	4466	4466	6666	6666
Business area						
Maintenance planning plant	*	*	*	*	4151	4191
Credit control area	1101	1101	1102	1102	2000	2000
Account type	*	*	*	*	*	*
Controlling area	5101	5101	5101	5101	5101	5101
Warehouse number	100	200	300	300		
Storage type	*	*	*	*	*	*

Figure 4.3 Organization/Value Matrix

Your task in this step is to create the organization/value matrix, which controls the depth of detail warranted by the concept, and therefore the total resulting development effort. Because the contents of the organization/value matrix define all access to enterprise data, the principles of data ownership and function owner-ship also have to be considered, and formal acceptance from the persons responsible in the user departments and areas is essential. Data ownership can be defined at company code or distribution channel level; however, you cannot predefine a single solution that is best for all enterprises. It might be better, for example, to define organization value sets (*OrgSets*) for each individual composite role or for an entire module area (such as Accounting). This depends on the differences between the individual functions in each organizational area (labeled with Org1 and Org2 in figure 4.3). Figure 4.3 shows an example matrix.

The organization/value matrix also helps you to create and maintain new authorization roles in the SAP system during live operations. As such, this matrix is a template for filling the relevant organizational fields during authorization maintenance and must be adapted to fit any changes.

4.1.6 Implementation—Creating the Single Roles and Profiles

During the implementation phase, the defined roles are modeled in the SAP system and the field values provided in the SAP standard are defined adequately based on the organization/value matrix.

You use the naming conventions defined in the framework conditions to create the roles and profiles (see Section 4.3.6 for details). If guidelines for creating roles have been defined in the framework conditions, they too must be adhered to and implemented. In particular, you have to ensure that the defined separation of responsibility is administered and that you do not assign an unintentional combination of authorizations within a role or between roles that are assigned together. For a technical description, refer to Chapters 2 (overview of SAP technology) and 5 (implementing roles and profiles).

4.1.7 Implementation—Creating the Composite Roles

We recommend using *composite roles* to model enterprise functions in the SAP R/3 standard. They can contain one or more single roles and ultimately help to improve the structure of the authorization concept. In addition, using composite roles makes the control function much easier to perform, thanks to its clear visualization of the control function.

You can maintain the role menu at either the composite role or single role level. The menu of a composite role always contains the menus of the single roles that constitute the composite role. While role menus at composite role level can be maintained more easily, a disadvantage is that the complete composite role menu has to be reimported and adjusted each time a single role menu changes. You can avoid this step by maintaining the menus directly in the single roles and then importing them into the composite role. This method of maintaining the menus in the single roles not only demands an increased maintenance effort, but the individual menus also have to be coordinated with one another to ensure that a consistent menu appears in the composite role. For this reason, we recommend creating the menus in the composite roles and adapting them for later changes there. Another advantage of this method is that you can design a specific menu for each composite role without having to worry about the underlying transactions at authorization level—this only makes sense for transactions that can be executed with the authorizations assigned to the role.

4.1.8 Test, Documentation, and Review

All system settings and changes to the standard SAP R/3 System have to be tested prior to going live. The implemented authorization roles have to be tested as well. Because you cannot verify complete, correct coverage even when you use the SAP Profile Generator, it is absolutely imperative that you test the defined roles. Requirements for a successful test series include the following:

▶ Coordinated testing forms

▶ Experienced, competent process operator as tester

▶ Adequate amount of time

For a detailed description of the different test phases, see Chapter 5.

4.1.9 Configuring the User Master Records

Configuring the user master records and assigning them to the defined composite roles is the next-to-last step in your implementation of the SAP authorization concept. The knowledge transfer from the project team members (consultants) to the employees who will be responsible for ongoing user/authorization administration must commence at this step in the IBM Phased Model. Of course, some involvement beforehand is also beneficial. The project team members are responsible for training the future administrators of the authorization concept, based on examples of their tasks. These employees should also create the initial user master records themselves.

4.1.10 Defining a Support Concept

The *support concept* defines the future design of the administration and change management procedures. The activities in this phase should be conducted in parallel to the design and implementation of the authorization concept and adapted as necessary. The focus is on either centralized or decentralized administration, depending on the defined framework conditions. You should analyze the advantages and disadvantages of both options based on the necessary resources, tools, and processes. Finding the optimal solution for a given enterprise also depends on the quantity structure, the enterprise structure, and the previous processes in this environment (see Section 2.3.3 and Chapter 5 for more information).

4.1.11 GoingLive Preparation—Knowledge Transfer and Training

Once the results of the previous phases have been obtained, securing them in the long term requires a knowledge transfer from the project team members (typically consultants) to the operator of the SAP system (customers or external administrators). This can be achieved through constant involvement in the project, as well as through courses and workshops.

4.1.12 Rollout Support and GoingLive Support

During rollout support, any remaining difficulties must be eliminated and the systems stabilized. Generally, activities in the authorization system following the GoingLive phase include the following issues:

▶ Error identification and correction

▶ Instructional support of user administrators and requestors (introduction, assistance, individual single training)

▶ Support for business-related SAP questions that pertain to the authorization concept

▶ Post-documentation

Consider that your administrators will have to prepare themselves for a particularly heavy workload in the first several weeks after the new authorizations are assigned, which they often cannot deal with fully due to their new tasks. Please consider this factor in your resource planning.

4.1.13 Monitoring and Review

Lastly, procedures and methods for effectively monitoring the authorization concept and role assignments are developed and implemented as necessary. One possibility here is regular monitoring of the roles assigned to each user, in order to identify any improper combinations of roles or violations of the framework conditions (see Chapter 6 for a description of various technical possibilities). Tasks in this area can be carried out by internal auditors, the operating staff, or an external auditing company.

4.2 Involved Parties

4.2.1 General

Before a design for an SAP security concept (and an R/3 authorization concept in particular) can be described theoretically, the tasks and persons responsible should be documented in a project role description. At the very least, this information must be defined clearly for all the involved parties. Figure 4.4 shows one possible way to map the dependencies.

It is also imperative to foster an understanding of and acceptance for the necessity of a coordinated authorization concept among all parties involved in an SAP implementation project. The authorization team members must perform this task at the start of the project, that is, this important step must be positioned at an early phase, in order to be considered in any relevant design decisions.

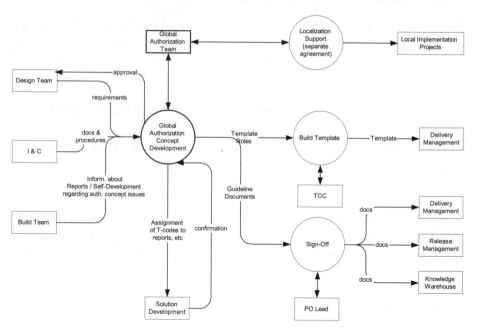

Figure 4.4 Responsibility Flow

This very aspect is one of the single most difficult tasks involved in actual project work, however. While all parties are often cognizant of the importance of authorizations, views on prioritization vis-à-vis other work packages—such as the actual Customizing or importing master data—tend to differ. One particularly difficult task is the reorganization of authorizations from an administrative perspective, due to an audit report from external auditors, for example, but without changing the authorizations for the employees. The user departments are faced with additional work that they perceive as already finished. In this case, the benefits for the entire enterprise must be clearly communicated.

It should be apparent that any authorization concept will be useless without a process design. However, the integration of authorizations should not be delegated to a downstream task; rather, they should take place concurrently with the defining of the new business processes to be modeled in the SAP system. By dealing with authorization issues early on, unnecessary additional effort (due to subsequent coordination and changes) can be reduced or even prevented.

The following sections briefly describe the parties that should be involved in designing and implementing the authorization concept.

4.2.2 Steering Committee

The activities of an established authorization team for a project are not directly affected by the decisions of a steering committee. Nonetheless, this group of individuals also has to understand that the implementation of an SAP authorization concept is one of the principal components of the security concept for the enterprise's IT processes, and therefore, a key factor for the security of the enterprise data. A clear management commitment is another essential prerequisite. Accordingly, when important project milestones are reached, the project managers should report and communicate this information on an as-needed basis.

Example: An enterprise consists of several business units (BUs) with plants that operate based on a profit center organization. Several staff functions (invoicing, marketing, and so on) and a holding company structure lie above this level. The plants report to their respective BU managers and consider their data (price calculations, cost of materials) as confidential and worth protecting. They reject giving access to departments from the holding company. This fact is to be modeled in the authorization concept, to ensure the effectiveness of the profit center organization as an internal control instrument. In contrast, the holding company insists on comprehensive access to all data available in the SAP system, based on its position in the corporation. Here, only a higher level can effect a decision: typically the steering committee, which either includes members of upper management, or at least reports directly to upper management.

Moreover, the steering committee should have the last word in certain design decisions involving the security strategy implemented in the authorization concept—for example, in deciding to grant data access through higher-level organizational units.

The steering committee should also temper the need for overly detailed protection requirements. For example, a specified requirement to implement protection for every single cost center can result in an inordinate development and (especially) administration effort, depending on the number of cost centers involved (some enterprises have several hundreds or even thousands).

4.2.3 Project Management

Project management plays a special role in developing and implementing the authorization concept, in addition to its already integrative character in coordinating the work packages. Project management must convey to the project team that it stands behind the implemented design decisions when questions arise; it must ensure suitable availability of the required resources and, lastly, it must be able to justify its activities before the steering committee.

4.2.4 Auditors

Auditors should be included in an "SAP authorizations" subproject from the start. Ideally, one (part-time) employee will accompany the tasks and rate them from the enterprise's perspective. In addition to the inspection-relevant aspects, this allows for smooth integration of the requirements of an internal auditing department in the concept. Involving the auditors will also help you to consider future needs for auditing the system controls (see Chapters 3 and 6).

Examples of auditing results include:

▶ Inspection plans for the SAP system

▶ Checklists for an authorization audit

▶ Additional, customer-written ABAP check programs for functions that are not covered by the standard SAP system

4.2.5 Module Specialists and Process Specialists

Because authorizations are a cross-component aspect of an SAP implementation project, the team that is in charge of designing the system controls requires the support of the project team (here: module or process team[4]). The project team's assistance is vital for the workshops whose goal is detailing the authorization con-

---

4 Here: module or process teams. When you design an organizational chart for an SAP project, you have to decide whether you want to structure the teams by SAP module or by the previously defined (main) business processes. Because there are advantages and disadvantages to both variants, different types of matrix organizations are frequently used.

cept. While the responsibility of the members of the authorization team is to influence the instantiation of the individual authorizations, specialists from the module and process teams are responsible for the specific requirements from the module or process perspective. If the creation of an authorization concept is not part of the system implementation, the user departments will be responsible for the development of this concept.

Therefore, the corresponding individuals should participate in the development of the authorization concept in the earliest possible project phase: in the determination of the utilized SAP functions. Their cooperation is also required in the definition of roles at the enterprise and, in the design of the SAP authorizations. Lastly, their support is essential during the role integration test, one of the later project phases.

4.2.6 Contact Persons from the User Departments

Input from the user departments is required for more than just the "Role definition (for an SAP authorization concept)" phase of a project. Even if there is reason to assume that all business processes to be modeled have actually been defined and accepted, practical experience has proven it beneficial—even essential—to once again involve the individuals who helped to describe the workflows at the enterprise. These individuals will enable you to identify the specific functions required and protection requirements at the data level based on the SAP transactions or, if the risk analysis has already covered this task sufficiently, at least rate it from the user department's perspective.

As previously mentioned, the user departments play a critical role in reorganization projects. They adopt and oversee the tasks that the project teams perform during implementation projects. Identifying the persons responsible or project team members required is much more difficult, however. The necessary support must also come from management or the steering committee.

In addition to their involvement in defining the roles, the contact persons must also accept the implemented roles, coordinating corresponding acceptance tests in their departments or conducting these tests themselves. Ideally, these contact persons will assume the function of *role owner* later on (see Section 4.4.2 for the tasks performed by this function).

4.2.7 User and Authorization Administration

It is particularly important for the employees who will be responsible for subsequent user and authorization administration to be included in the project at its inception, or at least, at the earliest phase possible. These employees are responsible for the seamless execution of the SAP authorization assignment and maintenance in the live system, and should therefore have a sound knowledge of the SAP Basis component, and, in particular, the details of the SAP authorization concept. For this reason, it is imperative that these employees be introduced to the subject and participate in detailed training courses at the start of the concept design process. Involving them in determining and defining the SAP authorization roles for the enterprise can also be very helpful.

4.3 Important Aspects in Detail

4.3.1 The Eleven Basic Rules

As already mentioned, the framework conditions form the fundamental foundation upon which the authorization concept is built. The eleven basic rules that every authorization concept must adhere to are listed below. These basic rules are both the starting point and the foundation of the framework conditions.

1. **The authorization concept is function-based**
   The defined authorizations must be based on the tasks and positions that exist at the enterprise, not on tasks that individual employees are responsible for due to their positions. Therefore, standardized roles should be used whenever possible.

2. **Need for authorizations**
   Each employee must only be granted the authorizations that he or she needs to carry out his or her responsibilities. Comprehensive, unnecessary authorizations must not be granted (no wildcard or full authorizations); however, non-critical authorizations (SAPoffice, display authorizations, and so on) can be granted as widely as possible.

3. **Detail depth and complexity**
   SAP provides an endless variety of options for restricting access to functions and data. For this reason, you should evaluate precisely whether the necessary depth of detail and the resulting intricacy of the authorization concept are really required, as too much detail can have an adverse effect on system administration and complexity. Proprietary developments in the authorization system should only be used in exceptional cases.

4. **Critical authorizations**
   Transactions defined as critical within the user departments (such as approvals, releases, master data, Basis area) should only be assigned to selected, qualified employees based on specific requirements. In particular, a wide range of authorizations (SAP_ALL, in case of emergency) must not be granted.

5. **User department input (processes and organizational structures)**

The value of an authorization concept is highly dependent on the inputs (processes, functions, and transactions) used to create it. Accordingly, early involvement by qualified employees from the user departments is essential. When developing the phased model, you should try to cover as many work steps with internal resources as possible.

6. **Functional separation**

Functions that are critical to the business process should be implemented in accordance with the dual control principle. You have to consider this prerequisite when designing your concept. All auditing requirements must be taken into account.

7. **Testing the authorizations**

Before authorizations are used in the live system, they have to be tested sufficiently and accepted by the employees in the user department (see Chapter 5 for a description of the various test steps).

8. **Documentation**

The defined authorizations must be adequately documented, in order to trace their creation and further development appropriately. This applies to both the user department-specific requirements and the technical implementation. Monitoring is therefore essential, and is also the purpose of an audit.

9. **Administration of users and authorizations**

You should already begin considering the subsequent administration of users and authorizations when you start designing the concept. This applies particularly to the chosen naming conventions. Early involvement of the appropriate employees will ensure that the knowledge transfer is effective and that employees are properly trained and able to assume their responsibilities.

10. **Project plan**

You should include the definition of authorizations in one of the first phases of the overall project plan, as the effort needed to perform this task is often underestimated. In order for the project to succeed, all tasks have to be organized in an efficient, timely manner. You should pay special attention to bottlenecks in your key resources (employees), who may play a key role in several projects or subprojects due to their special skills.

11. **Guidelines**

All the valid framework conditions and guidelines that apply to creating and administering users and authorizations must also be applied when developing the concept and the authorizations, in order to facilitate future comparison.

4.3.2 Framework Conditions

The framework conditions are your main document for recording the basic rules and analyzing the assumptions behind your concept. In particular, they should include the following aspects:

▶ Objectives, foundation, and validity of the framework conditions

▶ Organizational structure of the enterprise, along with the existing and planned system landscape of the SAP R/3 System (future release upgrades are important here)

▶ Information involving the degree of detail of the authorization concept (basic decisions)

▶ Description of the role-based approach

▶ Definition of responsibilities (decentralized versus centralized user administration, role/data administrator, communication channels, documentation)

▶ Definitions involving the separation of responsibilities within and between functions

▶ Definition of naming conventions for roles, profiles, user groups, and user IDs

▶ Requirements involving the documentation of the authorization roles

▶ Information regarding technical security that affects the authorization concept (such as instance profile parameters)

▶ Identification of possible constraints at module/object level and derivation of the desired functions

▶ Descriptions of version management and change management processes

Figure 4.5 shows one example of what a table of contents for such a document could look like (excerpt).

The next section deals with many—if not all—important issues inherent in the framework conditions.

Table of Contents

Figure 4.5 Global Authorization Guidelines (Excerpt from Table of Contents)

4.3.3   Degree of Detail of an SAP Authorization Concept

When you decide which basic characteristics a new design should have, you have to choose one of two opposing strategies or principles, which depend on the security needs of the enterprise:

▶ Authorizations will be defined *as loosely as possible* and *as restrictive as necessary*.

▶ Authorizations are implemented *as tightly as possible* (minimal authorization principle).

This decision should not be an arbitrary one; rather, it should follow your defined security strategy. An enterprise that promotes a culture of trust and fosters "empowered employees" would probably follow the first principle. This does not imply, however, that companies that follow the second principle perpetuate a culture of mistrust and powerlessness. Instead, such enterprises are generally restricted by tighter statutory regulations and rules than other enterprises (pharmaceuticals manufacturers, for example).

In addition to the comprehensive security strategy, you should also consider the following influencing factors when deciding on your degree of detail:

▶ Size of the company, number of named SAP users, and derived number of roles (number of defined OrgSets in the organization/value matrix)

▶ Presence of externals (such as customers, vendors, joint venture partners, external service providers, and consortium partners) in the system

▶ Ease of and responsibility for administration (in-house versus outsourcing)

▶ Scope of utilization of SAP functions, especially for "critical" data

▶ Enterprise organization (such as profit center-based organization)

The decision as to which principle the authorization concept will follow is a basic one, and must be coordinated among all levels of responsibility, right up to top management. Communication with all parties involved is a necessary first step.

This definition lays the path for developing the roles (profiles) to be defined in the system. If you use the "as tightly as possible and as widely as necessary" strategy, you have to define the authorization roles down to the transaction code level—often defining each exact field value for the organization objects. The first strategy ("as loosely as possible and as restrictive as necessary") is much different. In this case, you concentrate on the areas identified as critical, especially critical transactions. This information is available in the SAP Security Guidelines (for Basis authorizations) as well as other sources such as the Internet or third-party databases (auditors, enterprise consultants).[5]

As mentioned, you don't have to analyze the individual transactions in order to define the roles. Instead, definition at the task or submodule level (such as the "Shipping" task in sales or the Event Management submodule in HR) has been proven to be more effective. The selection must be drafted in suitable form to document cross-module coordination and, ultimately, future auditability. Nonetheless, it may make sense to include the transaction level for particularly sensitive areas (such as payments).

---

5 An outstanding overview of critical authorization objects in various SAP modules (so far BC, FI, and CO) is published periodically by Christoph Wildensee on the Internet at *http://www.it-audit.de*.

In addition to the standard ASAP tool provided by SAP, the *Business Process Master List*, the utilities for developing and documenting the authorization roles (described in the next section) have proven to be very effective for day-to-day project work.

4.3.4 Documenting the Authorization Roles

From the auditing perspective, the documentation of the authorization roles is especially critical, as it is a component of both the system documentation and the procedure documentation. On the one hand, you must describe the initial structure of the roles from a business and technical perspective. On the other hand, all subsequent changes have to be traceable for third parties, especially auditors (external auditor, QA, other committees, etc.).

SAP R/3 provides some support for the business documentation. For example, descriptive fields are available at certain places in the development environment, especially in the Profile Generator. Because a change history for long texts or even version management for documents is not supported by the SAP system, however, you should record this information in documentation that is separate from the system and procedure documentation. Figure 4.6 shows the screen for entering role descriptions in the Profile Generator.

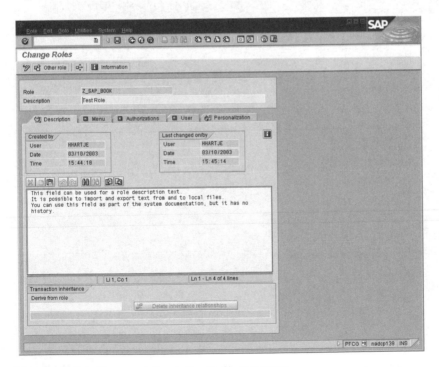

Figure 4.6 Role Documentation in the Profile Generator

Since the introduction of the SAP Knowledge Warehouse (SAP KW), SAP offers its customers the option of linking the role documentation directly with the KW. An additional button in the Profile Generator enables you to link with content, which means that external storage of additional documents (outside of the SAP system) is no longer required. This solution requires the use of the SAP KW, however, which is not reasonable if you don't plan to use it for other purposes as well.

Third-party solutions have proven to be practical solutions for this purpose, such as the ARIS® process documentation tool offered by IDS Scheer. Using this product, you can define business roles in addition to the detailed process descriptions, and describe their tasks exactly. The direct link to the subprocess allows you to locate relationships between an SAP transaction code and the role through existing reports in ARIS®.

If you must generate full documentation of the system settings (in this case, the authorization profiles defined for the roles), however, you will once again have to resort to an external solution. SAP does not provide a technical documentation tool. To back up the current settings, SAP merely offers an option for exporting (downloading) the roles to a proprietary format. Figure 4.7 shows the corresponding Download menu option in the Profile Generator.

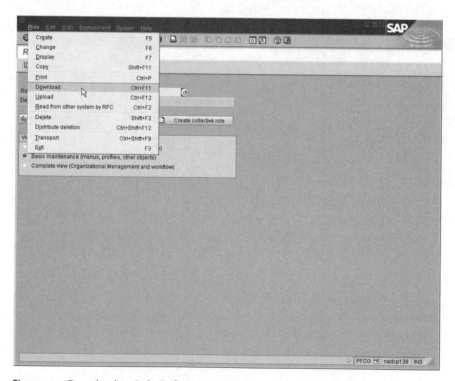

Figure 4.7 Downloading Role Definitions

This download enables you to copy roles quickly and easily to another system, without requiring an RFC or ALE link, or restore the initial state of roles at a later time. If you import backed up roles from an older version, however, all changes made to the newer version of the system since the download will be overwritten. The direct extraction or selection of individual data for comparison or further processing is not supported.

SAP R/3 provides a *journal function*, which means changes are logged. This logging enables experienced users to determine which employees changed which data and when; however, it only applies to the profiles defined for the authorization roles. The corresponding tables, with the change history data, were mentioned in Chapter 2. In contrast, SAP R/3 does not currently feature change documents for the actual authorization roles. You have to analyze the respective profiles to determine changes to the roles, which can be prove to be quite complicated in some cases.

In addition, the underlying reason for implementing a change cannot be documented. Such requirements can generally only be met through integrated change management tools (such as those available in the SAP PS module) or through third-party solutions. In the simplest case, changes to authorization roles are processed in a live SAP system through an established *change request procedure*, which analyzes the justification for the change, the persons responsible, and the effort required. For a detailed description of the change request procedure, refer to Chapter 5.

In practice, documentation consisting of the following components has proven helpful in developing an SAP authorization concept.

▶ Framework conditions (as described in Section 4.3.2)

▶ Business role description (contains work center-like descriptions that can be derived from the process documentation)

▶ Role/transaction matrix (contains the reference between an authorization role and its assigned SAP transactions)

▶ Data access matrix (describes the data accesses at authorization object level)

▶ Separation of responsibilities matrix (contains internal relationships between authorization roles and lists prohibited combinations)

▶ Administration manual (describes the day-to-day work of an authorization administrator with regard to the other documents listed above)

4.3.5 Template Approach

The *derivation function* is available for creating roles in SAP Release 4.6 and later, which means that one role can transfer certain characteristics—such as the contained transactions, the menu structure, or even certain field values—to another role. This transferring of characteristics makes it possible, based on a single role—the *template role*—to define various other roles that only differ in a few specific field-value entries. Accordingly, you can apply the same template role to different organizational units—such as company codes or distribution channels—with minimal effort, by merely configuring the characteristic values differently for each derived role (see Figure 4.8 for more information). In this respect, the derived roles adopt all the transactions, the menu, and all authorization-relevant constraints at field level from the template role. The derived roles only differ in one or more organizational levels (different distribution channels in the example in Figure 4.8). Therefore, derivation is especially useful in those examples where the function definition identifies a series of functions whose intrinsic tasks are identical, but which have to be defined differently at different organizational levels.

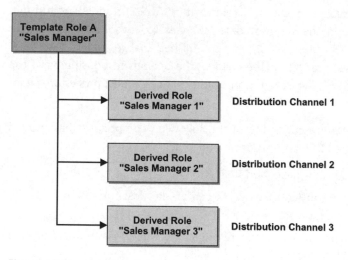

Figure 4.8 Template Role Concept

Therefore, using the derivation function within the framework of a template approach gives you many benefits in complex organizations, for example, role creation and maintenance is greatly simplified. If inheritance isn't used, the defined roles must be copied and configured appropriately for each additional organizational level. The maintenance effort required for changes increases exponentially, because each copied role would have to be changed manually. This method is inevitably more error-prone; moreover, it poses the risk that a previously homogeneous authorization concept may unravel due to the incomplete adaptation of the roles to be copied. In contrast, this risk is nearly negligible using the template method. All role changes that are not relevant for the organizational level are made exclusively in the template role and are copied simultaneously and directly to all derived roles. Changes that are implemented exclusively in the template role include adding or removing transactions, maintaining the role menu, and maintaining all authorization fields that are not relevant to the organization. If any such role changes are made directly in a derived role, whether inadvertently or intentionally, they will be overwritten the next time the corresponding template role is maintained. This differentiation of role changes (that is, those that are relevant to the organization and those that are not) simplifies the control over the roles, thus making your authorization concept both more uniform and less apt to unravel. In this case, maintenance of the derived roles is restricted to the field values of the organizational units. We recommend defining organizational value sets that are based on the enterprise's organizational structure (also see organization/value matrix). These sets then contain all the permissible organization values for each area, thereby defining the framework in which data can be accessed. The individual sets will differ in exactly those organization values in which the different derived roles will be delineated. You can then seamlessly configure the derived roles in the system based on these organizational value sets. Figure 4.9 illustrates the basic procedure for using the derivation function. The definition of a new role (through a task/function matrix, for example) is used to implement a corresponding template role in the system. All non-organizational field values are maintained in the template role, which then serves as the foundation for deriving the various single roles, each of which has to be configured in accordance with the different organizational value sets.

Please note, however, that the derivation function can only be used for single roles. Nonetheless, derivation is also extremely helpful when composite roles are used. In this case, the single roles defined at the task level are created as template roles and the single roles derived at the organizational level are grouped together into composite roles (see Figure 4.10). Ideally, your composite roles should only contain various single roles created within the same organizational value set, as only this method will ensure that the access privileges of the composite role are restricted to the same value set.

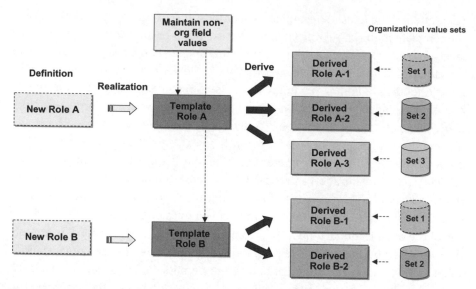

Figure 4.9 Creating Derived Single Roles

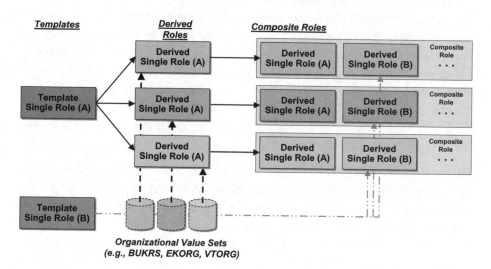

Figure 4.10 Template Functionality for Composite Roles

4.3.6 Naming Conventions

Separate names have to be defined for all elements of the SAP authorization concept that the enterprise creates itself (i.e., single roles, composite roles, tables, ABAP/4 reports, and so on). You should address the issue of naming conventions at the start of the authorization project, not only regarding the implementation of authorizations in the system, but also pertaining to the ease of administration and the clarity of the authorization concept—such as, defining clear rules for name assignment and ensuring that there is adherence to these rules.

In general, naming conventions in the authorization area should meet the following basic requirements:

▶ Clear delimitation from the SAP standard through the assignment of a unique (customer) namespace

▶ Fulfillment of uniform sort criteria (organizationally and technically)

▶ Clear delimitation among the various objects within the authorization concept itself

▶ Clear representation of module/business process assignment of the object

▶ Possibility to model the defined administration processes

In addition to these requirements, whose purpose is largely pragmatic, SAP also defines certain constraints; for example, technical names for authorization roles cannot start with "SAP", and an underscore "_" cannot be used as the first or second letter.

Depending on the complexity of the SAP system in question, it may be advisable to implement naming conventions for all relevant areas of the SAP authorization system. Specifically, these areas include:

▶ SAP authorization roles

   ▶ Composite roles

   ▶ Single roles

   ▶ Long texts of role names

▶ SAP authorization profiles

   ▶ Collective profiles (do not use in Release 4.6 and later)

   ▶ Single profiles (optional)

▶ Authorizations (optional)

▶ Customer-defined authorization objects

▶ Authorization groups

▶ Customer-defined tables

▶ Customer-defined programs

▶ Customer-defined transactions

▶ User names and user groups

In particular, the separation of certain tables, programs, and transactions is relevant not only in terms of the authorization concept. Naming guidelines often already exist at an enterprise (in programming guidelines, for example), which of course have to be considered.

When designing the naming conventions, we recommend that you pay close attention to the authorization-relevant workflow processes that will be established subsequently, to make it possible to restrict user administration accordingly through suitable namespaces. One such possibility would be to restrict role assignment by decentralized administrators to the roles of the corresponding organizational units and users that are assigned to certain user groups.

Naming conventions for authorization roles and profiles are defined as examples. The most important aspects that have to be considered in these examples are:

▶ Selection of the customer namespace by using Y or Z as the first letter of the technical name

▶ Unique identification of the role category: single role or composite role

▶ Identification of the SAP system in case of a distributed system landscape or when Central User Administration (CUA) is used

▶ Categorization of the role, for example, as required in a shared service center environment: Global or local role

▶ Definition of a higher-level organizational unit that the role can access

▶ Identification of the task of the single role in accordance with the task/function matrix

▶ Access type (activity: read or create) of the single role in accordance with the task/function matrix

▶ Name of the composite role

To meet all these requirements, you need a sufficiently complex naming system with a large number of differentiation criteria. While this naming system may seem quite complex at first, it is necessary to meet all the requirements of naming conventions listed above and it also offers several other important benefits. See Figures 4.11 and 4.12 for examples of naming conventions for single and composite roles respectively.

Using a characteristic for single and composite roles, for example, will greatly simplify role administration in the Profile Generator (in the above example, a colon ":" is used for single roles and an ampersand "&" for composite roles). If you operate several SAP systems that can be administered from a single instance or via Central User Administration (CUA), you must include the system names as well.

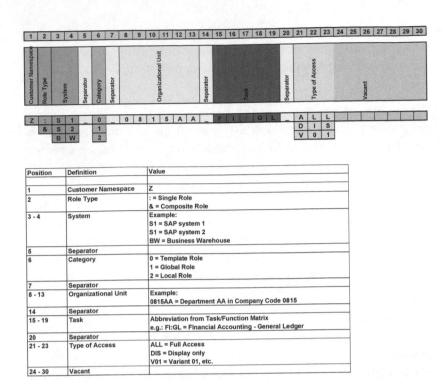

Figure 4.11 Sample Naming Conventions for Single Roles

Position	Definition	Value
1	Customer Namespace	Z
2	Role Type	: = Single Role & = Composite Role
3 - 4	System	Example: S1 = SAP system 1 S1 = SAP system 2 BW = Business Warehouse
5	Separator	
6	Category	0 = Template Role 1 = Global Role 2 = Local Role
7	Separator	
8 - 13	Organizational Unit	Example: 0815AA = Department AA in Company Code 0815
14	Separator	
15 - 19	Task	Abbreviation from Task/Function Matrix e.g.: FI:GL = Financial Accounting - General Ledger
20	Separator	
21 - 23	Type of Access	ALL = Full Access DIS = Display only V01 = Variant 01, etc.
24 - 30	Vacant	

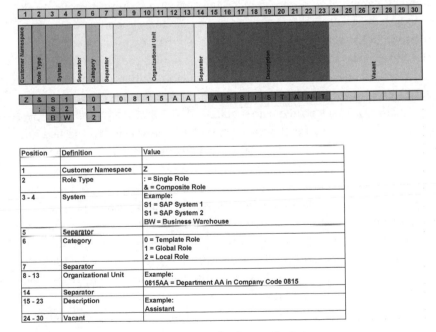

Figure 4.12 Sample Naming Conventions for Composite Roles

Position	Definition	Value
1	Customer Namespace	Z
2	Role Type	: = Single Role & = Composite Role
3 - 4	System	Example: S1 = SAP System 1 S1 = SAP System 2 BW = Business Warehouse
5	Separator	
6	Category	0 = Template Role 1 = Global Role 2 = Local Role
7	Separator	
8 - 13	Organizational Unit	Example: 0815AA = Department AA in Company Code 0815
14	Separator	
15 - 23	Description	Example: Assistant
24 - 30	Vacant	

You can categorize roles into *global* and *local* roles, for example, to distribute role administration responsibilities among several administrators, or to restrict local administrators to accessing "their own" roles. The same also applies to the organizational unit.

We recommend using mnemonic names wherever possible—for all name components—and avoiding abbreviations (use a conversion table instead). This technique enables you to be flexible when reorganizations and renaming occur within the enterprise. In addition, naming organization values in role names can be misunderstood, confusing, or simply insufficient as a differentiation criterion. If the company code and distribution channel are included in the role name as differentiation criteria, you will encounter problems when, for example, two areas in the same company code and distribution channel differ by a third criterion, or when roles do not contain either of these two differentiation characteristics. The "_" characteristic has been inserted as a separator in several places for increased transparency.

The sequence of individual criteria within the role name is also important; for example, the sort of identification criterion that is most important to the enterprise should appear first within the naming conventions, followed by less important criteria. This is highly dependent on the role administration requirements and can vary widely from project to project.

Fortunately, by extending the names of single roles and composite roles to 30 characters, SAP made it much easier to cover all these naming convention requirements in Release 4.6A. Please note, however, that the profile generated by the Profile Generator is still limited to 10 characters, which means a 1:1 reference within the naming conventions is no longer sustainable. When you generate the authorization profiles with the Profile Generator, the R/3 System proposes profile names automatically. These profile names start with the prefix "T-", followed by a two-place alphanumeric key for the SAP system ID (corresponds to the first and third place, such as T5 for system T65), along with a counter that is managed in a separate table and that increases by one for each new profile (see Figure 4.13). You can overwrite this proposal with a manual entry during creation, but you cannot change it subsequently. We recommend using the SAP system proposal for the profile name in traditional one-system landscapes when you assign the authorization roles in the user master record. A different solution is required in landscapes, where the first and third position of the system ID can be identical (e.g., systems T65, T75, and so on), to prevent unintentional overwrites from transports between systems. In this case, you should omit the hyphen following the letter T and use the full, three-character (and thus unique) system identifier instead.

If you use the Profile Generator, you cannot name the authorizations according to your own definitions. The technical name of an authorization is generated automatically from the profile name (see Figure 4.14).

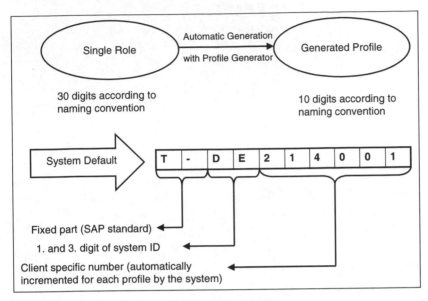

Figure 4.13 Naming Conventions for Generated Profiles

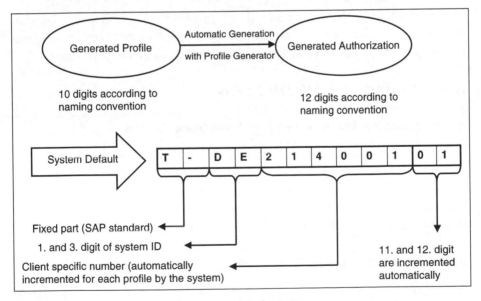

Figure 4.14 Naming Conventions for Generated Authorizations

The field lengths listed in Table 4.1 are generally available in Release 4.6A and later for the naming conventions of the various authorization-relevant elements.

	Number of places	
	Technical name	Short text
User	12	
Alias name	40	
Transaction	20	36
Transaction variant	30	30
Variant transaction	20	36
Authorization objects	10	68
Authorizations	12	58
Authorization profile	10	57
Single role	30	61
Composite role	30	61

Table 4.1 Available Field Lengths for Naming Conventions

Defined naming conventions are a component of the framework conditions, and require cross-project coordination with all involved parties. In particular, programming guidelines and standards have to be synchronized with the requirements of the authorization concept and accepted by all parties involved.

4.4 Definition of Work Areas

4.4.1 Defining the Utilized SAP Functional Scope

Prior to defining the authorization roles, you must define the utilized SAP functional scope. The goal here is to define which functions in each module are actually utilized at the enterprise. Although existing process documentation can be used as an aid, developing it with the support of the process team or the user departments is both faster and certainly more complete.

4.4.2 Procedure for Defining Roles at the Enterprise

Before you can begin implementing the SAP authorization concept, you have to define the actual roles. Now, you have to determine and analyze the business relationships. You can refer to job descriptions from the Human Resources (HR) department or reference manuals from the user departments (the latter describe which activities an enterprise employee performs—independently of applications, which position he or she holds at the company, and what type of interaction that employee has with other company employees (i.e., this can be used for the functional separation).

Remember that this status assessment necessarily records the status quo, which may differ from the new processes to be modeled in the SAP R/3 System. Nonetheless, this type of information is essential at this stage of a project, to define a consensus between the roles that will be modeled in the authorization concept and the "living" roles from future daily operations. Because terminology is very important to the subsequent administration process—that is, the process of granting SAP authorizations—it is essential to assign the authorization roles names that already exist within the organization and that will be accepted by employees. Harmonization with established names at the enterprise, even department-specific in the extreme case, has proven to be nearly ideal.

When defining the role names, we once again highly recommend holding workshops with the corresponding knowledge owners (i.e., selected department managers and employees from the enterprise organization). The foundation for such workshops is built by the descriptive documents introduced above (to the extent available), the participants' process knowledge, and, in particular, the best practice expertise of the external consultants. Accordingly, the procedure for determining roles at an enterprise requires the following steps:

▶ Reaching a uniform understanding of the role by defining terminology and the necessary degree of detail—in particular, the difference between SAP's definition of a role and other common definitions is particularly important

▶ Identifying similar areas of activity in each department, based on process descriptions and direct involvement of the knowledge owners

▶ Naming the identified activities with mnemonic names, ideally terms that are already defined and in use at the company

▶ Selecting the role definitions in accordance with their actual use in the SAP system (role/system reference)

▶ Naming the individuals responsible for roles at the enterprise

These steps for determining roles at an enterprise are described in detail below.

Reaching a Uniform Understanding of the Role

When conducting workshops, especially with regard to authorizations, it's extremely important to define the terminology from the start and to provide a comprehensible overview of the general context. In particular, the term *role* often has several definitions at an enterprise, each with a different meaning. For example, the term *role* can refer to a position in the organization (such as a department manager), or, it can refer to a specific activity (such as accounts payable). It is imperative, however, to bring about a uniform understanding of the term *role*. The introduction of terms, functions, and tasks seems to be the best solution here, as it frees you of having to use the term *role* and therefore avoids any misunderstandings that may arise.

Now, we recommend defining the degree of detail of the roles—that is, their "size." Companies with few employees and flat hierarchies generally use a role approach with a low number of roles (activities), because the activities will be distributed among fewer people, which means their individual scope is much larger. At such enterprises, the principle of *functional separation* can only be followed in especially critical areas. In contrast, employees of large corporations are usually highly specialized, and their jobs require a much smaller range of activities. Accordingly, the necessary number of single roles and composite roles differs significantly. Table 4.2 shows the different degrees of detail for role definition, using the Accounting area as an example.

Small to mid-sized enterprise: Accounting—existing functions	Multinational corporation: Accounting—existing functions
Accounts payable/receivable clerks	Accounts payable clerks
General ledger and petty cash clerk	Payroll accounting clerks
Controller	Accounts receivable clerks
Specialist for year-end closing activities	Key account manager
	Person who releases master data changes
	G/L clerk without sensitive accounts
	Specialist for G/L accounts
	Petty cash clerk
	Controller, cost center planning
	Controller, reporting
	…

Table 4.2 Different Degrees of Detail for Role Definition

Identifying Similar Areas of Activity

A role-based authorization concept builds on the activities supported by the ERP software, not the hierarchical structures. It is not always possible to completely omit the hazard of mixing organizational and functional role definitions. Department heads and other upper management use SAP nearly exclusively for approval procedures and reporting; their activities in the IT system are restricted to the functions of an end user. Therefore, when identifying the activities, you must both describe similar workflows in the sense of a function within a department and allow for consideration of the organizational structure at an enterprise.

Naming the Identified Activities

As previously mentioned, we recommend that you use existing terms within the enterprise, as this will make the detailed description and authorization assignment easier later. In most cases, however, especially at large companies, activities with the same content have different definitions in different areas or departments at the enterprise, resulting in a different understanding of the functional scope of these activities. Therefore, the real task here is to standardize the designations and increase acceptance of the newly introduced role names. If all else fails, this standardization must be enforced at the management (steering committee) level.

During the analysis of the enterprise organization, similar areas of activity must be identified and coordinated with employees from the user departments. These areas of activity are then assigned to the appropriate role names.

Selecting the Role Definitions

In the next step, you have to identify which of the defined roles are relevant for use in the SAP system. Existing process descriptions from the SAP implementation project can be used here. Roles that cannot be assigned to an SAP function can be ignored when you must define the detailed contents. Table 4.3 shows one possible selection form.

Role name	SAP functions contained in role
Accounts payable clerks	Yes
Payroll accounting clerks	No
Accounts receivable clerks	Yes
Key account managers	Yes
Person who releases master data changes	Yes

Table 4.3 Selecting the Relevant Roles

Role name	SAP functions contained in role
G/L clerks without sensitive accounts	Yes
Specialists for G/L accounts	Yes
Petty cash clerks	Yes
Controllers, cost center planning	No
Controllers, reporting	Yes
...	
Solution designers	No
Master data administrators	Yes
Change managers	Yes
...	

Table 4.3 Selecting the Relevant Roles (Cont.)

Naming the Individuals Responsible for Roles at the Enterprise

At this point in the coordination process, it is the optimal time to define the persons responsible for all roles. In some projects, the person responsible for the role is also called the *role owner* (similar to the *process owner* for business processes). The person responsible for the role has to do the following:

▶ Decide on the initial definition of a role and accept it.

▶ Evaluate, accept, or reject change requests that affect a role after its completion.

▶ Coordinate with other role owners when a function (a transaction) is contained in more than one role.

▶ Depending on the defined procedure, possibly approve when a user in the live system is assigned the role (control during role assignment) and when he or she is involved in controlling processes (for example, role assignment check or consideration of critical combinations)

▶ A helpful approach is to name persons responsible who actually come from the respective user departments and who know which subprocesses are associated with the role (e.g., strategic buyer → corresponding person responsible for the role: head of the central purchasing department. If necessary, the identified persons responsible or their assistants will have to be trained for their later activities. In some cases, however, it makes sense to link these tasks with existing hierarchies or areas of responsibility at the enterprise, in order to lend the appropriate weight to the decisions.

Holding Role Design Workshops

In conclusion, this chapter offers a short guide on using workshops to process the project steps described so far.

To fill the fields of the task/function matrix, you must consolidate the information from all the subteams of the SAP project—one way in which to do this is to hold *draft workshops* for each subteam. Each area chooses one or more contact persons, depending on the size of the subteam, who is the intermediary between their subteam and the authorization team. One proven method is to distribute the tasks to three workshops for each subteam, with the following sequence:

First Draft Workshop: Role Requirements

In the first draft workshop, the subteams are provided with an initial, general overview of the authorization concept, as the other project team members usually aren't sufficiently familiar with this area. It is especially important to clarify pertinent terms such as role (or activity group), authorization, profile, and so on, to avoid communication problems caused by a confusion of terminology.

This initial workshop will investigate which roles are needed, without actually deciding on their content. The role definitions can be developed from job or activity descriptions, as well as from the business descriptions of the processes to be modeled in the SAP system. You must pay special attention to the interfaces and delimitations between individual roles. It is also important to identify which subprocesses should never be combined in a single role—for example, these subprocesses can include approval or release strategies that require the dual-control principle.

Second Draft Workshop: Role Definition

Now that the roles to be created have been defined, you can determine the exact content of these roles in the second draft workshop. The function matrix is now extended to a task/function matrix. The subteams define the transactions or menu tree nodes that have to be included for each role in their respective areas of responsibility. They also determine which authorization (display, maintain, and so on) the roles should have at activity level for the corresponding transaction. This decision has to be made for each individual role. In the process, you have to ensure that the delimitation between the roles is achieved as defined in the first workshop.

Should a business process or subprocess have an exact description down to the transaction level, you can use the previous matrix (which indicates the relationship between roles and subprocesses) as an aid. You can easily move from this matrix to the task matrix by simply replacing the subprocesses with the corresponding transactions in the system.

Third Draft Workshop: Coordination Across Module and Subteam Boundaries

Once the major part of the work has been completed in the second workshop, the roles can now be coordinated between the individual subteams in this final phase—the third draft workshop—that ensures that no single subteam sees a specific transaction or area of the menu tree as "its property"; rather, the transactions are also used in other roles without the owner's awareness.

The completed task/function matrix makes it easy to coordinate roles across module and subteam boundaries: simply check the entries in the individual rows and columns.

Accordingly, the matrix is the main working document for the third workshop. By the end of the draft process, there must be a consensus of approval among all subteams and the corresponding persons responsible for individual as well as all roles.

In the next chapter, we will show you how to implement the defined design requirements in the SAP system, as well as which other factors you have to consider when implementing an authorization concept.

5 Procedure Model for Implementing an Authorization Concept

Now that you have defined the design requirements of the authorization concept, we will describe the actual implementation process. This chapter provides you with an overview of the organizational and technical procedure for implementing the authorization concept and making the transition to regular live operations.

5.1 Overview

The IBM Phased Model, which was described in the previous chapter, outlined the individual steps that must be taken and the milestones that must be met in an authorization concept project. So far, you have read about the project preparation phase and the design of the authorization concept, both of which correspond to the first four phases of the phased model. This chapter will focus on the implementation of the authorization concept.

Whereas close cooperation among the authorization team, the individual subteams in the project, and other involved parties is imperative when drafting the authorization concept, the authorization team can, on its own, execute most of the steps in the implementation phase. User department involvement is not necessary until the role tests. Of course, you have to ensure that the schedule of the implementation is synchronized with the schedule of the overall project.

To enable the authorization team to work independently, it is essential that all critical documents such as the task/function matrix and the organization/value matrix are complete and have already been coordinated with all involved parties. The actual implementation of the single roles and composite roles in the SAP system (Phases 5 and 6) is described in detail in Section 5.2.

At the end of the implementation phase, the roles have to be tested in order to correct as many errors as possible before going live. Before you test the roles in the system, you should ensure that the Customizing tests have already been successfully completed. Because any and all errors in the R/3 Customizing have been corrected, you can ensure that any errors identified during the role tests are due to the roles themselves. The role test (Phase 7) is described in Section 5.3. The role implementation phase cannot be considered complete until all the tests have been successfully executed.

Although this chapter focuses primarily on the implementation of the authorization concept, the following sections also describe the activities that will be part of your GoingLive preparations, and the administration of users and authorizations in a live SAP system.

5.2 Implementation

Do not make the description of the implementation of the authorization concept into a manual for the role/profile administrator. Instead, use it to provide an overview of the technical means that are available in the SAP system and that are used for implementing and testing the roles. To answer detailed and practical questions, we recommend that you refer to the book *Authorization Made Easy* (see Bibliography), which should prove helpful.

5.2.1 The Profile Generator—Overview

The main tool for implementing roles in the SAP R/3 System is the *Profile Generator* (also called the *Authorization Profile Generator*; see Figure 5.1), which was introduced in SAP R/3 Release 3.1G. Many new functions have been added since this first version, however. You use transaction code PFCG to call the Profile Generator. To activate the Profile Generator in a newly installed SAP system, you have to set profile parameter *auth/no_check_in_some_cases* to *Y*. This is the default value in the delivery system in Release 4.6C and later.

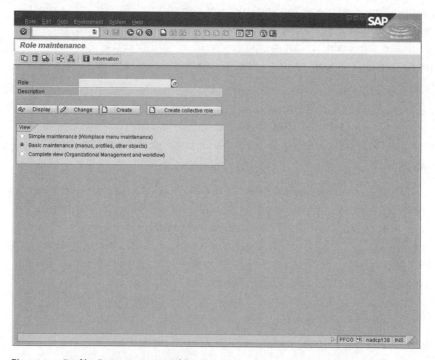

Figure 5.1 Profile Generator—Initial Screen

You can use the Profile Generator to create both single and composite roles. The basic difference is that composite roles are merely groupings of single roles. No separate profiles or authorizations are generated for composite roles. Instead, the profiles of the single roles, which are contained in the composite role, are summarized in the composite role.

During the creation of single roles, the Profile Generator is primarily responsible for generating the appropriate authorization profiles for the role menus, which contain the transaction codes defined in each role.

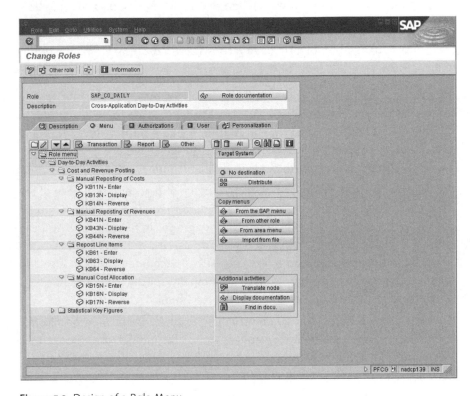

Figure 5.2 Design of a Role Menu

Unfortunately, even a powerful tool like the SAP Profile Generator does not support the complete automation of this task, which means that a fair amount of manual postprocessing is always required. Although the "manual" editing of authorizations and profiles in Transactions SU02 and SU03 has become superfluous in newer releases of the SAP R/3 System, comprehensive expertise is still required to verify, correct, and supplement the authorization values proposed by the Profile Generator. In unfavorable circumstances, simply using all the proposals from the system can result in large gaps in your authorization concept, because the generated profiles can contain more far-reaching authorizations than you originally planned when designing the role. Conversely, the tests following the role implementation can take an unnecessarily long time if the profiles do not already contain all the authorizations required to execute the transactions properly.

Creating Single Roles

In order to implement a role, the transactions that are to be contained in this single role must be defined. These transactions can be specified by indicating a corresponding menu node in the task/function matrix, for example, or directly as a list.

The technical configuration of a single role consists of two steps, which are briefly described, as are several details of this procedure:

1. After you create a new role and fill in the descriptive fields, you must first define the user menu (see Figure 5.2). All the transactions that are to be executable in the role are added to the user menu. Both individual transactions and menu tree nodes with several transactions can be added manually, or from other menus (SAP standard menu, role menu, or area menu).

   The design of the role menu, that is, the grouping, outline, and sequence of the transactions, is not linked with the SAP standard menu in R/3 Release 4.6 (in contrast to the transaction selection in activity groups in Release 4.0). You can insert, delete, or rename any menu node. You can move menu items around anywhere within the menu using the Drag&Drop technique. You can also add Internet addresses or documents (such as company-specific Help texts or contact persons) directly as a menu item in the role menu.

2. Once the menu is complete, you must generate the authorization profiles for the transactions contained in the menu, as well as the individual authorizations (see Figure 5.3). When the profiles are generated, the information that pertains to which authorizations are required for which transaction is extracted from the various tables (tables USOBT_C and USOBX_C). After the automatic generation, you must comb through the authorization data in the tree structure of the Profile Generator and check it manually. All the fields that the Profile Generator has not yet filled must be maintained. You can also add authorizations to or remove them from any authorization object.

   The Profile Generator flags the individual authorizations with traffic lights (see Figure 5.4): a red traffic light indicates an authorization with at least one organizational level that has not been maintained; a yellow traffic light indicates that at least one field of an authorization has not been maintained; and a green traffic light indicates that the authorization has been fully maintained.

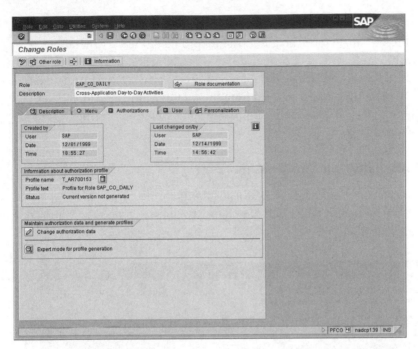

Figure 5.3 Maintenance of Authorization Information for a Single Role

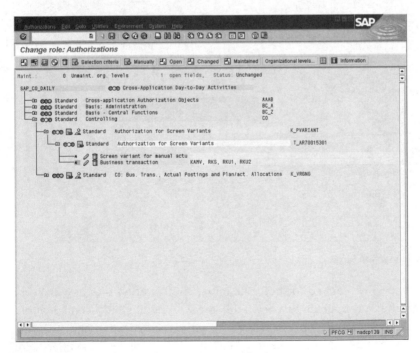

Figure 5.4 Manual Change of Authorization Field Values

Creating Composite Roles

In contrast to the single roles, no authorization profile has to be generated to create composite roles. Instead, a composite role is a collection of all the single roles that compose it. This assignment is derived from the task/function matrix. The menu of the composite role is derived from the menus of the individual roles, but can also be modified in the composite role itself as described further in the following sections.

5.2.2 Initializing the Profile Generator

Before you can use the Profile Generator for the first time, you have to initialize several customer-specific tables with SAP default values. You do so in Transaction SU25 (see Figure 5.5).

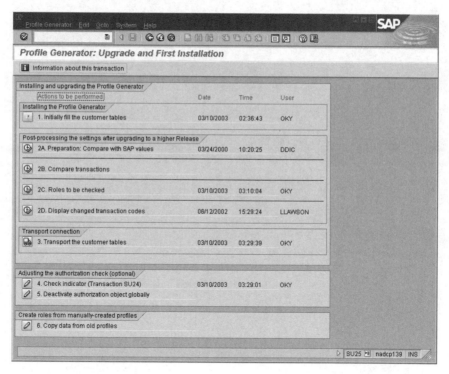

Figure 5.5 Transaction SU25

This initialization is required for both the initial configuration of a new delivery system and after any upgrade to a newer release. During the initial configuration, you only have to execute Step 1 in Figure 5.5, and possibly Steps 4 and 5. During an upgrade, the emphasis is with items 2A-2D and 6, if profiles exist in the system that were not generated with an earlier version of the Profile Generator.

The individual steps are as follows:

1. In the first step, you copy the SAP default values for tables USOBT_C and USOBX_C from tables USOBT and USOBX. These tables control the response of the Profile Generator during the generation of authorization values. The tables contain definitions for nearly every transaction code that pertains to which authorization objects the Profile Generator adds to the profile for a role contained in that transaction. You can also define customer defaults for field settings, in order to further automate the profile generation process.

   It is important to note that this information initially is not relevant to which objects are actually checked during the transaction. Regardless if an object is not entered in table USOBT_C, it will be checked if the corresponding check is programmed in the ABAP source code of the transaction. The converse also holds true, that is, an object will not be checked simply because it is entered in table USOBT_C. Therefore, there is no direct link between the table of default values and the underlying ABAP source code for the transactions.

   Because the tables determine only the behavior of the Profile Generator during generation, existing profiles are not affected by the settings. If you generate existing roles again after a modification or repeat initialization of these tables, however, the changes will affect the authorization profiles, which may require subsequent revision of the authorizations.

   When you upgrade an existing system, use this step with caution, to avoid overwriting existing, customer-specific modifications to the SAP standard.

2. Steps 2A through 2D involve the comparison of existing roles (and activity groups) that were created with earlier versions of the Profile Generator and that will continue to be used after a release upgrade.

   Step 2C displays a list of all the roles in which the authorization values in the profile assigned to the role do not agree with the default values in table USOBT_C. You have to revise these values manually. In particular, this step is always required when new authorization objects have been added to the system due to a release upgrade. These objects are not yet present in any roles and now have to be maintained.

   After a release upgrade, existing transactions are often replaced by newer or different transactions. Step 2D highlights all the roles that contain transactions for which new or changed transactions exist with other transaction codes. These new transactions can either be added to the role menus automatically, or inserted in the roles in place of the old transactions.

3. Step 3 is used to transport the customer tables you filled in Step 1. Roles and profiles are not transported here; they have to be added to a separate transport request.

4. Step 4 is optional. It calls Transaction SU24, which can be used to change the contents of tables USOBT_C and USOBX_C (see Chapter 2).

5. Step 5 includes a reference to Transaction AUTH_SWITCH_OBJECTS, which you can use to deactivate authorization objects globally. We do not recommend using this option, however. See Section 5.8.2 for more information on this subject.

6. Step 6 requires that you copy data from old profiles (i.e., manually defined profiles from previous SAP versions for which no role or activity group exists from the old release). You can have a new role generated automatically for each profile. In turn, the role generates the exact existing profile. You only need to perform this step if you have created profiles without the Profile Generator in an earlier version of SAP R/3, and want to retain these profiles after the release upgrade and administer them with the Profile Generator.

In order to convert a profile to a role, the profile must contain object S_TCODE (object for starting the transaction), which means that the concept you want to migrate must already be transaction-based. Profiles that only contain authorization objects without a reference to a transaction are only converted to the extent that the Profile Generator creates a role that only contains manually added authorization objects. In this case, you cannot generate a role menu with reference to table USOBT_C.

5.2.3   Roles Provided by SAP

SAP provides a large number of single roles in Release 4.6C of the standard SAP R/3 System. It is usually possible—with some restrictions—to use these roles to implement an authorization concept. Depending on the business process flows and distribution of tasks at your enterprise, however, the SAP roles will most likely be too insufficient to meet the demands of an authorization concept. Therefore, you should think of the SAP roles as sample templates rather than as "finished material" for the implementation. Of course, authorization administrators who don't have much experience in creating roles may find it useful to analyze the roles provided by SAP, in order to learn how to implement their own roles.

Should you or your administrator decide to use some of the roles provided by SAP in your system, although we expressly advise against doing so, be sure to create copies of the roles under separate names. Roles in the SAP namespace can be overwritten during each system update, nullifying any changes that you have made. Again, we generally do not recommend using this procedure.

5.2.4 User Menus

Starting in Release 4.6, users can elect to display a user menu after they log on to the system. The menu contains all the transactions from all the roles currently assigned to the respective users. Therefore, each user sees a predefined selection of the possible transactions, largely eliminating the need to search through the paths of the SAP standard menu. This option can also be deactivated if desired. In this case, each user's display is limited to the SAP standard menu (or an area menu), even if a different menu is defined in the respective roles. Role menus with flexible configuration options are available in Release 4.6A and later.

When you define a role, you also determine the menu that is linked with that role. We recommend that you follow several basic guidelines when designing the role menus:

▶ Each transaction should only appear once within a menu branch. If a transaction logically belongs to several areas, however, it can appear several times in the menu tree (as is the case in several places in the standard SAP menu).

▶ The positions of the individual transactions should be standardized across all the roles in a system, enabling users to find them easily even if the menu changes due to the addition of other roles. One way to ensure this standardization is to arrange the transactions in the user menus in accordance with their positions in the standard SAP menu tree. You do not necessarily have to follow this transaction sequence, however.

▶ All transactions for a certain activity area or task should be arranged in the same node of the menu, in order to enable users to find related transactions easily.

When a composite role is created, the menus of the single roles that make up the composite role are combined to form the menu of the composite role. The Profile Generator simply lists each single menu consecutively. Redundant or identical menu nodes are neither detected nor changed. The same situation occurs when a user is assigned several roles. The menu that the user sees after a logon corresponds to the set of the menus of all the roles in his or her user master record. This method is not always ideal, however, as it does not promote the creation of clear menus, for example, when identically named branches of the menu tree exist in several places.

One solution, albeit an extremely time-consuming one, is to manually rearrange the menu of each composite role when you define it. This solution also makes administering the roles more difficult, because when you change the menu of a single role, you also have to revise the menus of all the composite roles that contain that single role.

Accordingly, the SAP system features various options for automatically reassigning and condensing the menus after logon. The parameters of client-independent table SSM_CUST that are listed in Table 5.1 below affect the structure of the user menu (also see SAP Note numbers 203994, 321965, 357877, and 357693).

ID	SAP standard	Description
CONDENSE_MENU	No	All redundant information is condensed, both for transactions and menu texts.
SORT_USER_MENU	No	All menu nodes are to be sorted in alphabetical order.
DELETE_DOUBLE_TCODES	Yes	Transactions that appear several times in different menu paths are only displayed once.

Table 5.1 Customizing Switches for the Display of the User Menu

5.2.5 Generating the Authorizations

After you have created the user menu for a single role, you have to generate the corresponding profile and the related authorizations. To do so, switch to the **Authorizations** tab page in the Profile Generator.

Please note that the authorization data of a role is initially only saved in the role itself. You cannot use the authorizations until you *generate* the authorization profiles. If you change the authorization data of a role without generating the corresponding profile, the changes will not take effect. When you press the pushbutton **Change authorization data**, the Profile Generator generates the profile automatically based on the role menu.

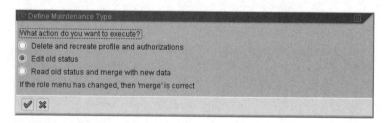

Figure 5.6 Expert Mode Options

Press the **Expert Mode** pushbutton to change the processing mode. The following options are available (see Figure 5.6):

▶ All existing information is deleted and the authorization data is generated again for this role. Select this item with caution, as it will cause all existing settings to be lost.

- The old status is edited. The authorization data is displayed as currently defined in the role and can be edited manually.

- If the menu of the role has changed, you must merge the authorization data with the new menu. When you select this option, existing authorization data is retained to the extent possible. The necessary authorizations are inserted for new transactions that have been added to the menu. You must always select this option when the role menu of an existing role has changed.

The Profile Generator now generates the authorizations that are required to execute the transactions contained in the user menu of the role. The necessary information is extracted from tables USOBT_C and USOBX_C, which are filled during the initialization of the Profile Generator as described previously.

Unfortunately, the Profile Generator cannot fill all the fields that are required in the authorizations completely or correctly. Organizational restrictions to the roles, for example (see the organization/value matrix) always have to be maintained manually. These fields, which are particularly important when maintaining the field values of the authorizations, are called *organizational levels*.

Do not enter the organizational levels directly in the fields of the authorizations. Instead, when authorizations with organizational level fields exist, the Profile Generator automatically displays a window (see Figure 5.7) in which you can maintain the field values for the organizational levels globally for a role. This method ensures that these values are recorded uniformly in all the authorizations of a role. Only rarely does it make sense to restrict an authorization object of a single role to a certain company code, personnel area, or similar organization, for example, while restricting a different object within the same single role to a different area. Accordingly, the values of the organizational levels are extremely important for the inheritance of roles, as described further below.

The standard SAP system automatically determines which fields the Profile Generator considers as organizational levels. You use Transaction SUPO to display and maintain all the organizational levels defined in the system. If you need to create new organizational level fields that are not supported in the standard SAP system, SAP Note number 323817 contains instructions and several tips for doing so.

When you maintain the organizational levels for a role, you see the view in Figure 5.3 of the authorizations created by the Profile Generator, in which you can maintain the field values of the individual authorizations. You have to fill and check the field values in accordance with the framework conditions and the organization/value matrix (see Chapter 4).

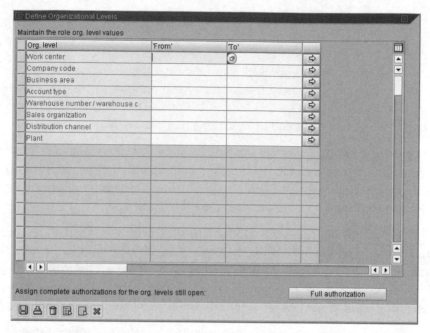

Figure 5.7 Maintenance of Organizational Values

Which authorizations the Profile Generator creates automatically depends on the contents of tables USOBT_C and USOBX, as described above. During the manual check of the automatically generated authorizations, you may find that too many authorizations, which are not relevant to the privileges defined for the role, were generated. You also may discover that certain authorizations required to execute the transactions contained in the role are missing.

If the Profile Generator has generated authorizations that are too broad or inappropriate for the role, you will have to delete them from the profile. There are two options for doing so:

▶ When you delete an authorization manually in the Profile Generator, it will not be contained in the generated profile. As soon as the profile is generated again for the role, however, the Profile Generator will add the authorization again (in accordance with the current settings in table USOBT_C), which means that you have to delete the authorization again.

▶ To prevent this occurrence, we recommend that you simply deactivate the authorizations that should not be contained in a role rather than delete them, and not change the Profile Generator proposals in the individual fields. In this case, the information for this authorization will remain saved in the role. The authorization will not be added to the generated profile, nor will it be added to the role again during the next profile generation.

If necessary authorizations are missing, you can add them manually. Manual post-processing is essential, especially when transactions with a large number of functions are involved, because the different roles often use different segments of the overall range of possible variants for a transaction.

When you manually maintain the authorization data generated by the Profile Generator, the status that is displayed for each authorization indicates which authorization fields and objects have been changed and which fields still have to be maintained.

The values have the following meanings:

▶ **Standard**
The authorization is in line with the SAP standard, as generated by the Profile Generator (fields filled with default values from table USOBT_C).

▶ **Maintained**
At least one field of the authorization that the Profile Generator did not fill has been maintained by the administrator.

▶ **Changed**
At least one field of the authorization that the Profile Generator filled with a default value has been changed.

▶ **Manually**
An authorization was added manually. No corresponding default value was defined.

Should you determine that an authorization is required in all roles that contain a certain transaction, or conversely that an authorization must not be present in any role that contains a certain transaction, you can define this globally by changing table USOBT_C.

After you have maintained the authorizations for a role completely, you can generate the authorization profile for that role. To do so, press the **Generate** button in the authorization view. The system automatically proposes a profile name, which you can typically use as the default, without changing it. To simplify the assignment of profiles to roles, you can also use the name of the role (or one derived from the role name) for the profile. For more information on naming conventions, see Section 4.3.6 in Chapter 4. Please note, however, that the length of generated profile names is limited to 10 characters (in comparison: the technical names of authorization roles can be up to 30 characters long).

5.2.6 Copying Roles and the Inheritance Function

Depending on the organizational divisions of the enterprise to be modeled in the SAP system, you may need several roles that contain the same functions but which access different data areas. Two different procedures, each with their own advantages and disadvantages, are available for creating these roles.

Copying Roles

You can create any number of copies of an existing role in the Profile Generator. After you copy a role, there is no link between the original role and the copy. You can also copy the user assignment of the role during the copy operation. This means that all users who were assigned the original role are also assigned the copy of the role in their user master records; however, this behavior is not recommended.

After you copy the roles, you must change the individual fields of the authorizations to create a functionally identical role with different data access authorizations.

This first method is very simple to implement. However, it can result in both consistency problems and an unreasonably large administrative effort if you have to subsequently change the functions of the role. Furthermore, if no external documentation exists that documents the relationship between the roles, you cannot ensure that the copies of the role will remain functionally identical.

Inheritance Functions for Roles

The second method deals with the inheritance or derivation of roles. You must first create a *reference role* that contains the required functions. This reference role is merely a template and is not typically assigned to users directly. Accordingly, you do not have to generate the authorization profiles for this role, because it is not used.

The role that is used as the template for inheritance passes its user menu onto the derived roles. If a new transaction is added to the reference role, it appears automatically in all the derived roles (see Figure 5.8).

In Release 4.6B and later, you can also maintain authorization data in the reference role. All the authorization information maintained here is passed onto the derived roles, with the exception of the *organizational values*. The organizational values are maintained for each derived role and enable the distinct assignment of organization-specific data access.

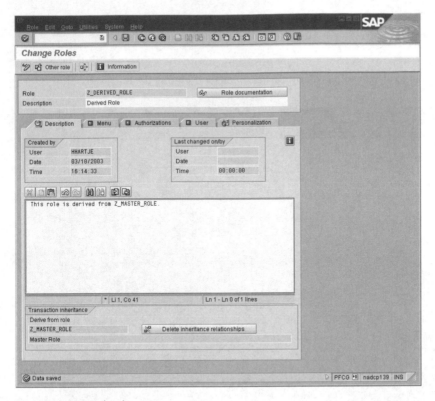

Figure 5.8 Derived Role

The inheritance method ensures that the link between the reference role and the derived roles remains even after changes are made. You can also disassociate the derived roles from the reference role. To do so, press the **Delete inheritance relationships** button in the derived role. In this case, the system creates an independent copy of the role from the derived role, which you can then maintain further as described in the previous section on copying roles. Please note, however, that once you delete an inheritance relationship, you cannot reestablish it.

5.2.7 Composite Roles

As described, you must first implement single roles, which only contain a few transactions each in accordance with a specific task. You then combine these single roles to form composite roles, which correspond to the business roles (functions).

To do so, you first create the single roles in the Profile Generator. You then create the composite role that will contain the single roles. You cannot assign transactions directly to the composite role. Instead, the composite role uses the user menus from the single roles. For information on eliminating any redundancies that may arise when forming composite roles, see Section 5.2.4.

It is neither logical nor technically possible to nest roles over multiple levels. You can only add single roles to composite roles (see Figure 5.9).

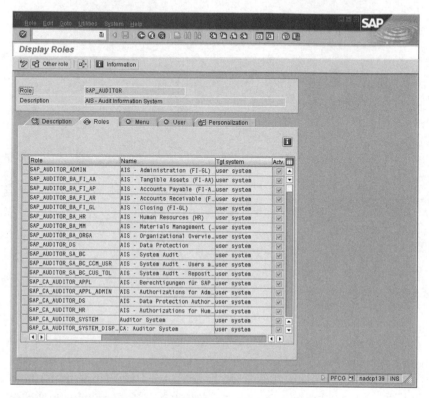

Figure 5.9 Adding Single Roles to a Composite Role

5.3   Testing the Implemented Roles

5.3.1   Requirements

It is essential to test the roles at the conclusion of the implementation phase. These tests must be coordinated with the progress of the other development and implementation activities in the system.

We do not recommend that you test the Customizing settings and the roles concurrently, because many error messages do not clearly indicate whether a Customizing error or an authorization error is at fault. Even when the SAP system clearly reports an authorization error, it is possible that the error might be caused by an incorrect or incomplete Customizing configuration—for example, when the wrong organizational values are checked.

When you test the Customizing settings, testing the business processes that you have implemented in the SAP system for the first time, we recommend that you use user IDs that have all authorizations (profile SAP_ALL) to ensure that no errors can arise due to authorization problems. Once the full functionality has been tested successfully, you can begin testing the roles.

At the start of the role test, you must have drafted test schedules. The schedule must list all the roles to be tested. You can use the business description of each role and its technical description (at transaction code level from the task/function matrix) to determine which functions can be performed with the role and therefore must be included in the test.

The authorization tests are divided into positive and negative tests:

▶ During the positive test, you test whether or not the transactions defined in a role can be executed, and whether the appropriate data can be accessed.

▶ During the negative test, you verify that those transactions, which are not contained in the role, cannot be performed, and that no data outside the range authorized for the role can be accessed. You should also ensure that transactions that are only supposed to allow read access to the corresponding data do not permit the data to be maintained, created, or deleted. Of course, you cannot perform the negative test for all possible transactions and data that are not contained in a given role. Instead, it is best that you restrict your testing to critical transactions and data.

The test is divided into three phases: unit test, role integration test, and user acceptance test—each of which must meet different requirements.

5.3.2 Unit Test

The *unit test* is conducted immediately after the implementation phase, and is a prerequisite for the integration test of the authorizations. The objective of the unit test is to compare the defined roles with the requirements of the task/function matrix and to ensure that the technical implementation functions properly. Employees in the authorization team can conduct the unit test.

The unit test enables you to eliminate obvious errors at an early stage, which, in turn, will make it much easier to conduct the actual integration test. If your schedule is tight, you can even conduct the unit test concurrently—while the implementation process is still underway. In this case, you must assign the defined composite roles to a specific test user ID and test them as soon as each role is complete. The unit test is a positive test, which means that you only verify that the transactions contained in the role are executable, but do not need to verify that explicitly excluded or critical transactions are inaccessible. The latter task is part of the integration test.

5.3.3 Role Integration Test

Once the unit test has been completed, the roles are ready for the *role integration test* phase. While the objective of the unit test is to ensure that the role functions properly—that is, that the transactions contained in the role can be executed—the integration test goes much further, involving both the expected results at the data level and the integration aspects.

Responsibility for conducting the integration test usually rests with the user departments. The tests themselves should be held by specially trained end users (key users, power users) who are intimately familiar with the business processes upon which the tests are based and who should have at least a basic understanding of the SAP technology used for authorization assignment and checks. The role integration test is a positive/negative test: it involves checking that the transactions are executable, that the data is processed correctly, and that the results are output properly, as well as confirming that certain critical transactions are not executable and that data access is restricted to the correct organizational values.

We recommend that you draft detailed test documents for this purpose. These documents should be based on the defined business processes or derived from the test cases in the existing *Business Blueprint*. The integration aspect—that is, the interaction between various roles within a business process—is also important here. If the Business Blueprint indicates that the individual steps of a business process have to be executed by different roles, this information has to be reflected throughout the test documents for the integration test.

5.3.4 User Acceptance Test

This step is optional; however, it is a useful addition from the change management viewpoint. In this *user acceptance test* phase, selected employees in the user departments can familiarize themselves with their intended roles and request any necessary changes before you go live with the system. Such requests could include rearranging the role menu, or adding user-developed transactions, reports, or table views.

5.3.5 Final Review

Because roles that have already been approved by the user departments can be modified during the testing process, all performed modifications have to be documented properly and sufficiently. During this *final review* process, you should also complete and conclude your work on the framework conditions.

The completion of this project phase involves another review of the authorization concept and the implemented roles. In particular, you should ensure that the framework conditions have been implemented properly and that all auditability aspects of the concept have been satisfied. It makes sense for the user departments to approve and release the roles formally for production use.

The authorizations are not assigned to the user master records until all tests and reviews have been concluded and the documentation has been finalized.

5.3.6 Technical Implementation of the Role Tests

When you encounter errors during the tests of the implemented roles, you must clarify whether missing or incorrectly assigned authorizations are responsible for a given error. To determine whether authorizations are missing in a role and if so, which ones, you can use the following options:

▶ Displaying a failed authorization check (Transaction SU53)
▶ System trace of all authorization checks (Transaction ST01)

Displaying a Failed Authorization Check

When a user encounters a missing authorization while testing a role, it will not be possible to execute the requested action. Although the SAP system displays an error message, this message does not necessarily indicate whether an authorization problem is actually involved.

In this case, you can use Transaction SU53 (or menu path **System · Utilities · Display Authorization Check**) to display the result of the last failed authorization check. As Figure 5.10 shows, the authorization that was checked, but is not present in the user master record is displayed first, followed by all the existing authorizations for the corresponding authorization object in the user's master record. Please note that the latter listing may be blank.

It is critical to call this display *immediately* after the failed authorization check, as only the last object that failed the authorization check is saved.

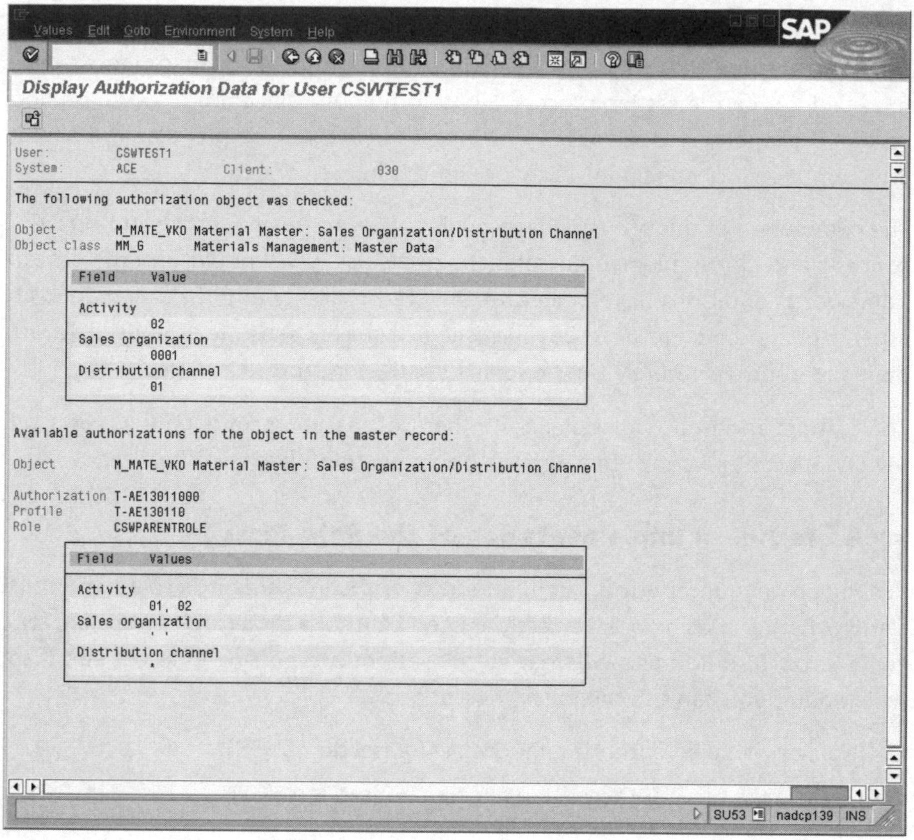

Figure 5.10 Display of Authorization Data

System Trace

The other option is the system trace (Transaction ST01). The system trace enables users to record various actions and results in the SAP system and then evaluate the resulting log. The authorization checks are the relevant objects here. Set the check box of the same name in the initial screen of Transaction ST01 to record them. When the trace is active, all authorization checks are recorded, together with the respective field values and the result of the check (see Figure 5.11).

Because the system trace can place a heavy load on your system, depending on the scope of data to be recorded, you should only activate it in test or consolidation systems, not in live systems. If you absolutely have to perform the trace based on master data or transaction data that is only available in the live system, you should select the filter criteria for the trace carefully in order to keep the resulting data volume to a minimum. For example, the various menu options will allow you to limit the system trace to a specific user ID.

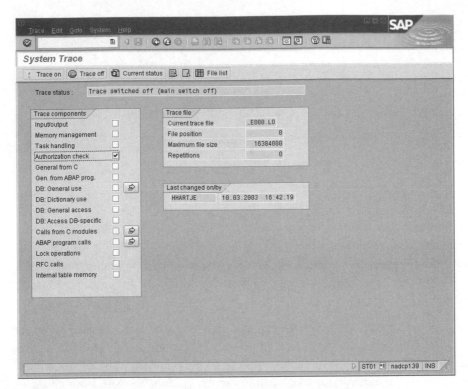

Figure 5.11 System Trace with Transaction Code ST01

Please also note that the trace is always restricted to one single application server. For example, if you execute the trace with an administrator ID in order to log the authorization checks performed for a different user ID, you have to ensure that both users are logged on to the same application server.

After you activate the system trace, you must perform the system actions (transactions, reports, and so on) that you want to trace. When you deactivate the trace at the end of the transaction, the results of the trace are available as a file for analysis.

Now, you should only examine the file entries generated as a result of the authorization checks. One line is written to the log file for each performed authorization check. Each line starts with a status value that indicates the result of the check. This result value is followed by the checked object with the corresponding field values. The start of a transaction in the trace file is indicated by the check of object S_TCODE with the corresponding transaction code.

ST01 code	Description
0	Authorization check passed
1	No authorization
2	Too many parameters for authorization check
3	Object not contained in user buffer
4	No profile contained in user buffer
6	Authorization check incorrect
7, 8, 9	Invalid user buffer

Table 5.2 Status Values During the Authorization Check

The status values for the authorization check are listed in Table 5.2. You will usually only see the values 0 and 1. Higher values can indicate programming errors in the authorization check or a table inconsistency in the user buffer or user master record.

To conduct an authorization system trace, proceed as follows: use a test user ID that definitely has blanket system authorizations (assign profile SAP_ALL to the test user ID, for example) to execute the transaction that you want to check. Then perform all the required functions within the transaction. The SAP system logs all the performed authorization checks. When you evaluate the log, a list of all the checked authorization objects is generated along with the respective field values required for each check. Based on this list, you can determine whether a role already has the correct values for all the checked authorizations.

5.3.7 Maintaining Authorization Data Manually

Even if you don't use the Profile Generator, you can still create authorizations and authorization profiles independently of roles. To do so, use Transactions SU03 (maintain authorizations) and SU02 (maintain profiles). Although SAP does not recommend using this transaction in Release 4.6C and later, it is still possible. Please note, however, that you cannot use these transactions to maintain profiles and authorizations that were initially created with the Profile Generator. These automatically generated profiles and authorizations are flagged with a **Generated** identifier.

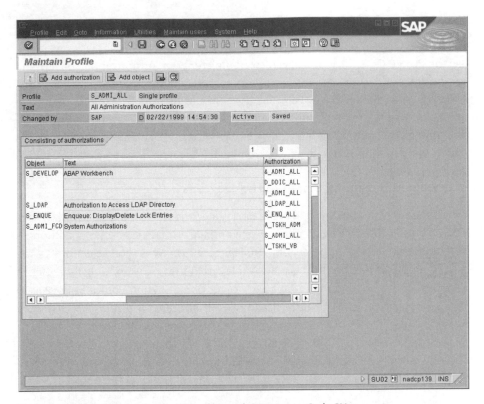

Figure 5.12 Manual Maintenance of Profiles with Transaction Code SU02

Maintaining Profiles Manually

To maintain profiles manually, you use Transaction SU02 (see Figure 5.12). In this transaction, you can create, maintain, and delete single and composite profiles. For single profiles, the names of the authorization objects are displayed (and entered) in the first column, as shown in Figure 5.12, and the names of the authorizations for the corresponding object appear in the last column. If several authorizations exist for an object, the object in question is only listed once. The administrator can now add individual authorizations to the profile or delete existing ones.

If you want to add manually defined authorizations to a profile, you have to create them in Transaction SU03 first (see below) before you can enter them in the profile.

When you manually delete profiles or authorizations with these two transactions (SU02 and SU03), the SAP system ensures that the objects to be deleted are no longer used in any profile or user ID. If they are, the objects cannot be deleted.

Maintaining Composite Profiles Manually

The Profile Generator does not generate composite profiles automatically. If you use the Profile Generator exclusively to administer your authorization concept, no composite profiles are needed. You have to create them manually, if necessary. Although it is technically possible to use composite profiles as components of other composite profiles—thus creating nested, multilevel profiles—we highly discourage you from using this option, as SAP does not guarantee that such constructs will function properly in all circumstances.

Manually Maintaining Single Authorizations

You can use Transaction SU03 to maintain, create, and delete single authorizations. When you start the transaction, the system initially displays all classes of authorization objects that exist in the system (see Figure 5.13). When you select one of the classes, all the objects in that class are displayed in the corresponding list. You can also display the documentation for each object here. When you double-click to select an object, a list of all authorizations for that object is displayed (see Figure 5.14). The flag in the *Ty.* (type) column indicates that the Profile Generator has generated this authorization. All authorizations without this flag were created manually. Any authorizations that were not generated automatically can be maintained or deleted. You can also create new authorizations for the selected object.

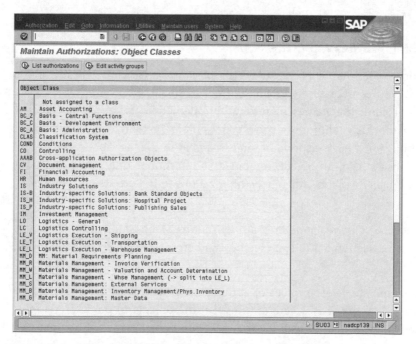

Figure 5.13 Authorization Object Classes in Transaction Code SU03

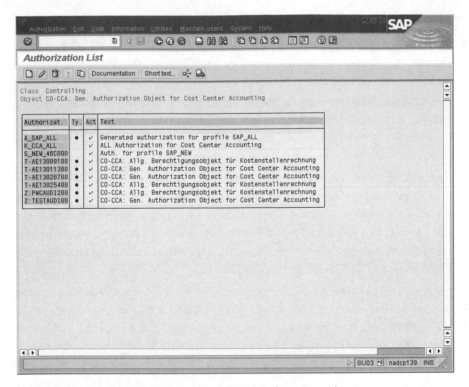

Figure 5.14 List of all Authorizations for a Selected Authorization Object

5.4 Configuring the User Master Records

Before you go live with your system, you have to create the necessary user IDs with the corresponding authorizations. To create the user IDs, you must use Transaction SU01. To do so, you have to enter the user data—in particular, the name and initial password are required fields that you have to enter before you can save a new user master record.

The link between a user master record and the corresponding authorizations is established through the authorization profiles (single and composite profiles) recorded in the user ID. During the logon to the SAP system, all the authorizations in the profiles for the user ID are loaded into the user buffer. All the authorization checks performed in the system then use these authorizations saved in the user buffer. Accordingly, when profiles are added to or removed from a user ID, or existing profiles are modified, the user in question has to log onto the system again for the changes to take effect.

To enter profiles in a user ID, you can choose from the following two options:

▶ You can enter manually defined *composite* and *single profiles* in the user ID directly in Transaction SU01. Generated profiles can also be added directly, however, the SAP system responds to such attempts with a warning message.

▶ The recommended method is to assign *roles* instead of profiles to the user IDs. You can either enter roles for a user ID in Transaction SU01 or assign user IDs to a role in Transaction PFCG. The result is the same in both cases: a link is established between the user ID and the role.

Please note, however, that simply entering the role in the user ID does not mean that the user has the associated authorizations, because the profile for the role (or profiles in case of composite roles) has not been recorded in the user ID yet. This recording of the profile in the user ID occurs during the user comparison, which you can either start manually or schedule automatically with report PFCG_TIME_DEPENDENCY.

Because you can specify a validity period for each role, we recommend that you schedule the report PFCG_TIME_DEPENDENCY to run each night. When the validity period of a role commences or expires, the profile for that role is automatically added to or removed from the user ID during the next user comparison.

The manual assignment of generated profiles is a critical process: during the next user comparison, all generated profiles will be removed from the user ID if no corresponding role has been entered. Therefore, if you manually assign generated profiles, you must never use the user comparison.

5.5 Going Live

Once the user roles have been tested and entered in the user IDs, nothing else stands in the way of your *going live*—at least from an authorization standpoint.

Despite all your tests and reviews, however, it is still almost inevitable that you will discover mistakes in the granted authorizations in the first few weeks. Even if you exercise the greatest of care in defining your roles and authorizations, because of the complexity of the authorization concept, errors are unavoidable. Therefore, going live with the system marks the start of an intensive support phase, which usually lasts four to six weeks.

As administrators have to deal with an increased number of error messages and change requests from users, they also have to simultaneously become familiar with working with the corresponding tools—such as the Profile Generator and the System Trace—even if they were already involved in implementing or testing the user roles previously. Therefore, the presence and support of the members of the authorization team (usually the consultants) are required to ensure a seamless live start. In the first few weeks after going live, the primary responsibilities of these individuals include:

▶ Quickly localizing and correcting any errors discovered after going live

▶ Evaluating the change requests submitted by the users and implementing them where appropriate

▶ Helping the authorization administrators get started with their new responsibilities and providing them with the necessary skills and knowledge required for regular operations

▶ Adjusting the documentation to reflect subsequent changes

▶ Assisting in the establishment of an end user support organization (setting up a support hotline, for example)

5.6   Regular Operations

5.6.1   The Authorization Concept in a Live System

When you begin to implement an authorization concept, you should already consider the technical and administrative workflows inherent in the future live system. This is a key aspect that should be discussed from the start of the project, as described in Section 4.3.2. In most cases, existing processes and employees' areas of responsibility change over time. Ultimately, the naming conventions used for the authorizations (composite roles, roles, and profiles) that will be assigned to the users are critical for the division of responsibilities in user and authorization administration.

This user and authorization administration is only one part of system operations. Overall, the following areas can be identified as additional examples:

▶ User care and support organization

▶ System operating and batch support

▶ Quality management

▶ Cooperation with SAP in dealing with error messages

▶ Support of the technical infrastructure

  ▷ Networks

  ▷ Operating systems

  ▷ Databases

  ▷ Web links

- ▶ Server support
- ▶ Client support
- ▶ Hardware support
- ▶ Interface support

These operational functions are not described in any detail here, however, as this chapter focuses on the design of user and role administration.

5.6.2 User and Role Administration

The tasks of user and authorization administration should be kept separate in live systems. Different methods are available for implementing the necessary functional separation:

Variant 1

SAP recommends splitting the administration functions into three areas of responsibility:

- ▶ The *user administrator* assigns roles to the users and adds the corresponding profiles to the user master records (user comparison).
- ▶ The *authorization data administrator* creates the roles and maintains the role menus and authorization data for the respective roles. The authorization data administrator should not be authorized to generate the authorization profiles, however.
- ▶ The *authorization profile administrator* generates the authorization profiles from the roles.

The underlying authorization objects—that is, the technical background—were mentioned briefly in Chapter 2 and are listed in detail in Appendix A, together with the relevant fields.

A separation into two areas of responsibility is also usually sufficient. In this case, the responsibilities of the authorization data administrator and the authorization profile administrator are combined, and you only need to differentiate between authorization administrator and user administrator.

Some authors also recommend separating the assignment of roles to users and the resulting assignment of authorization profiles (user comparison). This separation of role assignments and authorization profiles enables you to implement the *dual control principle* both in the definition and assignment of authorizations.

Variant 2

Another option for implementing functional separation also consists of dividing the tasks into three groups, each with different tasks:

▶ The *user administrator* defines the users in each user group based on approved requests, and changes the corresponding user master data and address data. He or she can also assign single and composite roles to user master records, as long as these roles are not critical and are assigned to each user automatically. The user administrator is not authorized to assign department-specific authorizations or create single or composite roles in the system.

He or she can also perform periodic monitoring activities. The user administrator is faced with additional responsibilities when Central User Administration (CUA) is used, as it is this individual's responsibility to check the distribution logs (Transaction SCUL) and correct any errors.

▶ The *authorization developer* creates the single and composite roles in the system, based on approved requests from the user departments (role managers), and changes existing authorization roles. The authorizations are placed in a role pool for the respective authorization administrator, based on the defined naming conventions. Developers are not authorized to create or change user master records, or assign authorizations to users.

▶ The *authorization administrator* assigns authorizations to the users, based on approved requests from the user departments. However, this only applies to the single and composite roles that lie in his or her area of responsibility, as defined by the naming conventions. The authorization administrator is not authorized to change user master records, create users, or create authorizations in the system.

If CUA is used, the authorization administrator also has to check the distribution of assignments, using Transaction SCUL.

This variant can also be split into two roles instead of three, if your resources are limited. In this case, you would combine the user administrator function with the authorization administrator function. As a minimum requirement, however, both of these functions should be kept separate from the function of the authorization developer.

In addition, an *authorization superuser* has to be created for security reasons; this user maintains the administration roles, which must be assigned to user group SUPER. The administrators should not be allowed to maintain their own authorizations or master records. The functions of the superuser can be added to the authorizations of an emergency user or a system administrator, for example.

A detailed concept is required to divide the individual tasks (such as the blocking/unblocking of users or the resetting of passwords) among the three functions.

5.6.3 Change Request Procedure

Once an authorization concept is implemented, it does not remain static. Just like the organization and structure of an enterprise, the roles and profiles have to be adjusted to reflect changes in the way you do business. Moreover, staff fluctuation, reorganizations and transfers automatically require changes to existing user master records and authorizations. Both users and authorizations have to be modified continually, with the corresponding versions documented.

Formalized change management procedures, which define both the process flows and the corresponding areas of responsibility, have to be established for these processes. Deviations from these procedures should be avoided and only used in case of an emergency. The objective of such procedures is to inform and include all the involved parties promptly, while concurrently ensuring that each change to the system is documented in an auditable manner.

The user IDs and authorizations are only one component of an enterprise-wide change management procedure. Similar rules should also apply to the transport system, to Customizing (system settings), and to the import of R/3 HR Support Packages, and other Support Packages (patches). This section only deals with the options relevant to user IDs and authorizations, however. The necessary process steps should be described in a second step.

Change Request Procedure for User Master Data

In the user master data area, the defined change processes should consider the following possibilities and regulate them accordingly. Different administrators are responsible for performing the various tasks, depending on which variant was selected.

▶ **Creating a new SAP user ID with appropriate authorizations**
Typically, a user request should contain all the information required to create the user and the corresponding composite roles. This case deals with new employees not previously employed by the enterprise. In most cases, a reference user that performs the same function is used to define the authorizations.

▶ **Changes to a user master record (without authorizations)**
When employees are transferred, undergo address or name changes, or other changes to the master data, no changes to the authorizations are needed.

▶ **New assignment of/changes to authorizations in a user master record**
This example also applies to changes in authorizations, even when nothing

changes for the user within the user master record. Examples here include enhancements to a function or the assumption of additional responsibilities by a user.

▶ **Blocking/unblocking users (resetting passwords)**
Change requests of this type can result from temporary employment or tasks. It is also frequently necessary to reset passwords that users have forgotten, or that the system has blocked due to repeated failed logon attempts.

▶ **Deleting master records**
When an employee leaves an enterprise, the corresponding user ID in the system should also be deleted. This example not only involves security aspects; because license fees are based on the number of named users, only active users should exist in the system.

▶ **Procedure for technical users**
The rules for requesting technical users, such as those rules used for handling interfaces or batch runs, are often ignored. These users have to undergo a change management process just like dialog users.

Change Request Procedure for Authorizations

In addition to changes to the user environment, all possible reasons for modification have to be identified with regard to the corresponding authorizations and integrated into the change management procedure.

▶ **Additional authorizations for existing roles**
Necessary changes can result from the addition of new authorizations—that is, additional transactions, authorization objects, or field values—in a single role. Such changes could be due to new requirements or discovered errors.

▶ **Additional roles**
When new organizational units or new responsibilities are defined at an enterprise, new single roles have to be defined to meet these requirements within the authorization concept. The defined procedures should be used to develop the new roles.

▶ **Additional functions (composite roles)**
When new functions (or work centers) are described with a new task structure, the corresponding authorizations—composite roles and the corresponding single roles—have to be generated for these functions. The defined procedures should also be used to develop the new composite roles.

▶ **Creating new roles and composite roles**
The generation of new roles or composite roles can be defined as another step. The change request procedure also has to consider this case.

▶ **Adding a new role to an existing composite role**
Functional enhancements result in the addition of a new single role to an existing composite role. The enhancement can be due to an additional transaction code or field value.

▶ **New composite role with new and old single roles**
New functions do not have to be implemented completely through new single roles. Thanks to the component structure described above, some of the tasks can be covered by existing single roles.

▶ **Changes to existing roles and composite roles**
You do not always have to create new single or composite roles to meet new requirements. In some cases, existing roles can be adapted to meet the new requirements.

▶ **New transactions**
If the role already contains all the authorization objects that are necessary for the additional transaction, as well as the corresponding field value settings, no further adjustments are needed. If not, you can add a new single role to an existing composite role.

▶ **Changes to field values**
When a new field value (such as a new company code or distribution channel) is added, this value merely has to be added to the corresponding authorization objects.

▶ **Existing roles in existing composite roles (functional enhancement)**
This simplest case of an adjustment results from a reorganization of existing single roles in an existing composite role.

A change request procedure must include all the previously listed examples. The following defined steps apply to each adjustment request:

1. A user authorized to submit a request (such as a defined key user) requests that a role or user be changed in the SAP system. This request is recorded by the responsible organization (hotline, support team). The request can be submitted as a printed form or via a workflow tool (the latter is recommended at large enterprises with a considerable number of change requests).

2. When users are involved, the line manager has to approve the creation/change of the user master before the action is performed.

3. If additional authorizations are involved, the person responsible for the role must be informed (see Section 2.13.2). This individual estimates the effort required to change the role and decides whether the request will be implemented. When a role is to be supplemented with functions that are already contained in (or reserved for) other roles, the person responsible for roles has

to contact the other responsible persons and coordinate the role modification. The person responsible for the role approves the change to the authorization (or authorization assignment).

4. Depending on which variant of user and authorization administration is used, the responsible administrators may also process the approved change requests.

5. The requests must be documented and stored appropriately. If a tool is used, this step can be performed automatically.

The definition of this change request procedure and the role assignment procedure must be fully known to all users and administrators before the authorizations go live, in order to avoid delays. Therefore, it is imperative that you start identifying and defining the processes at an early stage in the project.

5.7 Emergency Concept

5.7.1 Background

Despite the detailed configuration of an SAP R/3 authorization concept, it may become necessary to use emergency authorizations (you can also define emergency users). Such authorizations can be necessary in exceptional situations that require direct intervention in the live system, usually in case of inconsistencies in the system or system data. These comprehensive authorizations are also required in day-to-day operations, however, such as month-end closings and special production flows.

Because you first have to define what truly constitutes an emergency for an enterprise, you also have to develop authorizations for these emergency cases. You should avoid having to assign these far-reaching emergency authorizations to deal with minor problems. Therefore, it is recommended that you establish an emergency concept with several levels, in order to respond to requirements with a greater degree of flexibility. If a user cannot execute a process at a given level, he or she can be assigned the next-higher level (of course, if the situation is a true emergency, you can skip this procedure).

You also have to define appropriate naming conventions for the various emergency authorizations, both to delimit these special authorizations from the functional authorizations and to identify the various emergency levels.

5.7.2 Multilevel Emergency Concept

To restrict the premature assignment of SAP_ALL or similar authorizations in case of problems, the emergency authorizations should be divided in line with the underlying problems. Specifically, an authorization problem can have the following causes: insufficient field values or insufficient organizational levels.

1. In the *first emergency level*, you can correct such problems by defining the existing functional authorizations with a full organization for the organizational/field values (generic approach). Therefore, an accounts payable clerk who is restricted to one company code would be permitted to execute all authorized transactions without restrictions.

2. When transactions are missing, users are not capable of executing a functional process (that is, not a Basis-related process).

   One way to correct such problems is to create *area emergency authorizations* in the *second emergency level*. Based on the SAP menu areas (e.g., Financial Accounting, Treasury, Plant Maintenance, Materials Management), all the transactions in these areas are placed in a respective composite role, which is then granted full authorization for the authorization objects. This enables you to grant an emergency authorization that is restricted to one functional area, without Basis authorizations. You should also add all the namespaces for customer-defined transactions to these profiles.

3. If the error occurs due to processes involving a Basis component (batch input sessions or IDoc management, for example), the user does not need functional authorizations.

   Extremely critical Basis authorizations (such as client copy via SCC4) should be defined together with the internal auditing department. These authorizations should be excluded from *emergency level three* ("far-reaching Basis authorizations"). All other Basis authorizations should remain executable.

4. If the error still persists, you should define the *highest level* as an emergency authorization that corresponds to the SAP_ALL authorization.

5.7.3 Flows and Processes for Requesting and Logging

The use of such critical authorizations must be sufficiently recorded and audited, with respect to both request and assignment and during use by the requesting employees. You can do this using *system logs* or the *Security Audit Log*. In addition, a request procedure should enable you to determine which employee requires an emergency authorization for which activities at which time. You should only use this procedure from the third level onwards, however, to avoid making the system resources and workflows unnecessarily complicated.

5.8 Technical Details

This section describes several technical details that are relevant to implementing and administering the authorization concept.

5.8.1 "Authorizations" Information System

Nearly all information involving roles, profiles, authorizations, and user IDs can be queried and displayed in the "Authorizations" Information System (see Figure 5.15). You use Transaction SUIM to call the "Authorizations" information system. Like the Profile Generator, the "Authorizations" information system is available in Release 3.1G and later. Starting in Release 4.6, you can also reach the authorization information system through area menu AUTH.

The "Authorizations" Information System features numerous reporting options. In addition to numerous reports that list the roles, profiles, and users by various selection criteria, the last two menu items deserve special mention: **Where-Used List** and **Change Documents**. The where-used list is available for profiles, authorization objects, authorizations, and authorization values in Release 4.6 and later. You can display change documents for users, authorizations, and profiles, but unfortunately not for roles.

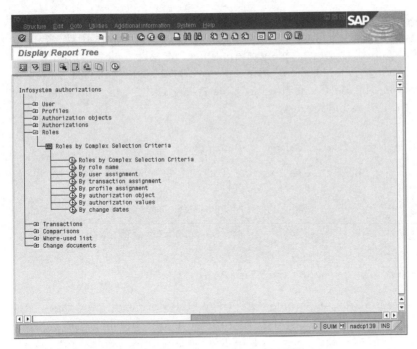

Figure 5.15 The "Authorizations" Information System (SUIM)

5.8.2 Reducing the Scope of Authorization Checks

Transaction SU24, which calls for table USOBX_C, enables you to reduce the scope of authorization checks. You can also use Transaction AUTH_SWITCH_ OBJECTS to deactivate authorizations globally, if they will not be used at your enterprise. The Profile Generator does not add any authorizations to the generated roles for deactivated authorization objects. Therefore, if you deactivate and then reactivate an object, you may have to revise a many roles or profiles. For this reason, we do not recommend deactivating objects. Authorization objects that start with S_ and P_ (Basis and HR areas, respectively) cannot be deactivated globally. Transaction AUTH_DISPLAY_OBJECTS displays a list of the globally deactivated objects. The application log (Transaction SLG1) records the global activation and deactivation of objects under object name PRGN_LOG_OBJ.

5.8.3 SAP_ALL and SAP_NEW

Profile SAP_ALL contains full authorization (that is, wildcard (*) authorization) for all the existing authorization objects in the system. Therefore, a user ID that has profile SAP_ALL can execute any transaction in the system. This profile should never be present in a user ID in SAP systems with production data. For information on using SAP_ALL for emergency authorizations, refer to Section 5.7.

When new authorization objects are added or existing ones changed, you must generate profile SAP_ALL again. To do this, you can use report RSUSR406 (in Release 4.6 and later), which regenerates profile SAP_ALL for the current client. To generate SAP_ALL for all clients, use report AGR_REGENERATE_SAP_ALL. Furthermore, you can use the settings in table PRGN_CUST listed in Table 5.3 to influence the generation process.

Field	Default	Description
ADD_ALL_CUST_OBJECTS	Yes	Add customer authorization objects (namespace Y, Z) to SAP_ALL
ADD_OLD_AUTH_OBJECTS	No	Add outdated objects (class AAAA)
ADD_S_RFCACL	No	Add full authorization for S_RFCACL to SAP_ALL

Table 5.3 Relevant Customizing Switches in Table PRGN_CUST

In addition to the SAP_ALL profile, SAP_NEW is also of major importance. It is required for release upgrades of the SAP system. A corresponding partial profile exists in SAP_NEW for each release of the R/3 System. These partial profiles contain wildcard authorizations for all authorization objects that are required in this release for functions *that already existed in the previous release*. In contrast, SAP_NEW does not contain authorizations for *new* functions in the new releases. For more information on this profile, refer to SAP Note number 28186.

6   Auditing SAP R/3 Authorization Concepts

Due to the complexity of the SAP R/3 authorization concept, checking the production roles and composite roles is not a simple task for third parties and is also extremely time-consuming. Fortunately, several tools and check programs are available that can reduce the effort required.

As you have already deduced from the previous chapters, access authorizations in the SAP R/3 System and its components are highly complex. The complexity of the R/3 System exceeds that of other, comparable ERP systems because the access authorizations are freely configurable and also because some processes require authorization objects from several different modules. In some instances, the authorizations already include information for subsequent administration and change management (for example, through the naming conventions for the roles and composite roles and the development responsibility for certain critical areas). Due to the high degree of integration within the SAP R/3 System, users from different areas can access the same set of information (master data, for example), which makes it difficult to delimit the functional areas. Moreover, the same security mechanism protects both system management functions (e.g., batch input sessions, job control) and application areas.

Furthermore, authorization concepts can vary widely between enterprises, even if the same development method is employed. These differences among authorization concepts stem from inherently different basic assumptions and design decisions at the technical level, as well as divergent organizational structures and the associated differences in positions at the enterprises. Another influencing factor here is the desired degree of control and functional separation (integration of business processes versus the necessary separation of responsibilities according to security aspects).

Up-to-date documentation and adherence to the defined framework conditions and development requirements are essential to ensure the uniformity and comprehensiveness of the authorization concept and to enable authorization developers to work properly.

Accordingly, both internal and external auditors have to expend a great deal of effort (both cerebral and technical) to adequately check the detailed authorization concepts for several thousand users and develop suggested improvements, especially in light of the difficulty of designing detailed audit checklists posed by the differing concepts. Due to the major importance of access authorizations, however—after all, such accesses determine the data integrity—audits of authorization concepts are crucial. Accordingly, tools for supporting auditors' work have been developed by SAP, as well as by auditing firms and other enterprises.

In this chapter, we will first describe the SAP standard tools and then identify several developments from external providers. Due to their inherent complexity, however, most of the external developments are provided as components of consulting services, rather than tools.

6.1 User Information System

6.1.1 Structure

This section briefly describes the standard user information system (UIS) for authorizations in the SAP system. You use Transaction SUIM (or menu path **Tools · Administration · User Maintenance · Info System**) to reach the "Authorizations" information system (Figure 6.1), which displays report tree AUTH.

This report tree contains a selection of standard reports and transactions for SAP R/3 users and authorizations for the objects used in this environment:

▶ Users by selection criteria

▶ Profiles by selection criteria

▶ Authorization objects by selection criteria

▶ Authorizations by selection criteria

▶ Roles/activity groups by selection criteria

▶ Transactions by selection criteria

A where-used list and a comparison (role comparison, for example) are supported for nearly every object. All change documents are recorded and retained until the objects (such as profiles) are deleted. Each subtree can be expanded further and contains detailed analyses of the respective node area.

As with all SAP reports, the selection of the search criteria can affect system performance (Figure 6.2). SAP Note number 85344, which involves the AIS (Audit Information System), contains the following recommendations:

> *"As long as the selection parameters are within a reasonable range, there should be no noticeable differences in the performance ... as compared to the normal usage ... in the functional departments."*

Because the reports necessitate searching large tables, the system response time depends on the auditor's expertise in setting the selection criteria.

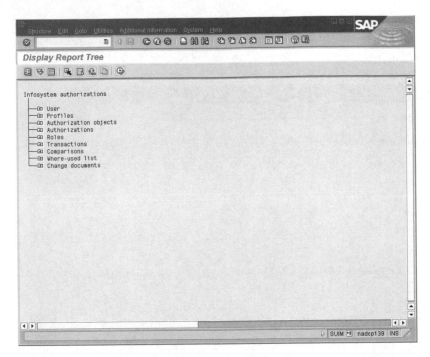

Figure 6.1 User Information System (SUIM)—Initial Screen

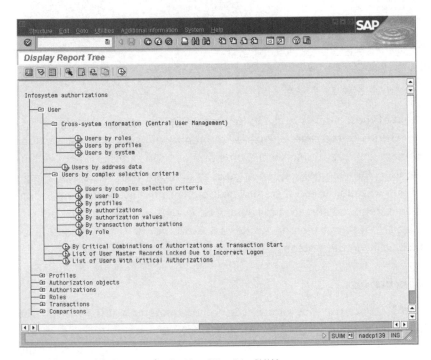

Figure 6.2 Possible Reports for Section "User" in SUIM

The results are displayed in a list that you can print or save in a local file. In addition, newer SAP releases feature direct integration with standard office applications, enabling you to display and edit the results directly in an Excel table.

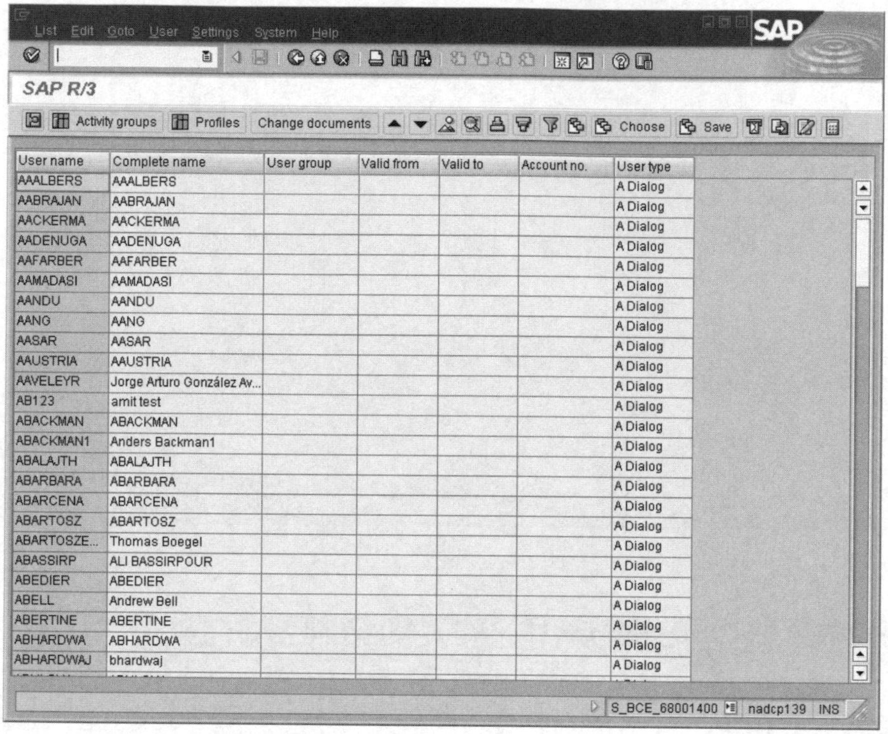

User name	Complete name	User group	Valid from	Valid to	Account no.	User type
AALBERS	AALBERS					A Dialog
AABRAJAN	AABRAJAN					A Dialog
AACKERMA	AACKERMA					A Dialog
AADENUGA	AADENUGA					A Dialog
AAFARBER	AAFARBER					A Dialog
AAMADASI	AAMADASI					A Dialog
AANDU	AANDU					A Dialog
AANG	AANG					A Dialog
AASAR	AASAR					A Dialog
AAUSTRIA	AAUSTRIA					A Dialog
AAVELEYR	Jorge Arturo González Av...					A Dialog
AB123	amit test					A Dialog
ABACKMAN	ABACKMAN					A Dialog
ABACKMAN1	Anders Backman1					A Dialog
ABALAJTH	ABALAJTH					A Dialog
ABARBARA	ABARBARA					A Dialog
ABARCENA	ABARCENA					A Dialog
ABARTOSZ	ABARTOSZ					A Dialog
ABARTOSZE...	Thomas Boegel					A Dialog
ABASSIRP	ALI BASSIRPOUR					A Dialog
ABEDIER	ABEDIER					A Dialog
ABELL	Andrew Bell					A Dialog
ABERTINE	ABERTINE					A Dialog
ABHARDWA	ABHARDWA					A Dialog
ABHARDWAJ	bhardwaj					A Dialog

Figure 6.3 Display of Results List for All Existing Users

Development of these reports began in Release 3.0D. The results list (Figure 6.3) from early versions of the reports, such as the report of executable transactions for a user/role, were fuzzy or incorrect. Some of the reports are static and are limited to one user. More complex queries (such as different field values for a large number of authorization objects) are not possible with the available tools. Some of the queries required for an audit, such as change documents for activity groups/roles, are not available prior to Release 4.6C, nor have they been implemented technically in the system.

6.1.2 Conclusion

While the UIS can be used for audits, it is not adequate as a singular tool. The information system is better suited for administrator support than it is as an auditing tool. The authorization information system contains new reports for roles and activity groups in Release 6.10 of the Web Application Server.

6.2 Audit Information System

6.2.1 History

SAP introduced the *Audit Information System* (AIS) in Release 3.1I. It is a standard Basis component in Release 4.6A and later, and can be imported as an add-on for older releases (3.0D and later; see SAP Note number 100609).

6.2.2 Audit Approach

Auditors of an SAP R/3 System require a variety of reports and analyses to perform their duties. However, it is not always easy to define the exact scope and corresponding transactions or menu paths of the required evaluations and reports, in order to define the corresponding authorizations for the auditor—not to mention a detailed audit approach. Many enterprises have not defined a specific role or position for an auditor.

Based on this requirement, SAP developed the AIS as a utility for auditors, in order to "improve the audit flow and audit quality."[1] The goal was to create "new, methodical approaches."[2]

To achieve this goal, existing SAP standard programs were grouped together in a new structure. You can define default settings for variables that are used in multiple reports, which simplifies analyses for the following areas and respective users in charge:

▶ Business/tax auditors

▶ Internal auditors/data protection officers

▶ Controlling

▶ System auditors

Interfaces to other software packages (such as ACL and IDEA) are already available.

6.2.3 Structure

Prior to Release 4.6C, the only way to call the AIS was through Transaction SECR (Audit Information System display—see Figure 6.4).

---

1 Schiwek/Buchholz, P. 4, compare Watkins, Chapter 1.10
2 Schiwek/Buchholz, P. 4, compare Watkins, Chapter 1.10

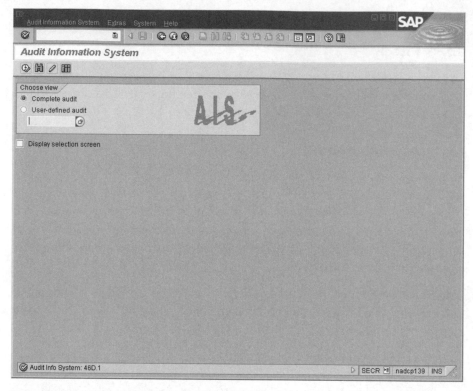

Figure 6.4 Transaction Code SECR—Initial Screen

The auditor can select from two different views:

▶ **Complete audit**
This view encompasses the full set of reports and analyses within the AIS.

▶ **User-defined audit**
You can also define a selection of available analyses, which corresponds to a specific audit request. This enables you to exclude reports that are not required for the audit. In addition, a user-defined audit enables you to conduct precise post-audits in subsequent years, as the audit can be considered a work program.

As previously mentioned, the system performance information from SAP Note number 85344 also applies to the AIS.

The full audit is divided into three main areas (choose **Complete audit** in SECR), which are shown in Figure 6.5.

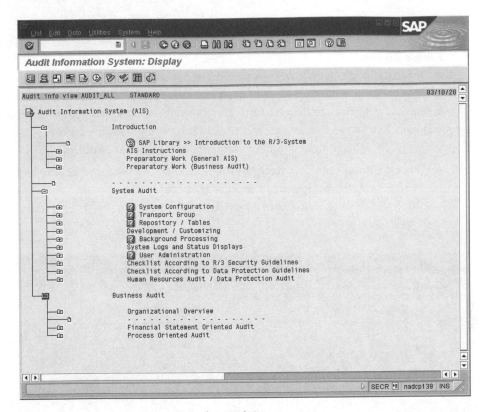

Figure 6.5 AIS Reporting Tree—"Complete Audit"

▶ **Introduction**

In addition to general Help information and instructions for use, you can use this section to define global settings for the underlying AIS. This applies to both the general settings (user authorizations or user-defined parameters via Transaction SU3 in the Introduction section) and to the variables used in the different reports (such as the report year in the **Business Audit** section):

▷ Maintain Table TVARV for the fixed values of the selection variables (see below)

▷ Maintain the user groups for running queries

▷ Maintain the constants for executing balance sheet analyses in Bilanzdaten Baetge

▷ Maintain separate user settings

▶ **System Audit**

This subtree groups together all the functions from the general system area. Figure 6.5 shows all the additional nodes (such as **System Configuration**), which, in turn, contain the individual reports and analyses. One part of the system audit is **User Administration**, which is described in more detail in Section 6.2.5.

▶ **Business Audit**

The **Organizational Overview** section provides auditors with an overview of the organizational definition of the enterprise structure. The analyses contain the relevant organizational units from Customizing (such as company codes and quantity structure of accounts and documents) along with the corresponding keys (such as account assignment elements and document controls).

The **Financial Statement Oriented Audit** contains all the year-end closing and balance sheet-related analyses and reports that provide information required by auditors (such as final balances, key figures, extrapolations, master data, update tasks, and so on).

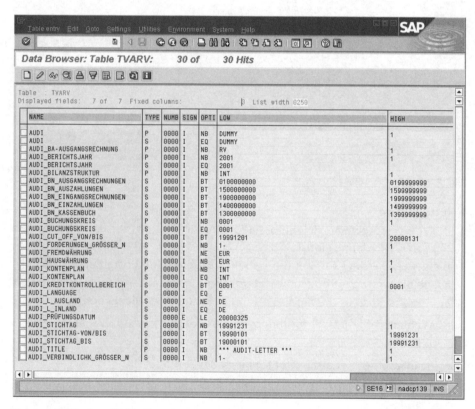

Figure 6.6 Display of Table TVARV

The **Process Oriented Audit** provides auditors with information regarding the generic enterprise processes (such as accounts receivable, retail, sales, and so on) and the corresponding areas required for auditing in SAP R/3. Please note, however, that information is not available for all processes (the icons are mere empty shells, without any other information). Because many parameters of a business audit will remain identical throughout an audit period (such as the reporting year, document number intervals, or charts of accounts), you can define them in a table (TVARV) in the **Preparatory Work** section (see Figure 6.6). These parameters then apply to all analyses and reports of the audit itself.

The respective parameters are stored in the table as variables. The naming conventions require these variables to start with the string "AUDI_BERICHTS JAHR", such as for the period examined in the audit.

In addition to these fixed values, you can also define *selection variables*—upper or lower thresholds for displayed receivables within an analysis—AUDI_FORDERUNGEN_GRÖSSER. The default settings of the individual variables for both areas upon AIS delivery and installation are described in SAP Note number 77503.

The business audit is not described in more detail, because user administration is part of the system audit.

6.2.4 System Audit

The reports, transactions, and analyses that are grouped together in the AIS System Audit are all the standard SAP programs for system management and monitoring. The reports, which are distributed among multiple report trees and menu excerpts within the Session Manager, are divided into ten areas. They can correspond to a single, delimited audit request or individual audit steps in a full system audit:

▶ **System Configuration**
Helps auditors navigate through the system and provides comprehensive information about the technical and organizational content of the system (parameters, clients, programs, tables, and so on).

▶ **Transport Group**
Checks the regulated release between development and production environments, and the adequate documentation of all changes to system objects (tables, programs, screens, documentation modules, and so on).

▶ **Repository/Tables**
Contains information on tables, including access authorizations, change documents, and access statistics in the R/3 Repository Information System.

▶ **Development/Customizing**
Documentation of enhancements and extensions to the SAP standard (transactions, programs, and so on), concept of Customizing settings.

- ▶ **Background Processing**
  Checks conventional job control in the system (such as payment runs, dunning runs, MRP runs, and so on) through the request procedure, documentation, and logs.

- ▶ **System Logs and Status Displays**
  Contains a variety of the monitoring and evaluation logs that exist in the system, such as the application log, Security Audit Log, database and system logs, and server status.

- ▶ **Checklist According to R/3 Security Guidelines**
  Contains the ten audit sections described in the individual chapters of the SAP R/3 Security Guide, including the audit questions defined in the checklists in each area. This section also includes questions regarding the R/3 authorization concept and its implementation—questions such as "Do you integrate authorization checks in your own developments?"

  - ▶ User authentication
  - ▶ R/3 authorization concept
    A total of 18 questions that pertain to areas such as administrative tasks or authorization checks
  - ▶ Network infrastructure
  - ▶ Protection of the operating system
  - ▶ Protection of access to the database
  - ▶ Protection of the live system (change and transport)
  - ▶ Remote communications (RFC and CPI-C)
  - ▶ Secure store and forward mechanisms and digital signatures
  - ▶ Logging and checks
  - ▶ Special topics

- ▶ **Checklist According to Data Protection Guidelines**
  In accordance with the data protection guidelines, auditors can receive additional information for this audit area, including introductory information.

- ▶ **Human Resources Audit/Data Protection Audit**
  This area covers all the HR-related analyses and reports.

- ▶ **User Administration**
  Because this section contains the audit of the SAP R/3 authorization concept, user administration is described in detail in the next chapter.

You can display additional information for some of these sections by clicking on the corresponding Help function (question mark icon). In the user administration area, for example, this information includes general background information and helpful tips with regard to correct parameter settings, as well as development objects such as activity groups, roles, and profiles (see Figure 6.7).

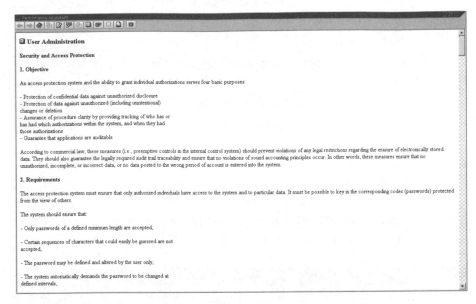

Figure 6.7 User Administration Help Function

6.2.5 AIS Subtree "User Administration"

The **User Administration** section includes all the standard information tools in the SAP R/3 System that an auditor can use to examine authorizations in a live R/3 System. The following areas are listed in detail:

▶ **Authentication**
Analyses for password and logon rules (for example, password length, allowed passwords, lockout and automatic blocks) as well as for standard users (such as SAP*, DDIC) and special users (such as emergency users, developers, and administrators)

▶ **Information System: Users and Authorizations**
This node corresponds to the report tree from Transaction SUIM (see Section 6.1).

▶ **Authorizations**
This section contains the analyses of the system parameters (Table RSPARAM) and the transactions for the authorization check (SU53) and user buffer check (SU56). It also contains an initial screen for starting traces of the authorization checks (ST01).

▶ **Profile Generator**

In addition to direct access to the Profile Generator (Transaction PFCG), this section also contains the client-independent settings for the authorization checks within the Profile Generator:

▶ User master comparison

▶ SAP settings for check indicators (SU24)—Authorization Object (Check Under Transactions)

▶ Customer settings for check indicators (SU24)

▶ Comparison of check indicators with SAP proposals (SU25)—Upgrade Tool for Profile Generator

▶ **Overview of Users**

To enable statements about the users and their timeliness, this section contains analyses regarding the users contained in the system (number, SM04 or AL08 for users logged on globally or locally) and their respective logon status (users never logged on, users not logged on in the last 30/180 days, etc.).

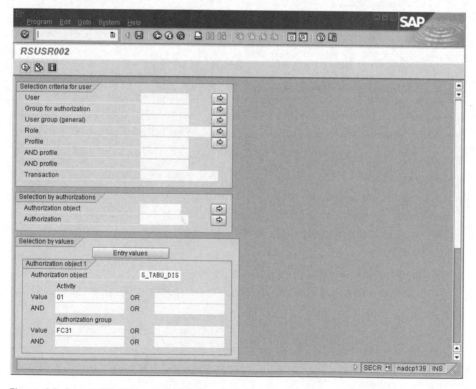

Figure 6.8 Report RSUSR002 Including Search Criteria

► **Which User Is Allowed to...?**

Default settings for selection criteria of standard reports are already included as a template for investigating critical authorizations for users. All the reports contained in this section refer to the Report RSUSR002 and contain information regarding the authorization objects and their field values. Figure 6.8 shows "Users who can update accounting periods."

These default values are examples for checking critical transactions and authorizations with the Report RSUSR002. The degree of critical authorizations can vary depending on the level of risk that is used. Generally, however, the following areas within an audit are considered to be especially critical processes (selection):

► Remote access (definition of the concept and design of the remote authorizations)

► Batch processing, transport management, and ALE concept

► Program changes and table access

► System operation (definition of responsibilities and designation of the corresponding authorizations; operating-system commands, access to database and operating system)

► Administration of users and authorizations (underlying concept of functional separation and designation of the corresponding authorizations)

► Financial transactions (functional separation for payment/posting)

► Human resources (access to critical infotypes such as basic pay)

► Master data (change authorizations for central data, defined responsibilities for each area)

► Internet users
Special evaluations regarding the administration of Internet users

► Central User Administration
Reports regarding the implemented structure of Central User Administration (CUA) (distribution model and logical systems) as well as user distribution and the corresponding distribution logs (transaction code SCUL)

6.2.6 Authorizations for the AIS

Until the conversion to the role-based menu structure in Release 4.6C, the standard system contained a composite activity group called SAP_CA_AUDITOR, which included the following single activity groups (the following example reflects Release 4.6A; older releases can contain other single activity groups with regard to the precise naming conventions):

- SAP_CA_AUDITOR_APPL_ADMIN_AG
  CA: Audit Administration

- SAP_CA_AUDITOR_APPL_AG
  CA: Auditor SAP applications (except HR)

- SAP_CA_AUDITOR_DS_AG
  CA: Auditor: Data Protection

- SAP_CA_AUDITOR_HR_AG
  CA: Auditor HR

- SAP_CA_AUDITOR_SYSTEM_AG
  CA: Auditor System

These single activity groups contained the required authorizations for each audit area. The structure proved to be complex and difficult to comprehend, however, and many adjustments were required. In addition, auditors were granted a wide range of access authorizations in the system.

6.2.7 AIS Role Concept

Starting in Release 4.6C, the AIS is a component of the core R/3 System for the financials and logistics modules (see SAP Note number 451960). Support Package SAPKH46C27 converted the previous report tree (which can still be called in Transaction SECR) to a role-based structure in the Profile Generator. This process corresponds to the general conversion of report trees to role menus during the migration of older SAP R/3 releases to Release 4.6. Report trees created with Transaction SERP (Release 4.5 and earlier) can be converted to area menu structures for Release 4.6 in Transaction RTTREE_MIGRATION.

All further developments take place exclusively in this new environment, which has had a major impact on the authorizations required to use the AIS.

The previous single and composite activity groups have been replaced by the new composite role "SAP_AUDITOR—AIS, Audit Information System." This composite role contains all the newly defined single roles for the menu (see Figure 6.9).

With the introduction of the role concept, SAP also split the *transaction roles* from *authorization roles* in the AIS. The menus shown in Figure 6.9 are the transaction roles and contain only the transaction codes required to execute the corresponding reports, transactions, and analyses. In contrast, the authorization roles do not contain any menus. Instead, they contain the authorization objects required to start the transaction, including proposals for the underlying field values. The **Roles** tab page contains all the single roles assigned to the composite role—that is, all the transaction and authorization roles (see Figure 6.10).

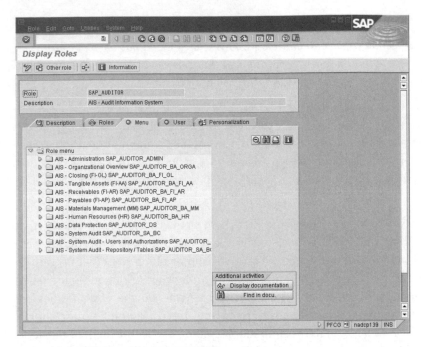

Figure 6.9 Composite Role SAP_AUDITOR

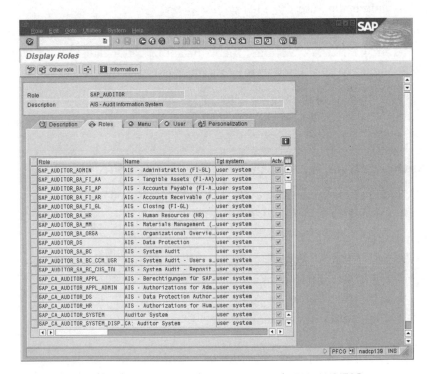

Figure 6.10 Single Roles Assigned to the Composite Role SAP_AUDITOR

SAP defines this relationship as follows:

"The transaction roles contain a menu, however, they do not have authorization values. The authorization roles contain authorization values, but no menu. All roles are delivered without an authorization profile name."[3]

Several transaction roles can be used for one authorization role, and vice versa. The options are defined in the respective role descriptions. According to SAP Note number 451960, this is intended to prevent the "...unintentional addition of authorization default values with change authorizations during a later correction or enhancement of the roles...". Therefore, it is now much easier to maintain clearly delimited roles.

To use the SAP roles, you have to transfer them to the customer namespace (that is, replace the "SAP" prefix with "Z"). You then have to modify both the transaction roles (with regard to the menus) and the authorization roles (with regard to the authorization data) in accordance with the underlying customer requirements and generate the corresponding profiles. Depending on the audit request or scope, you can then create composite roles from the corresponding single roles, test them, transport them to the production system, and assign them to the auditors there. The user master records of the individuals involved in the audit must be classified as information users (*limited professionals*).

Enhancements to existing roles (through new functions) should then be created in new roles first and generated in a profile. Then, the authorization data of the generated profile should be transferred to the respective authorization role.

SAP also recommends creating additional transactions in a special AIS namespace (such as Z_AIS*) and assigning this generic namespace to the AIS roles once in authorization object S_TCODE.

6.2.8 Authorizations for Auditing Authorization Concepts

Of the existing templates for AIS single and composite roles, you can use the following roles to audit an SAP R/3 authorization concept:

▶ **Transaction role**
SAP_AUDITOR_SA_BC_CCM_USR

▶ **Corresponding authorization roles**

▷ SAP_CA_AUDITOR_SYSTEM
AIS authorizations for system audit (full)

▷ SAP_CA_AUDITOR_SYSTEM_DISPLAY
AIS authorizations for system audit (display only)

---

3 SAP Note number 451960

You can also use the former of the two authorization roles to audit the Repository and the complete system.

The menu of the transaction role corresponds to the **User Administration** section of the report tree, as indicated in Figure 6.11.

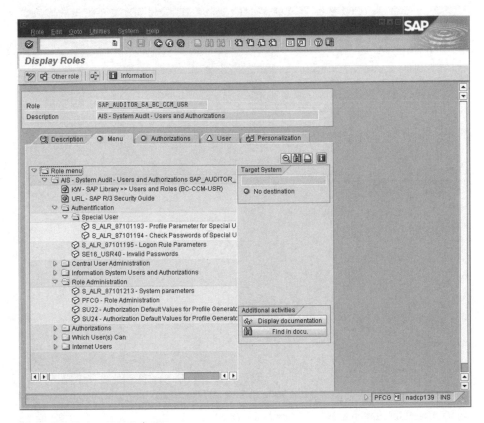

Figure 6.11 Transaction Role Menu

The authorization role contains the authorization objects required to execute the transactions, reports, and programs defined in the menu. As previously described, some of the SAP templates are missing the organizational levels (indicated by the red traffic lights in the Profile Generator—see Figure 6.12) and other field values. You have to adjust these values in accordance with the existing structures and organizational definitions at your enterprise.

It is imperative that you test the configured authorization values to ensure that they function properly. You can define two different authorization roles to differentiate between active and display authorizations.

We recommend that you coordinate with internal and external auditors in order to develop composite roles that correspond to the individual audit requests. This will accelerate the auditing process and relieve the workload for both system administrators and authorization administrators during the audit.

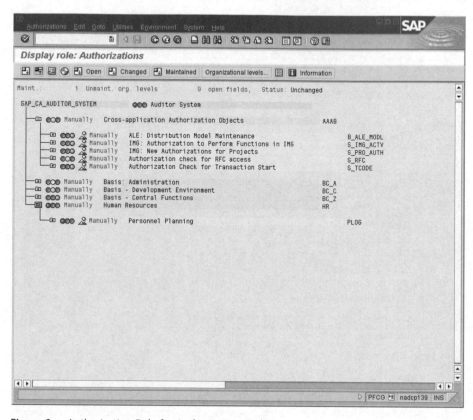

Figure 6.12 Authorization Role for Authorization Audits

6.2.9 Data Collection and Evaluation Techniques

The **User Administration** area almost exclusively contains reports and transactions in the role menus. Accordingly, most of the data is collected from information systems (user information system) and the corresponding reports with the underlying ABAP programs (for which the auditor can generate variants). Several options are then available for processing the results lists further:

▶ On-screen display

▶ Printed list

▶ Transfer to the analysis software via flat file

The AIS also provides a variety of other evaluation techniques, especially for the business audit, which include:

▶ **Queries**

Queries (custom queries to the SAP database) enable users to create reports that are not provided in the standard SAP system. Users do not require any ABAP programming skills to create and run queries. Results can be printed in a list, displayed in dialog, broken down (drilldown), and downloaded for stochastical audit functions, reporting, and balance-sheet creditworthiness checks.

The auditor can determine the selection criteria for the query from the specified InfoSets (use Transaction SQ02 to administer the InfoSets) for the audit-relevant data fields (layout of the evaluation). You then use Transaction SQ03 to define user groups and functional areas and assign them to one another. To use queries, users must be entered in user groups /SAPQUERY/AU (Audit) and /SAPQUERY/AM (Asset Manager).

Users in a query user group can then use Transaction SQ01 to start any query of their assigned user group. Please note that queries are not described in any detail here.

▶ **Report**

Sufficiently qualified and authorized auditors can write their own ABAP reports and run them in the system. This will only rarely be possible, however, as auditors usually lack the necessary comprehensive system authorizations.

▶ **Drilldown Reporting**

SAP Drilldown Reporting is a dialog-based information system. Because the various analyses and key figures are displayed in a uniform manner, it makes it easier to create comparative analyses of assets, finances, and profits. You can transfer balances and balance-sheet data via an open interface to external auditing software or balance-sheet creditworthiness rating through Baetge & Partner. Because this is almost exclusively relevant for the business audit, however, this function is not described in any detail here.

▶ **Download**

Results from queries of the SAP database can be processed further by other applications (such as ACL, IDEA, Microsoft Excel, and so on). Possible download formats are .asc, .bin, .dbf, .ibm, .wk1, .dat., and .xls, or unconverted .dat and .rtf.

6.2.10 Conclusion

The current status of the AIS in the SAP system is a vast improvement over earlier releases. Its major advantage is its sensible grouping and structuring of the relevant information systems and reports, including the required authorizations for the auditors.

Its fixed structure does not permit detailed queries across multiple authorization objects or combinations of transactions, however. Additional audit software is required to perform such tasks. In this context, the internal/external auditors could also cooperate with the development department to create enterprise-specific analyses in the authorization area. Auditors can also retrieve certain information directly from the corresponding authorization tables.

Nonetheless—and especially because it is available free-of-charge in the standard SAP system—the AIS is a useful, logical catalog from which the auditor can select the necessary reports. The collections of relevant reports and analyses within each area are particularly beneficial.

6.2.11 More Information on the AIS

▶ More information on the AIS is available in the SAPNet for customers and partners under *http://service.sap.com/AIS*.

The most important SAP Notes with regard to using the AIS are listed in the Appendix B.

6.3 Direct Table Access

Experienced auditors may find it easier to retrieve the relevant information directly from the tables that contain the authorization data. To do so, they need to have display authorizations for Transactions SE16 and SE17 in their master records. In a subsequent step, the generated Excel lists are imported into an analysis/database program (such as Microsoft Access or ACL) and then analyzed based on the underlying selection criteria. The advantage of direct table access is that very few quantity restrictions apply. The depth of detail of the analysis, however, is limited.

The underlying tables (naming conventions US* or AGR*) were discussed in Chapter 2 and are therefore not described in detail here. Please note, however, that you will have to link various tables and the information they contain in order to perform an analysis.

Example: Table AGR_1251 contains all authorization objects (and values) for each single role. Table AGR_AGRS lists all the single roles in each composite role. An auditor can therefore analyze the link between these two tables to compile and evaluate all the authorization objects (and values) for each composite role.

To do so, auditors need to have detailed knowledge of the underlying tables and their relations.

6.4 Supplementary Audit Areas

In addition to the technical aspects just described, auditors should also analyze other areas with regard to the SAP R/3 authorization concept. Because most of these areas are described in detail in Chapters 2, 4, and 5, they are listed only briefly here:

▶ **Documentation**
The entire concept must be documented adequately and clearly from the start of the project. Aside from the coordinated framework conditions, this documentation applies especially to the task/function matrix and the organization/value matrix. All information relevant to decision-making should also be documented.

▶ **Naming conventions**
Naming conventions not only help auditors to categorize the roles and composite roles, but also control the administration of these authorizations. Auditors should investigate the logic of the naming conventions for roles, composite roles, profiles, user groups, and so on.

▶ **Design**
The authorization concept should be developed with a role-based approach. Moreover, there should be a logical ratio between the number of functions or composite roles in the system and the number of employees at the enterprise. A ratio close to 1:1 is indicative of a person-specific authorization concept instead of the sought-after function-oriented concept. Another issue is the depth of detail—that is, the number of protected levels. Here, as well, auditors should ensure that the authorization concept is not subdivided into too much detail, in order to prevent the proliferation of too many authorizations.

▶ **Adherence to the framework conditions**
Auditors should check whether the authorizations were developed based on the defined framework conditions, or whether variances can be found. Enhancements to the concept—due to acquisitions, for example—have to be drafted in accordance with the existing guidelines.

► **Change management procedures**

To ensure that the authorization concept is maintained and enhanced properly and consistently, it is imperative that uniform, well-known change procedures are established in order to avoid deviations.

► **Other**

The auditing of related areas, such as database/network security and the infrastructure, is not described here.

6.5 Other Audit Tools

Both the complexity of the SAP R/3 authorization concept (described in the previous chapters) and the standard tools for auditing authorization concepts (described in this chapter) invite the need for a significant number of additional, third-party tools and software packages that support both auditors and enterprises.

The goal of the vendors of such tools is to define the additional benefits of using their products. In many cases, these benefits compensate for the weaknesses of the User Information System (SUIM—see Section 6.1.2) and the Audit Information System (AIS—see Section 6.2.10).

The main advantage of these products is that analyses are not restricted to a single user or a limited number of combined authorizations. Therefore, the tools are typically very powerful and often require some preparatory work.

The solutions described below only represent a small selection of the tools available on the market. Their mention does not imply a positive rating or recommendation on the part of the authors. The list is merely intended to sample the available wares and briefly describe the functionality of each product. For detailed information on the software packages, refer to the corresponding Web site listed for each. Sources of information that list other products are also listed.

6.5.1 SAPAudit—CheckAud

Until recently, this product was distributed under the name *SAPAudit*, which has been changed to *CheckAud* in the current release. The underlying structure of the software has not changed, however.

The tool "was developed with the objective of making the authorization concept much more transparent and easier to analyze."[4] The authorizations managed in the system are imported through a scan tool and can then be analyzed by the auditor in a separate evaluation module, independently of the administrators. The

---

4 Functional principle of "CheckAud for SAP R/3 Systems," *http://www.checkaud.com*

scan takes place for each system and client and is based on the information stored in the authorization tables (see Chapter 2). The analyses are then based on the authorizations that exist in the scanned client, and are divided into the following sections:

▶ Automatic analysis of standard reports

Examples:

   ▶ Users blocked after failed logon attempts

   ▶ Users who have not logged on yet or who are not assigned to groups

▶ Automatic analysis of system parameters

Analysis of RSPARAM and PSPFAR, including descriptions, characteristics, and current settings

▶ Analysis of R/3 tables (accesses and default settings)

Examples:

   ▶ Access to authorization groups

   ▶ Table buffering

▶ Analysis of elements in the authorization chain at higher/lower-level tree structures

▶ Analysis of authorizations at transaction level, including the underlying application authorizations

▶ Analysis of critical freely definable authorizations and critical authorization combinations

▶ Delta analyses since the last scan of client-specific authorizations

More information on this tool is available at the Web site *http://www.checkaud.de* (*http://www.sapaudit.de* is forwarded automatically).

6.5.2   ACE

ACE stands for *Automated Controls Evaluator* and is a product of Pricewaterhouse-Coopers (PwC). It was introduced in 1999 and has since been enhanced for each new SAP release. ACE is based on a Microsoft Access database.

The defined objective of ACE is to provide all the information required to audit security settings, system parameters, and configured controls simply and flexibly. ACE enables the definition of complex search criteria for all users and authorizations. The query results can be displayed in various hierarchies and overviews, thereby making it easy to use the formatted data in an audit report. ACE features the following five analysis reports:

▶ **Information lists**

Queries in ACE, partially standardized, of all the information that was extracted from the SAP system

Example: Number of clients, number of users, and so on

▶ **Object lists**

Relationship between users and authorization objects

Example: Query of users who have specific field values in the corresponding authorization objects

▶ **Transaction lists**

Relationship between users and executable transactions

Example: Query of users who can execute specific transactions, based on the assignment of authorization objects and the corresponding field values

▶ **Linkage lists**

Combination of all lists (object, transaction, and other linkage lists) through "and" and "or" operators

Example: Analysis A contains all users with the authorization to maintain central customer master data (Transactions XD01, XD02).

Analysis B contains all the users who can release credit memos or create customer orders (VA01, VA02).

When analyses A and B are linked with an "and" operator, linkage list C contains all users for which both A and B apply.

▶ **Hierarchy lists (tree lists)**

Relationship between users, profiles, and authorizations in hierarchical form

It is also possible to define *evaluation groups* to exclude certain data from the selection—for example, to not display any users who have the SAP_ALL authorization, to avoid falsifying the analyses. According to PwC, the main advantages of this tool are its lack of dependence on a specific release and the fact that it is operated outside of the SAP system.

ACE requires you to upload two ABAPs into the system to be audited. These ABAPs control the download of the relevant authorization tables (500 to 600) into the ACE tool, for example, into the Microsoft Access database. The sequential processing of the download is intended to keep the system load as low as possible. The duration of the download depends, among other things, on the number of analyzed modules, the number of users, and the release (a download with five modules and around 2000 users takes about an hour).

All check and analysis activities are then carried out directly in the ACE, without any further connection to the SAP system. All downloaded tables are listed in a log for control purposes.

6.5.3 APM

APM is short for *Authorization and Profile Management* and is a product of *real-time AG*. The main focus of this product is to simplify the administration of SAP users and authorizations. APM has been developed based on ABAP and, according to the vendor, "can be implemented without any modifications in a minimum amount of time."[5] The settings in the APM tool are synchronized automatically with those in the Profile Generator in SAP R/3, which means parallel maintenance in both systems is possible (although the vendor recommends limiting maintenance and development to a single tool).

With regard to the subsequent audit of the authorizations developed in APM or SAP R/3, this tool features several reports and analyses in addition to the standard SAP reports:

▶ Consideration of SAP audit guidelines for the MM and FI modules via *pre-Customizing settings*

▶ Specific control of special users and contingency authorizations in the different security levels (system log with a complete recording of all activities, including special user functions)

▶ Periodic analyses of audit-specific information

▶ Definition of risk analyses for creating and maintaining SAP R/3 authorizations

▶ Analysis of process chains

▶ Logging of security-relevant aspects (such as failed logons, terminated update runs)

APM also generates documentation of the SAP profiles. For more information about this tool, visit the vendor's Web site at *http://www.realtimegroup.de*.

6.5.4 More Tools

In addition to the tools already described, several other vendors offer similar tools and software packages that have a different focus, but can still support certain aspects of user and authorization audits. These tools include:

▶ **PSM (Parks Security Management) by Firma Parks Informatik GmbH** (*http://www.parksinformatik.de*)

---

5 See the realtime AG Web site: *http://www.realtimegroup.de*

This tool serves mainly to administer authorizations. Importing the defined SAP R/3 authorizations into this tool enables both "centralized authorization management" and "centralized reporting possibilities."[6] To do so, PSM transforms the SAP structure into its own structure roles, areas of responsibility, and hierarchies, and enables the graphic display of these elements.

▶ **Authorization Toolkit by SecurInfo** (*http://www.securinfo.com* or *http:// searchsap.techtarget.com/whitepaperPage/0,293857,sid21_gci848943,00.html*) The primary purpose of the Authorization Toolkit is to simplify the development of an SAP R/3 authorization concept. This tool "simplifies, accelerates, and controls the SAP security process."[7] Authorizations are developed in accordance with a predefined methodology in a separate authorization structure: the *information ownership*. This function and the change management tool integrated in the tool enable auditors to quickly create an overview of the roles and functions at an enterprise. Because risks inherent with critical authorizations and functional separation are considered from the project's inception, these factors are easy to check later.

▶ **TopMan®-Prüfset by agens Consulting GmbH** (*http://www.agens.com*) You export the data to Lotus Notes to transfer the SAP R/3 authorizations to a Notes database. This knowledge database already "translates privileges that have proven critical from *agens* experience into the SAP terminology (combinations of authorization objects with special field values)."[8] The preconfigured settings in the knowledge database are compared with the actual authorizations to create an automatic audit of critical privileges. Customers can also enhance these preconfigured settings flexibly to meet their specific needs.

6.5.5 Conclusion

The large number of tools and software packages available on the market would seem to indicate that the SAP standard is insufficient for an adequate audit of the SAP R/3 authorizations. However, this statement is not generally valid, depending on the enterprise's specific security needs. The authors have intentionally avoided rating and recommending individual products, as they are only partially comparable and because each has a different focus. Nonetheless, one or more of the tools described above may be useful for audit support. Of course, we recommend that you investigate the features of each tool in detail prior to making any purchase decision.

---

6 See the Parks Informatik GmbH Web site: *http://www.parksinformatik.de*
7 SecurInfo, P. 4f.
8 See the agens Consulting GmbH Web site: *http://www.agens.com*

7   SAP Enterprise Portal

The SAP Enterprise Portal is SAP's entry into the promising market for portal software. This technology makes it possible to seamlessly integrate all applications and components for a user and provide personalized, customized information. Access control is especially relevant in this context, as the portal is an externally accessible window to an enterprise's internal IT systems.

7.1   General Aspects

A *portal* is a *single point of access* to a specific dataset. It provides a window to an enterprise's internal information processing that permits controlled access to a variety of applications through a standardized user interface, the Web browser.

A portal can be used to access a wide variety of systems, such as enterprise resource planning software (ERP, i.e., the core SAP R/3 System), Customer Relationship Management (CRM), Supply Chain Management (SCM), groupware and workgroup applications, and even mainframe applications (see Figure 7.1). A portal means the consistent separation of the presentation logic from the application logic. Applications and information become accessible anywhere, at any time, with any type of computing device (desktop, laptop, PDA, cell phone, and so on).

A portal allows you to integrate different applications transparently and automate cross-enterprise business processes. A portal can integrate internal and external sources of information, personalize this data, and supply it to the user in a customized environment.

Portals enable and support e-business solutions at an enterprise. The following usage scenarios are possible:

▶ **Business-to-Business (B2B)**
Steelmaker ThyssenKrupp uses the *BuyForMetals* portal as a virtual marketplace to integrate its entire supply chain electronically (*http://www.buyformetals.com*).

▶ **Business-to-Employee (B2E)**
General Motors rolled out *mySocrates.com*, its employee portal, in 2001. The portal offers self-service applications such as registering for further training, reserving meeting rooms, local news, weather, sports, and so on. The portal is integrated with General Motors' HR systems.[1]

---

1   See InformationWeek, November 19, 2001

► **Virtual organization**

The U.S. Army uses a portal to integrate its global logistics activities. The portal is used to coordinate movements of troops and matériel by the Air Force, the Navy, the Marines, and the Army.[2]

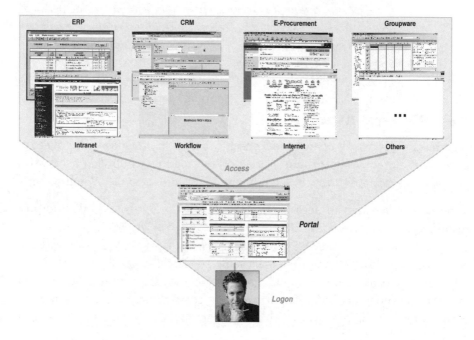

Figure 7.1 SAP Enterprise Portal — Principle

To summarize, deploying a portal at a company can help to realize the following usage potential:

► Internal applications can be made available globally in a secure environment.

► Costs can be cut via reduced administration effort and lower training expenses, as the users always work with the same user interface.

► Existing investments can still be utilized, as *legacy applications* can be integrated in the portal.

► Almost all end user devices are shipped with the graphical user interface (GUI) pre-installed: the Web browser. Therefore, no extra installation or distribution of the software is needed.

► Automating business processes across enterprise boundaries can increase efficiency.

► Providing structured, selective information can boost productivity.

2 See InternetWeek.com, March 21, 2001

- Splitting the application logic from the presentation simplifies the replacement of applications.
- The central point of access simplifies security administration.

Portals continue to increase in importance; their growth rate in Western Europe is projected at 39% annually through 2006 (CAGR according to IDC, a market research institute).[3]

Adequate consideration of security aspects is considered fundamental to realizing this growth scenario, especially since portals make it possible to access internal enterprise data from the Internet, which means an additional, external user level is added and has to be integrated within the enterprise.

7.2   Portal Components

A *portal* is the bridge between an enterprise's internal applications and the external world. Implementing the full functionality of the scenarios that we described requires complex interaction among various components that have to be added — in addition to the actual portal software.

7.2.1   Web Server

To deliver the HTML files to users, a *Web server* (also called an HTTP server) is required. The SAP Enterprise Portal works together with the *Internet Information Server* (IIS) from Microsoft.

7.2.2   Application Server

An *application server* is required to enable communications between the portal and the application (component system) in question. The application server converts protocols (from HTML to SAP GUI, for example), manages status information about the session (while HTTP is a status-free protocol that does not save any previous queries, applications and databases are strictly status-oriented), and manages logons to the component system.

The SAP Enterprise Portal requires the *SAP Internet Transaction Server* (ITS) or the *SAP Web Application Server* (Web AS). If you want to use the innovative *Drag&Relate* technology, you will also need to deploy a *Unifier*.[4]

---

3 See IDC, August 21, 2002
4 See SAP AG (4). This source contains important information for the subsequent descriptions.

7.2.3 Runtime and Development Environment

A *runtime environment* is required to run interface programs that access the component system (*iViews*). Because these programs are written in the Java programming language, a *Java runtime environment* (JRun or J2EE) is required for the portal to function properly. In addition, a Java *development environment* (JSDK) is required to develop and modify the interface programs.

7.2.4 Directory Service

The portal accesses a *directory service* to manage the user information. All information regarding the identity of the portal users is saved here, along with the synchronization information for the identities between portal and the various component systems. SAP Enterprise Portal works together with the LDAP-capable products *iPlanet Directory Server*, *Microsoft Active Directory*, and *Novell eDirectory*.[5]

7.2.5 Database

A SQL-compliant database is required to store the configuration settings for the portal, particularly the large quantity of personalized user configurations.

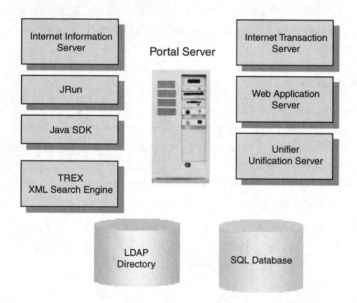

Figure 7.2 SAP Enterprise Portal—Components

---

5 See SAP AG (3), January 7, 2002. This source contains important information for the subsequent descriptions.

7.2.6   Search Engines

It is generally advantageous to integrate portals with content management software and search engines, as this makes it easier to access the required information. SAP Enterprise Portal uses the *Trex* software as its XML-capable search engine (see Figure 7.2).

7.3   Interaction between the Portal and SAP R/3

As mentioned, a portal can be used to access other systems directly, including ERP systems. SAP Enterprise Portal supports transparent access to all elements of the core SAP R/3 System. Users can access the full functionality from SAP R/3 via the portal, to the extent allowed by the enterprise's business processes and security policies. In addition, the portal expands the possibilities for accessing the R/3 System in several important aspects:

▶ Users can use a Web browser as the front-end software. Because no special SAP software, such as the SAP GUI, is needed to access the SAP R/3 System, this software no longer has to be distributed or installed.

▶ Users can access the R/3 System independently, locally via the Internet. Costs for expensive leased lines or long-distance calls are eliminated.

▶ The portal also supports the transparent integration of other applications that do not necessarily have to be from SAP. External information such as news feeds can also be integrated within the portal environment.

Specifically, the following four scenarios for integrating a portal with an SAP R/3 ERP system can be identified:

▶ Scenario 1
SAP Enterprise Portal is to provide access to the existing SAP R/3 transactions as they are available in the component system—that is, without any loss of functionality. SAP's Internet Transaction Server (ITS) is used in this case. The ITS uses a generator (SAP GUI to HTML) to automatically convert all dynpro-based SAP R/3 transactions to HTML coding and delivers them to the portal. SAP Enterprise Portal merely has to generate a standard iView to integrate the ITS in the portal.

▶ Scenario 2
SAP Enterprise Portal is to provide access to separate program calls that differ from the SAP R/3 user interface. In particular, a special interface program called a *Connector*, which is usually written in Java, is required to call *BAPIs*. The required iViews are Java Server Pages (JSPs) or Java iViews developed specifically for this purpose, which you can either purchase as finished products from

SAP or write, using the *Portal Development Kit* (PDK). In practice, self-written iViews can access one or more SAP R/3 Systems through the aforementioned *Java Connector* or with the ITS.

▶ **Scenario 3**

The SAP Web Application Server (Web AS) can also be used instead of the ITS. It is based on a different integration concept. *Business Server Pages* (BSPs) can be used to write ABAP-based and JavaScript-based Web applications on the Web AS. In turn, these applications can be integrated with SAP Enterprise Portal using iViews. This solution is preferred when data from both R/3 and non-R/3 systems is to be made Web-capable, because the Web AS—in contrast to the ITS—employs Java to enable non-R/3 connections.

This solution requires a greater programming effort, however. Web AS Release 6.20 does not currently provide an automatic generator (SAP GUI to HTML), nor does the current version of Web AS support Drag&Relate. According to information from SAP, these features will be supported in Release 6.3 of the Web AS.

▶ **Scenario 4**

It is recommended that the innovative Drag&Relate technology be enabled for use for more than calls of SAP R/3 transactions. This technology enables users to move individual data or entire data objects from one SAP R/3 transaction to another with the mouse. This scenario requires either an R/3 Unifier (for Drag&Relate between SAP R/3 transactions) or a Unification Server (for Drag&Relate between R/3 and non-R/3 transactions). If a unification server is used, a product-specific unifier must be available for each application (for R/3 and for Baan, for example). Because this function can be of great help in processing your day-to-day work, it is described in more detail in the next section.

7.3.1   Drag&Relate

Drag&Relate technology creates logical links between objects that can be saved in entirely different applications. For example, an order that exists in an ERP system can be linked with a customer from the CRM system at the click of a mouse—by dragging the data around as you would in Microsoft Explorer. SAP Enterprise Portal saves and manages this link, enabling far-reaching integration between different applications.

Drag&Relate requires an additional technical component that enables communication between the portal and the component systems. This additional data about relationships between objects from different applications is called *hyperrelational links*, and must be managed in an additional database.

The technical component that is responsible for interaction between the component systems and the portal is called the *Unifier* (see Figure 7.3). A separate unifier is required for each logical system. If only SAP systems are integrated, the *R/3 Unifier* is used, and works in parallel with the Internet Transaction Server (ITS). In general, all information sources that are linked with the portal via iViews can also be integrated in the Drag&Relate mechanism. In addition to various component systems and databases, Internet resources can also be integrated.

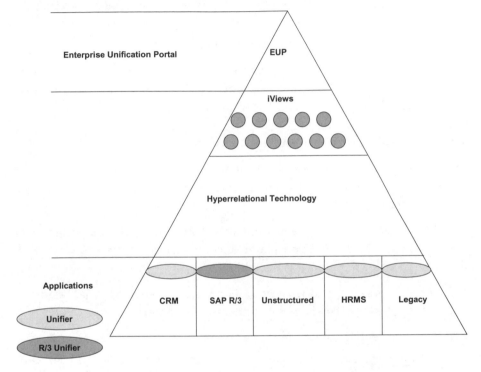

Figure 7.3 Unifier

In heterogeneous system environments, specific unifiers are used for each information source to be integrated. In this case, an additional component is required for synchronization: the *Unification Server*. This component is simply another unifier with type "Database access," which synchronizes the databases held in the various other unifiers.

7.4   Access Control and Administration

The principles for system *access control* (also referred to as authorization and authorization management) are identical in all environments. Access to internal resources (data, applications, and so on) should be granted in a controlled manner, in accordance with existing security policies. Authorized users should be able to access selected objects using a defined method.

To do so, the following main steps are required:

▶ Identifying the user, for example, based on the unique user name
▶ Authenticating the user, for example, based on proof or user verification (password) that the user has to provide
▶ Verification by the system whether the user is allowed to access the respective object in the requested manner, based on a set of rules
▶ Decision to allow or refuse the transaction or process

Because the basic terminology of authorization management has already been described elsewhere in this book (see Chapters 2, 4, and 5), the focus of the information that follows is on the portal-specific attributes.

7.4.1 Identification and Authentication

To identify a person in a system, either a user name or an ID is generally used. This name can be identical or similar to the name of the relevant person, or merely a random character string.

Modern directory services standardize user names in order to ensure their uniqueness worldwide. For example, mnemonic names can be appended with the name of an organization and a country ID.

The process of proving that the alleged identity is truly genuine is called *authentication*. There are three basic types of authentication systems:

▶ Based on knowledge, for example, by entering a password or code word
▶ Based on possession, for example, through the use of intelligent chip cards (smart cards)
▶ Based on physical characteristics, for example, fingerprint or other biometric data

Of course, combinations of these types are also possible, for example, issuing smart cards to employees and also requiring entry of a password (often called a *PIN* in this case) in the system.

SAP Enterprise Portal supports the following identification and authentication technologies:

▶ Combination of user name and password
▶ SAP Passport (X.509v3 certificate issued to SAP customers' end users)
▶ Third-party products

User Name/Password Combination

The simplest, but unfortunately most insecure authentication method is the combination of user name and password. SAP Enterprise Portal features its own management functions for users and their passwords (see Section 7.4). The user name in the portal can (but does not necessarily have to) correspond to the user ID in other systems. A mechanism for mapping the user IDs in other systems is provided (see Section 7.4.5). Alternatively, direct logon to an SAP component system or the Web Application Server is also possible. In this case, users can use their SAP R/3 user IDs and passwords. The portal forwards the logon information to the respective system and receives a response. If the response is positive, the user is admitted by the portal.

SAP Passport

The authentication process that utilizes the SAP Password is based on certificates. It is much more secure; however, it is also unfortunately much more complex to implement. Certificates contain information about the identity of a user, a cryptographic key, and information about the certificate itself—such as issue date and validity (see Figure 7.4). These certificates are issued by an electronic certification instance and digitally signed. Users can use these personal certificates to identify (i.e., authenticate) themselves anywhere in the virtual world, including portals and applications that support this technology. Therefore, the certificate is a kind of digital ID. The value of this personal identification rises and falls with the general acceptance of the authority that issued it.

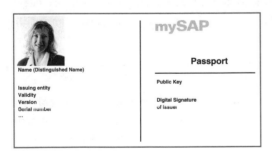

Figure 7.4 Certificate

In SAP Enterprise Portal, the certificate is included in the SSL handshake. In this process, the user authenticates him- or herself to the portal, while the portal, in turn, authenticates itself to the user with its own certificate. SSL (Secure Socket Layer) is a protocol that ensures the confidentiality and integrity of the transferred data, while supporting authentication of the communication partners. *Strong cryptographic keys* are used to fulfill these functions. SSL is the de facto standard for communication security in the Internet, supported by all widespread Web browsers and Web servers.

The major advantage of using certificates is that no confidential information such as passwords is transmitted or saved on the server side. The major disadvantage of certificates is the complexity of managing them. Every enterprise that wants to use certificates has to decide whether it wants to establish its own infrastructure (*public-key infrastructure*, PKI) or use the services of an established Trust Center. Therefore, certificates are much more secure than passwords, but are also much more expensive.

Third-Party Products

Third-party products are another alternative for identifying and authenticating users. Such products enable the implementation of both *one-time passwords* and *Single Sign-On systems* (see Section 7.4.6).

One-time passwords require an additional authentication server. They are only valid for a single logon and cannot be reused. The primary advantage of one-time passwords is that "eavesdropped" passwords cannot be used for electronic break-ins. The need to change passwords regularly is also eliminated, thereby greatly simplifying user administration.

An attack on this type of security system would require that one could determine the algorithm used to generate the one-time passwords, along with the initialization value. This is a much more difficult feat to achieve than hacking a single password, or a large set of passwords. One-time passwords are therefore an excellent alternative, as they increase security significantly, but cost much less than certificates.

7.4.2 User Administration

Considerable preparation is required to implement the method of access control. First, information regarding the identity of the admitted users (i.e., users that have access) must be saved and administered. This type of user administration can be centralized or decentralized; can occur separately for each system or integrated for all systems; and can take place in files, databases, or *directories* .

In addition, a process has to be defined that models the entire life cycle of a user in a system environment—from new hire to separation from the enterprise. It is especially important to define clear areas of responsibility for the individual steps, such as responsibility for creating new users. The definition of change management procedures (see Chapter 5) is also required in this context.

SAP Enterprise Portal supports Central User Administration (CUA) with its *corporate directory*. The information required for each user is saved here, in a central location, for the entire enterprise. Therefore, a corporate directory can be viewed as a type of enterprise-wide address book in the form of a hierarchical database. The hierarchy is modeled in a tree structure that enables globally unique user identification, for example, based on the hierarchy levels: *Country*, *Organization*, *Organizational Unit*, *Site*, and *Name*.

The current de facto standard for accessing enterprise directories is *LDAP (Lightweight Directory Access Protocol)*. Technically, LDAP is a reduced-functionality implementation of the X.500 standard, which uses the TCP/IP Internet protocol to access the directory data. LDAP directories can exist in distributed form, on multiple geographically remote servers. In this case, each individual server houses a branch of the same overall directory. This method for accessing directories is extremely beneficial to response times. The individual servers are in close contact with each other and have a mutual synchronization mechanism.[6]

The corporate directory can also be utilized by SAP component systems. In this case, LDAP capability has to be added to the respective system. The implementation of *Central User Administration* (CUA) is required to do so. CUA enables you to centrally store components of user information across different distributed SAP systems (see Figure 7.5). A synchronization mechanism distributes this centrally defined and maintained user data to the user administration functions in the individual SAP system. In this scenario, the receiving systems are called *child systems*. Updates are replicated in both directions, and can therefore be implemented centrally or locally (see Chapter 2 for more information). CUA also features a synchronization mechanism with LDAP directories in Release 6.10 and later. Updates are possible in both directions here as well.

Using enterprise-wide directories in centralized user administration simplifies administration processes and increases security—as a result, the following specific benefits can be reaped:

► Administration costs fall because redundant user maintenance is eliminated

► Inconsistencies are eliminated because users are only defined in one instance

► Automatic elimination of cases where employees have left an enterprise but still exist as valid users in the systems

► Faster integration of new employees in the system landscape and faster activation of changes

---

6 Also see *http://wp.netscape.com/directory/v4.0/faq.html*.

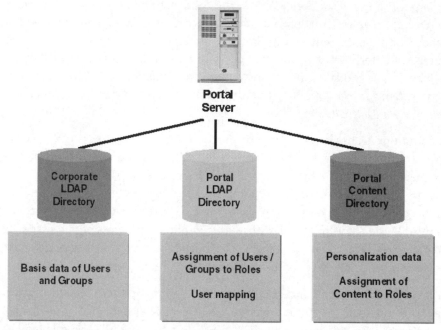

Figure 7.5 User Data Storage

In addition to the corporate directory, the SAP Portal also uses a separate portal directory. It saves certain user settings for each user for the portal itself. A third directory is also used: the *Portal Content Directory*, which contains the detailed personalization data for each individual user. This last directory is the largest in size and is therefore managed in a SQL-compliant database.

7.4.3 Role

A role at an enterprise corresponds to a job description and accordingly comprises the set of an employee's privileges and responsibilities. A user's role in the system maps the set of privileges that user has in the corresponding system (see Chapter 4 for information on designing an authorization concept).

The definition of a *role* is completely detached from the identity of a specific user. Instead, it corresponds to the task categories that can exist in a system. Each role can be assigned to one or more employees, or even to groups of employees. Examples of specific roles in the Accounting department at a large enterprise include: Controlling Clerk, Accounting Clerk, Controlling Department Manager, Intern, IT Coordinator, and so on. A role should contain the exact privileges that are required to perform the respective task. If responsibilities change, the corresponding role has to be modified.

The advantages of a role-based authorization system include simplified administration and increased security:

▶ Separation of responsibilities between user management and role definition, because no interdependencies exist between these two areas (see Chapter 5 for information on the separation of responsibilities in user and authorization administration)

▶ Prevention of accumulation of privileges, because the assignment to the old role is simply revoked when a user changes departments

▶ Reduction of complexity and administrative effort, because individual privileges don't have to be maintained for each user

SAP Enterprise Portal is role-based, just like the SAP R/3 component system. The *portal roles* define which information and applications users with the corresponding roles can access, regardless if an SAP component system or any other application is involved. This mapping of roles to access rights is implemented technically by defining the appropriate iViews that a user is authorized to call in the respective role. An *iView* is a connector that enables access to *backend applications*.

The detailed authorizations for the transactions and processes that a user is allowed to execute within a certain application, as well as which authorizations are excluded, are still saved in the respective authorization definition, not in the portal. The same applies to the mechanism for checking the corresponding authorization: the portal merely retrieves the existing information from the integrated component systems. Therefore, an authorization concept developed in SAP R/3 does not have to be modified or enhanced for use in an SAP Enterprise Portal; the defined roles, composite roles, and detailed authorizations are transferred to the portal identically.

The portal merely uses the respective users' roles to determine the initial selection of which users can generally access which applications. In a second step (based on an application-specific role definition, the SAP R/3 authorization concept in this case), the respective application is checked to determine which transactions a user is authorized to execute and which data that user can display.

The SAP Enterprise Portal manages the roles in the *Portal Content Directory*. Roles can be assigned to both individual users and groups. Roles already defined in an SAP component system can be imported. Any changes to the role definition can be reported back to the component system.

7.4.4 Personalization

A major feature of portals is their capability for *personalization*. Each user can be presented with a fully customized work environment, in accordance with his or her own preferences and/or work requirements. Enterprises can make different uses of this personalization, depending on how their portals have been deployed. The following two examples show possible uses of personalization:

▶ Public portals can use this type of customization to implement personalized marketing. Customers can be presented with exactly those products that are most likely to arouse their interest. The personalized environment can also be used for customer relationship management (CRM), to create a sort of meeting point between customer and vendor.

▶ Enterprises can provide their employees with personalized work environments and structure the necessary information logically, without overwhelming them with data overload.

Benefits include an increase in employee productivity and the targeted use of methods for selling your products or services.

All information regarding the user-specific settings of the portal is saved in the Portal Content Directory, which is not a separate directory service, but is located in a SQL database.

Examples of user-specific settings include display colors, visible menu items and links in a screen, screen division, and so on—in short, all aspects inherent in selecting the visual presentation.

7.4.5 Synchronization

When system environments have evolved over time, various different user and authorization management systems typically exist in parallel. Even when a corporate directory is used, *legacy systems* that cannot access this enterprise-wide directory might still be in operation, which requires redundant user administration. Checking the specific authorizations within an application, however, is still an integral responsibility of the application—this means each user has to have an ID in the application.

Because it cannot be assumed that a user will have the same exact ID in all possible systems, a *synchronization* method is required, and is implemented via the *user mapping mechanism*. Actually, this mechanism is nothing more than a table in which the portal identity of a specific user is assigned to the identity in the respective applications. Each user in the system has a row in this table, in which the user

IDs in the different systems are allocated and mapped to one another. The portal uses this user mapping to determine which user ID to use for which backend system.

Portal User:	SAP User:	Siebel UserID/Password:
Michael Schumacher	d040011	903845233, {Schumi}
Anna Kournikova	d052340	230982029, {Wimbledon}
Tiger Woods	d043536	324098211, {Handicap}
Cathy Freeman	d048347	202377724, {GoldMedal}

Figure 7.6 User Mapping

This *user mapping* in the portal (see Figure 7.6) is required in cases where no dedicated authentication server is available to support Single Sign-On for all applications (otherwise user mapping is managed by the SSO server).

7.4.6 Single Sign-On

The standard SAP Enterprise Portal supports a Single Sign-On mechanism. *Single Sign-On (SSO)* is a technology that enables users to access many different systems with a single logon. Duplicate requests for identification or authentication are eliminated, although each system requires authentication on its own.

Single Sign-On boosts ease of use significantly. Your employees no longer have to remember multiple IDs and passwords, and navigation between systems becomes much easier. Moreover, SSO systems improve security, as the large number of IDs and passwords in heterogeneous environments tempts users to write them down or use easy-to-remember (and thus easy to guess) passwords.

A typical SSO system works with a dedicated server, the *authentication server*, where the user logs on at the start of the session. The authentication server verifies the user's identity and, if the verification is positive, issues a *ticket*. The user can use this ticket to access other applications and request access. The applications verify the authenticity of the ticket and, again if the validation is successful, grant access to the user in accordance with the defined role. This repeated check runs in the background and is completely transparent to the user. Only if the application does not accept the ticket, is the user notified and prompted to enter his or her password.

The SAP Enterprise Portal is based on this exact principle. It can assume the role of the authentication server in both homogeneous SAP environments and heterogeneous environments. When a user logs on to the portal, the portal verifies the logon information and issues a *SAP Logon Ticket* to the user. This ticket is saved as a cookie on the user's hard drive. Therefore, the user's Web browser must support cookies, and cookies must be active, in order to use this function.

The SAP Logon Ticket saves only the following (non-confidential) information:

▶ User's identity
▶ Validity period of the ticket
▶ Name of the issuing portal

The ticket itself does not contain any passwords. The portal's digital signature guarantees the authenticity and validity of the ticket (see Figure 7.7).

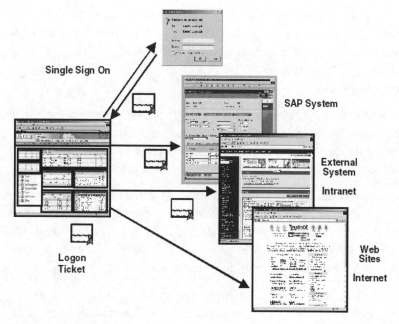

Figure 7.7 SAP Logon Ticket

The process of admitting a user to an SAP component system consists of two steps. In the first step, the component system checks the authenticity and validity of the digital signature in the ticket. If the digital signature comes from a trusted portal, the identity is used to log on. No password prompt is displayed.

The process is similar for non-SAP systems. In this case, however, you also need to add a *ticket verification library* in DLL format and the certificate of the portal server for the corresponding system (see Figure 7.8). This library, together with the portal certificate, makes it possible to use the SAP Logon Ticket to log on to non-SAP systems.[7]

---

7 SAP, January 7, 2002: SAP Enterprise Portal 5.0: Security

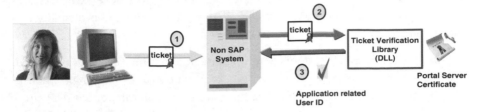

Figure 7.8 Single Sign-On with DLL

Alternatively, users can also be authenticated through a secure Web server. In this case, the Web server is enhanced with a *Web server filter* and the portal certificate, which enables it to validate the authenticity and validity of the ticket. In the positive case, the user identity is copied to a field of the HTTP header and sent to the non-SAP component system with an HTML document. Because this system trusts the Web server, the user is admitted (see Figure 7.9).

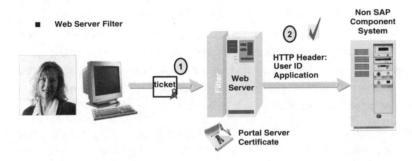

Figure 7.9 Single Sign-On with Web Server Filter

The SAP Logon Ticket has multiple layers of protection against manipulation. The most powerful tool here is the portal server's digital signature. If the ticket is altered in any way, either intentionally or inadvertently, it becomes void immediately. The digital signature is practically impossible to counterfeit, because it is based on *strong encryption algorithms* that have withstood comprehensive attacks in the past. The correct implementation of these procedures is a prerequisite for the security of the entire system.

Additional protection can be achieved by transmitting the ticket via the SSL protocol. SSL (Secure Socket Layer) is also based on strong encryption used in the transport layer of networks. All data sent via the TCP protocol can be encrypted and decrypted transparently.

Additional protection is afforded by the ticket's limited validity: potential attackers only have a limited window of time for manipulating the ticket, which is protected by various cryptographic methods that greatly reduce the probability of a successful attack.

If a non-SAP component system cannot be integrated in the scenarios described, another way to implement SSO is via synchronization (user mapping). The user identity and password for each application can be saved in the portal LDAP directory. When a user has authenticated him- or herself with the portal, the ID/password combination is simply read from the directory and forwarded to the respective system.

The major disadvantage of user mapping is that the passwords have to be saved in the portal directory, which poses an obvious security gap (also see Figure 7.10). In this case, comprehensive measures have to be implemented to protect the portal LDAP server.

You can also reduce risk by restricting the privileges of users who can access an application via the portal. In this case, you can define a group called *portal users*, to which each portal user is assigned automatically. This group possesses limited privileges in the respective applications, similar to guest users. Entering a password may not be required in all cases, which makes saving passwords in the portal directory unnecessary; however, it is not possible to provide the full functionality of an application with this method.

In heterogeneous application landscapes, SSO-capable products from third-party vendors are a feasible alternative. Products of this type authenticate the users on a centralized authentication server. This server is in permanent contact with all applications via interface programs, called *agents*, which ensure transparent authentication on all required systems.

7.5   Other Security Controls

7.5.1   Requirements

SAP Enterprise Portal provides a single point of access to an enterprise's internal information processing systems. Because this access point is usually on the Internet, it is visible to all Internet users worldwide. Therefore, the first security requirement of a portal is that there be comprehensive security measures to protect against electronic break-ins, hacking, and espionage. The internal IT environment must be protected against unauthorized access. The access control and authentication methods described must be supplemented with additional measures.

The second security requirement of a portal is permanent accessibility and availability. Business partners, customers, and employees will quickly lose faith in the portal technology if it is not always available. Threats to availability—that is, the failure of hardware and software along with potential disasters—have to be met in some way. Furthermore, the confidentiality and integrity of the communication relations have to be protected in order to maintain the trust of all users.

The supplementary security controls that are essential to running a portal are described in the next section, which is followed by a more detailed description of some of the risks.

7.5.2 Risks

SAP Enterprise Portal consists of several different software packages (see Section 1.2). Each of these packages has its own prerequisites for live operation. In addition, each of these packages has known and unknown flaws and weaknesses that can all increase risk for the portal. The known weaknesses are well-documented and disseminated on the Internet, and can therefore be easily exploited.

Potential attacks on the portal are primarily aimed at accomplishing the following:

▶ Unauthorized access to resources
▶ Execution of hostile program code
▶ Data theft
▶ Destruction of technical infrastructure

The basic structure of a potential network attack includes the following steps:

▶ Explore and select the target of attack
▶ Test the attack target for its known weaknesses
▶ Exploit the discovered weaknesses to gain access privileges
▶ Misuse these access privileges
▶ Erase the evidence

Various patterns of attack can be used against a network. Computer hackers or crackers typically attack the weakest link in the security chain. For example, crackers will hardly be able to eavesdrop on an SSL-encrypted connection and try to decrypt the data, in order to gain password and ID information. Instead, they will try to gain access to the server where the user IDs are saved, copy the corresponding file, and then leisurely crack the individual passwords in a dictionary attack using widely available tools.

Even easier: an attacker could call an employee at your company, claiming to be the Help desk, and ask for the password—on the grounds that it is needed for maintenance purposes.

Both "insiders" and "outsiders" represent potential attackers. *Insiders* are those individuals who are in direct contact with the respective enterprise and possess specific knowledge of that enterprise with regard to:

▶ Unmotivated employees (for example, employees laid off, passed over for promotions, or transferred involuntarily)

▶ Tight business partners with close relationships

▶ Suppliers and subcontractors

▶ Business partners and consultants

▶ Temporary employees

In contrast, *outsiders* are individuals who do not have a direct relationship with the respective enterprise:

▶ General business partners

▶ Competitors

▶ Hackers, crackers, and information warriors

▶ Professional industrial spies

Both insiders and outsiders can apply a multitude of attack methods against networks, although insiders frequently have the direct advantage of inside information, thanks to their immediate connection with the enterprise. Nonetheless, the implemented security measures have to provide protection against both internal and external attacks.

Figure 7.10 summarizes several of the most important threats and attack typologies of a portal. Now that the risks have been described, we will introduce the necessary supplementary security measures in the next section.

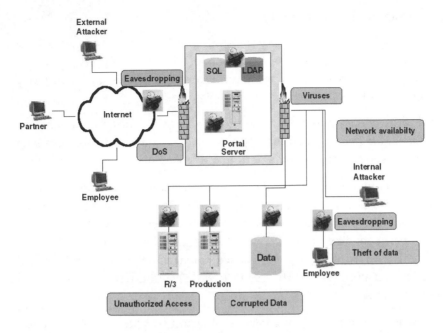

Figure 7.10 Portal Configuration Threats

7.5.3 Physical Security

Physical security encompasses all measures for protecting against unauthorized entry, theft, and damage due to forces of nature and catastrophes such as fires and plane crashes.

Typically, all SAP Enterprise Portal components should be located in a restricted-entry zone, such as a dedicated server room or computer center. This room should be equipped with the necessary fire protection, air conditioning, redundant power supply, and other safety features. The wiring and distribution should also be access-protected.

Measures for failsafe operations, such as redundant servers (distributed geographically in the ideal case) and communication links, have to be defined. A contingency plan should be defined, tested, and updated regularly. A comprehensive backup concept rounds out the physical security measures.

Please note that portal security is only part of the overall security concept for physical security. Therefore, it is not recommended that you define separate measures for physical and portal security.

7.5.4 Organizational Security

The importance of *organizational security* is often rarely appreciated; however, it is, in fact, one of the most important components of the overall security definition. Measures for physical and technical security cannot perform optimally unless they are sufficiently synchronized and planned.

If you fail to adequately inform your users of risk exposure, they may be tempted to short-circuit the implemented security mechanisms. The most famous example is the system password taped to the bottom of the keyboard.

An essential prerequisite is the definition of a security concept that clearly defines security objectives, risks, and areas of responsibility. This concept must exist in a document or manual that is accessible to all relevant user groups. Of course, the document will need to be revised periodically to reflect the changes to the system environment, as part of an ongoing change management procedure. Detailed guidelines should also describe which specific workflows have to be adhered to in which specific situations.

For the SAP Portal, for example, organizational security implies answering the following questions:

▶ Who will administer the portal and under which rules?
▶ Who has access to the server room?
▶ Who will be informed in case of an emergency?
▶ Which steps will be taken in case of an emergency system?
▶ Where are the backup systems located?
▶ Who is responsible for reporting security-relevant incidents?

Don't forget that incorrectly configured software can make your data easy prey for attackers. Therefore, system administrators must be thoroughly trained in the deployed systems. In addition, mechanisms for quality assurance and acceptance after installation and changes are also integral components of organizational security.

7.5.5 Installing Updates

To ensure the data integrity of the SAP Portal and the integrated systems, all programs have to be tested regularly for weaknesses. All available updates, patches, and hot fixes must be installed as quickly as possible.

7.5.6 Antivirus Software

Viruses are the most common threats to Web servers. Almost 50,000 viruses and variants are currently known. Many of them, such as the W32.Nimda.A@mm virus, exploit known weaknesses in the *Internet Information Server*. A comprehensive antivirus concept must be defined to protect the SAP Portal. The chosen antivirus software must support the automatic download and installation of the latest virus definitions and upgrades. If an unknown virus is encountered, the antivirus program must be capable of detecting typical virus patterns of attack. In such cases, the program should isolate the files automatically (place them in quarantine) and notify the system administrator.

7.5.7 Security Perimeter to the Internet

A typical method of protecting an internal network from Internet-based attacks is to create a security zone consisting of routers and firewalls to check both incoming and outgoing network traffic. Experts refer to such security areas as *demilitarized zones* (DMZ). Publicly accessible systems such as Web servers are typically run in a DMZ. The DMZ prevents direct access to the SAP Portal, as every communication passes through one or more filter systems. The filters limit the number of possible communication protocols, senders, and recipients.

The use of multilayered filter systems with components from different vendors has proven to be effective. If an unknown weakness in a component is discovered and exploited, the other components can mitigate the damage.

7.5.8 Intrusion Detection System

In addition to a security zone, it is advisable to deploy an *intrusion detection system* (IDS). An IDS uses a database with known attack patterns. It monitors selected servers or the network in real time and can issue an alert when it detects a suspected attack on the SAP Enterprise Portal. Depending on the selected configuration, the IDS can inform an administrator, reconfigure a component in the security zone, or execute another freely definable action—such as shutting down the server and automatically restoring a *backup image*. If a backup server can take over for this period, end users will not experience any downtime and the disabled server will quickly be accessible again.

7.5.9 Encryption and Integrity Verification

An *encryption protocol* is used to protect the integrity and confidentiality of communication between SAP Enterprise Portal and the end user, for example, to mitigate eavesdropping and manipulation. This protocol is called the *Secure Socket*

Layer (SSL)[8] and has become the global encryption standard for the World Wide Web (WWW). It enables users to uniquely identify both the server and, all sent and received information that has been encrypted. The SSL protocol negotiates the parameters for encryption and data integrity at the start of the communication. In addition to the server, users can optionally be identified and authenticated based on certificates.

The SSL protocol provides transparent security with the following features:

▶ The connection is private. Every data transfer is encrypted once the communication parameters have been negotiated.

▶ The connection is authenticated. The server is always authenticated; client authentication is optional.

▶ The connection is trustworthy. The data transfer contains an integrity check based on a cryptographic checksum.

SSL is used to protect Internet-based (HTTP-based) communication in the SAP Enterprise Portal. If SAP-specific communication protocols, such as *remote function calls* (RFC), *SNC (Secure Network Communications)* is used to integrate specific security functions. SNC is nothing more than a set of function calls that can be used in SAP systems. The actual security function—that is, specific algorithms for encryption and integrity protection—is defined in a standardized library that must also be present. This library must be compliant with the Internet standard *GSS-API* (*Generic Security Services—Application Programming Interface*). All details of the security functions, such as the algorithms and key lengths employed, are defined in the implementation of the GSS API-compliant library.[9]

7.5.10 Secure Operating System Configuration

Before you commission the portal, you have to ensure that the operating system configuration is secure. First of all, this means installing the latest updates at operating-system level. You also have to deinstall all the operating system components that are not essential to running the SAP Enterprise Portal. Every additional piece of software poses the danger of unknown security gaps that can be exploited. We strongly recommend that you pay special attention to the communication software, such as FTP servers. Also pay attention to the standard methods for secure operating system configuration: rename the administrator accounts, deactivate guest accounts, and lock out external hard disk access.

---

8 See RSA Laboratories, May 2000
9 See SAP (5)

7.5.11 Summary

SAP Enterprise Portal, as the "gateway to the world," requires supplementary security measures in addition to the mechanisms present in the portal software itself. These measures incorporate physical, organizational, and technical aspects. The portal must be operated in a suitable environment, with measures for controlling physical access and for protection against technical failure and catastrophes. A comprehensive security concept, supplemented with detailed guidelines on portal administration, is the foundation for planning and implementing all security measures.

When an SAP R/3 System is integrated, however, the portal does not check the users' authorizations for R/3; this task is relegated to the application. Here, the portal utilizes the defined roles and gives users extra functions such as Drag&Relate.

Other security measures, such as a security zone between the internal network and the Internet, automatic detection of attacks, virus protection, and encrypted communications, are essential to the secure operation of the portal.

8 Future Developments and Methods

As stated in Chapter 2, the SAP R/3 authorization concept has been modified often over the past several years. This pattern will likely continue in the near future. In order stay up-to-date, you need to pay attention to new developments and follow the information flow.

The previous chapters of this book described all the relevant elements of an SAP R/3 authorization concept in detail: the framework conditions, design, technical and organizational requirements, implementation options, check and audit options, and the extended features of an enterprise portal. Although this book is based on Release 4.6C, some information on future developments regarding the security available already exists. To keep this book as current as possible, this chapter describes several anticipated new features, both in the SAP authorization system and the SAP environment in general.

8.1 Preface

Countless enterprises around the world use SAP products to control their business processes and for business management in general. The core functions in Materials Management, Sales and Distribution, Financial Accounting, and Human Resources Management have been supplemented with numerous industry solutions and new components (such as Customer Relationship Management (CRM), Business Information Warehouse (BW), Advanced Planner and Optimizer (APO), and the Workplace) under the mySAP philosophy. Both enterprises and their employees are dependent on a properly functioning SAP system, and have every right to expect their systems to function accordingly.

At the same time, the global enterprise networks—both internal and external—that enable direct electronic links to customers, vendors, business partners, and employees pose a major threat, and demand flexible, effective security mechanisms for enterprise management, system administration, and system monitoring in daily operations. It has become apparent that inter-enterprise electronic business and services (see Figure 8.1), also called *collaborative business*), cannot be implemented without the necessary security and protection.

Therefore, this chapter will deal with the latest developments in enterprise-wide Central User Administration (CUA), access to enterprise directories (LDAP), authorization and role administration in the context of the SAP Web Application Server (Web AS), and user authentication.

Figure 8.1 mySAP Business Suite Collaborative Business—Cross-Company Processes

8.1.1   Access to Enterprise Directories (LDAP)

Enterprise directories, where information is stored centrally for the entire enterprise (also called *LDAP—Lightweight Directory Access Protocol*), are not only used within the Enterprise Portal, but can also be applied in the SAP component systems (see Chapter 7 for more information). This directory is a kind of enterprise-wide address book in a hierarchical database structure. You can use Transaction LDAP to link and integrate (Customizing) R/3 Systems with LDAP servers. This link is an improvement in the utilization of functions in CUA and the mySAP Workplace. Transaction LDAP was first introduced in Web AS Release 6.10; the LDAP functionality is the declared standard for Web AS and for future SAP developments in the area of EP 5.0+ products.

Transaction LDAPMAP supports the maintenance of the directory determination procedure and its mapping—for example, object class *Users*. To synchronize the datasets between the R/3 component systems and the LDAP directory, the two reports SLDAPSYNC_USER for user data and (since Web AS 6.10) SLDAPSYNC_ ROLE for role assignment, which you can schedule as a periodic synchronization run, ensure the quality and consistency of the data. Figure 8.2 illustrates the link and relations between the respective system components (SAP R/3 and others) and the LDAP directory.

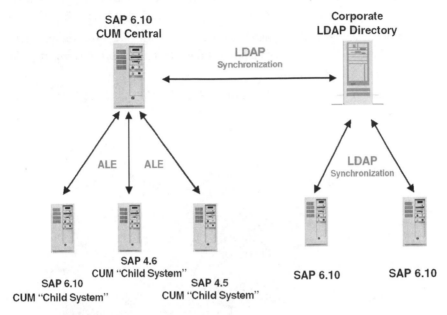

Figure 8.2 LDAP Synchronization

8.1.2 Central User Administration

Central User Administration (CUA—see Section 2.11 for more information) is a pre-requisite for deploying and using LDAP directories. CUA enables the storage and maintenance of central user information, which is distributed to the target systems (child systems) and back through a synchronization function (see Section 7.4.5 for more information). In short, it turns SAP users into portal users.

Synchronization consists of the following steps to exchange data between systems.

▶ **Mapping the directory determination procedure**

  ▶ Convert data

  ▶ Build complex structures

  ▶ Link data with specific directory attributes

  ▶ Assign data to specific object classes

▶ **Synchronization process**

  ▶ The synchronization process detects differences between the SAP system and the directory. The user data is divided into three work categories.

▶ The different data, which exists either only in the SAP system or only in the directory, is processed by the synchronization reports (see Section 8.1.1). You configure these settings before you run the report. During the synchronization process, the user objects are either created, deleted, or blocked.

▶ The reports execute the synchronization runs for the appropriate user objects, based on the Customizing settings. This function is supported in CUA Release 6.10 and later.

▶ Figure 8.3 highlights the functions of CUA and LDAP synchronization.

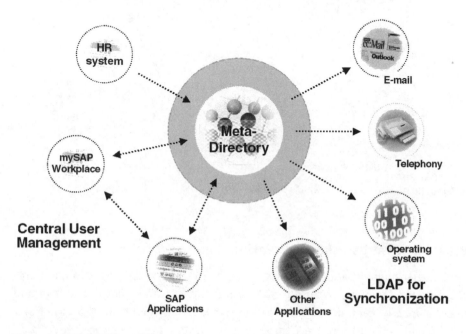

Figure 8.3 Central User Administration

8.1.3 Authorization and Role Administration (SAP Web AS)

Designing the Role Contents

The SAP R/3 role concept, which contains both single and composite roles, will be replaced by *worksets*. The links between the composite role and one or more single roles is no longer relevant for designing the authorization concept, as shown in Figure 8.4.

Semantic structure of role design

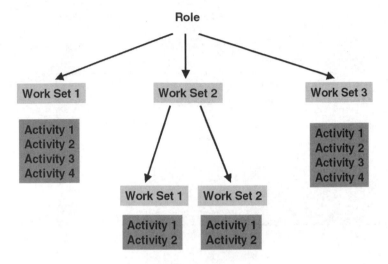

Figure 8.4 Structure of the Role Design

In this paradigm, the role is a "container" for one or more worksets, which are typical positions (jobs) at an enterprise. The respective employee therefore sees all the relevant information, data, and services. The workset contains a set of logical activities that belong to one or more work steps. These activities (i.e., work steps such as *Create order* or *Create promotion campaign*) are saved in the workset.

The workset structure is based on the following design:

▶ The role contains all relevant functions, information, and services that a user or group of users has to perform at an enterprise. In addition to the content, the role also contains the structure of the portal for each user.

▶ The roles must contain worksets. A *workset* is a collection of activities, information, and services, which form a homogeneous bundle of activities. The sales manager, for example, has the worksets *Team Leader* and *Promotion Manager*. The workset users can function as substructures for other roles.

▶ The workset's structure contains the individual activities that belong to a specific bundle of tasks. For example, *Create promotion campaign* and *Start promotion run* are activities that are contained in the *Promotion Manager*'s workset.

Figure 8.5 illustrates the integration of roles, worksets, and activities.

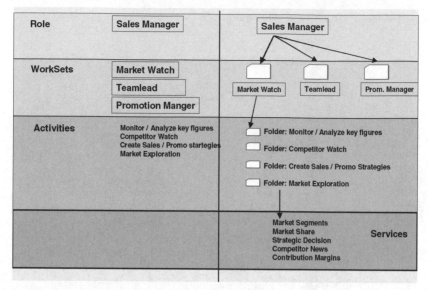

Figure 8.5 Role Structure of the Sales Manager

8.1.4 User Authentication

The identification and authentication of users in different deployed systems can be implemented through the Single Sign-On (SSO) procedure (one single logon for all systems). Further logons are not necessary. The configuration for user authentication and SSO (see Section 7.4.6 for more information) requires the configuration of the following parameters, which can be combined in three major groups:

▶ Parameters for passwords (see Section 2.2.4 for more information)
▶ Parameters for the SAP Logon Ticket (see Table 8.1)
▶ Parameters for the X.509 certificate logon (see Table 8.2)

SAP Logon Ticket parameters
login/create_sso2_ticket
login/accept_sso2_ticket
login/ticket_expiration_time
login/ticket_only_by_https
login/ticket_only_to_host
login/ticketcache_entries_max

Table 8.1 SAP Logon Ticket Parameters

SAP Logon Ticket parameters
login/ticketcache_off
ssf/name
ssf/ssfapi_lib

Table 8.1 SAP Logon Ticket Parameters (Cont.)

X.509 certificate logon parameters
snc/extid_login_diag
snc/extid_login_rfc
login/certificate_request_ca_url
login/certificate_request_subject

Table 8.2 X.509 Certificate Logon Parameters

Figure 8.6 shows the relevant options for SSO. You configure the user authentication and SSO in Transaction SSO2 in the SAP component system. In contrast, Transaction VUSREXTID links the SAP user ID with the external user ID.

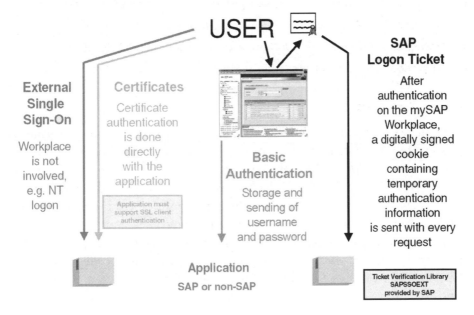

Figure 8.6 Single Sign-On—Options

8.2   Related Issues

Auditing, Logging, and Intrusion Detection Systems

▶ Configure security-relevant actions and activities

▶ Auditing and logging in every SAP component

▶ Alerts and information messages from the SAP GUI or Workplace Administrator

▶ Use and integration of monitoring and alert functions through intrusion detection systems via CCMS BAPIs

For more information on this subject, see Sections 7.5.8 and 7.5.9.

8.2.1   Other Transactions

The following transactions are relevant for service-level accesses (Web AS) and trust management:

▶ Transaction SICF: Protection against service-level accesses (SAP Web AS, Release 6.10 and later)

▶ Transaction STRUST: Trust manager

▶ Transaction STRUSTSSO2: Trust manager for *Workplace Single Sign-On*

▶ Transaction SSO2: Workplace Single Sign-On administration

▶ Transaction SSO2_ADMIN: Workplace administration SSO2 ticket

▶ Transaction STAT: Local transaction statistics

8.3   Outlook

As we already mentioned at the beginning of this chapter, throughout the various releases, the SAP R/3 authorization concept has been modified often. Functions such as areas of responsibility have been introduced and then deactivated again (in Release 4.5). It is therefore difficult to predict whether this pattern will remain in the "new R/3 world." Nonetheless, the basic constructs of the authorization check, authorization objects, and the corresponding transactions will likely be retained as the fundamental foundation. Therefore, the more that you focus on the system standard when developing your R/3 authorization concept, the less likely you will be to lose functions or convert authorizations after a migration or upgrade.

A   Authorization Objects

This appendix contains more detailed descriptions of the authorization objects listed in Section 2.3.9 (Table 2.6), which are relevant for user and authorization management.

Object and field	Description
S_USER_GRP	User master maintenance: user groups Object related to the processing of user groups in user administration
S_USER_GRP "User Group" field	The user administrator can define one or more user groups for maintenance here. This makes sense when your enterprise has more than one user administrator. In this case, you have to ensure that every user is assigned to a user group. Users that are not assigned to a group can be maintained by all user administrators.
S_USER_GRP "Activity" field	You can use this field to restrict what the administrator can do with the corresponding authorization. Possible values: 01—Create 02—Change 03—Display 05—Block, unblock 06—Delete 08—Display change documents 22—Add user to activity groups 24—Archive 78—Assign 68—Model Assign systems or activity groups to users as a model in user management, which enables you to derive the actual assignments from this model later.
S_USER_AUT	User master maintenance: authorizations Limits authorization objects and namespaces for authorization development
S_USER_AUT "Authorization Object" field	Enter the authorization objects for which the authorization developer can maintain the authorizations.
S_USER_AUT "Authorization Name" field	You can use this field to limit authorization developers to a restricted namespace for assigning authorization names, which makes sense if several administrators work on the system.

Object and field	Description
S_USER_AUT "Activity" field	You can use this field to restrict what the administrator can do with the corresponding authorization. Possible values: 01—Create 02—Change 03—Display 04—Delete 07—Activate 08—Display change documents 22—Assign authorizations to profiles 24—Archive
S_USER_PRO	User master maintenance: authorization profile You can use this object to limit the namespaces for profiles that administrators can access.
S_USER_PRO "Authorization Profile" field	Use this field to enter the authorization profiles that an authorization developer can maintain, or an authorization administrator can assign to users.
S_USER_PRO "Activity" field	You can use this field to restrict what the administrator can do with the corresponding profile. Possible values: 01—Create 02—Change 03—Display 06—Delete 07—Activate 08—Display change documents 22—Assign profile to users/cancel assignment 24—Archive
S_USER_OBJ	Authorization system: global deactivation of authorization objects When you save or deactivate the global deactivation of authorization objects, this authorization object is checked in the transaction (auth_switch_objects).
S_USER_OBJ "Authorization Object" field	Name of the authorization object that can be globally deactivated
S_USER_OBJ "Activity" field	Activity with the following possible values: 02—Change constellation of deactivated authorization objects 07—Activate constellation of deactivated authorization objects 21—Add the inactive (saved) constellation of deactivated authorization objects to a transport request

Object and field	Description
S_USER_SYS	User master maintenance: system for Central User Administration This object restricts the systems to which administrators can distribute authorizations for users.
S_USER_SYS "Subsystem" field	Recipient system for Central User Administration
S_USER_SYS "Activity" field	Possible values: 02 — Change 03 — Display distribution logs in the system 68 — Assign systems to users or activity groups as a model in user management, which enables you to derive the actual assignments from this model later. 78 — Assign system to a user (the user will be distributed to this system) 90 — Initial transfer of users from the system
S_USER_VAL	Authorization system: field values in activity groups Only the values that are defined in this object can be maintained by administrators in fields of authorization objects (except object S_TCODE)
S_USER_VAL "Authorization Object" field	Specify the authorization object. If a user administrator is to maintain organization level in an activity group, you have to set the full authorization * for this authorization field.
S_USER_VAL "Field Name" field	Specifies the authorization field to be protected
S_USER_VAL "Authorization Value" field	Permitted values for the field in the object that the user can enter or change in the activity group. If a user is to maintain intervals or make wildcard entries (a value ending with "*"), you have to set the full authorization * for this field.
S_USER_TCD	Authorization system: transactions in activity groups Only the transactions that are defined here can be entered in activity groups (intervals can only be maintained with full authorization for this object).
S_USER_TCD "Transaction Code" field	Transactions that authorization developers can assign to the activity group and for which they can grant authorization for starting the transaction in the Profile Generator
S_USER_WWW	User master maintenance: Internet users Restricts the allowed maintenance of Internet users

Object and field	Description
S_USER_WWW "Activity" field	01—Add or create 02—Change 03—Display 05—Block 06—Delete 23—Maintain password 39—Check 45—Allow 51—Initialize 90—Copy
S_USER_AGR	Authorization system: check for activity groups This object restricts which activity groups/roles an administrator can edit for a given activity.
S_USER_AGR "Activity Group" field	This field determines which activity groups the administrator can process.
S_USER_AGR "Activity" field	This field determines which activities can be performed with the activity groups. The following activities are available: 01—Create activity groups 02—Change activity groups 03—Display activity groups 06—Delete activity groups 22—User master comparison for activity groups. In this case, the profiles generated in the Profile Generator are copied to the user master of the corresponding users in the activity group. 36—This activity is not in use. It is intended for additional objects that can be maintained from within the activity group. 21—Transport activity groups 64—Generate 68—Model: Assign activity groups to systems or users as a model in user management, which enables you to derive the actual assignments from this model later. 78—Assign activity groups to systems or user groups in the main system, when Central User Administration is used. DL—Download UL—Upload

B SAP Notes

This appendix lists important SAP Notes involving the SAP R/3 authorization system, in addition to those already mentioned in the previous chapters (see Section 2.14).

Release	SAP Note	Application area	Title
46B—610	416549	BC-BMT-OM	Renaming users: owner link not updated
40B—46D	373672	BC-BMT-OM	Error deleting users in SU01 or SU10
46C	354227	BC-BMT-OM	RHPROFL0: Evaluation path PROFL0 is incorrect!
45B—46D	327680	BC-BMT-OM	RHPROFL0: Problems in data selection
45B—46D	324916	BC-BMT-OM	RHPROFL0: Error in list output of non-existent users
31H—40B	304130	BC-BMT-OM	Deleting end date error in IT 105 according to user
*	207862	BC-BMT-OM	No user menu in session manager
45B—46B	189260	BC-BMT-OM	RHPROFL0: "AG" object type not considered
30F—30F	99439	BC-BMT-OM	Activity groups: Termination during task maintenance
46A—46B	184165	BC-BMT-OM	Error message when deleting users
40A—40B	372549	BC-CCM-BTC	Missing check indicators for SM49
*	373347	BC-CI-WEBR	Authorizations for WEB Reporting
45A—46D	323636	BC-CUS-TOL-ALO	Log analysis: Table is not in authorization group
46C—46C7	205633	BC-CUS-TOL-TME	Authorization S_TABU_LIN: Records missing
46B—630	526616	BC-SEC-USR	SU21: Obsolete input help with F7 function
46B—620	519385	BC-SEC-USR	SU01: Additional information for note 503336 (EarlyWatch client)
620	517174	BC-SEC-USR	Missing company address when creating J2EE service user
45B—620	511192	BC-SEC-USR	CUA consistency check report

Release	SAP Note	Application area	Title
46B—620	503366	BC-SEC-USR	SU01: Correcting inconsistencies when maintaining addresses
620	492210	BC-SEC-USR	Service user for Java cannot be created by RFC
45B	490969	BC-SEC-USR	SUIM: CALL_TRANSACTION_LOCKED short dump if SARP is locked
45B—610	452476	BC-SEC-USR	Where-used list for authorization object in programs
46B—630	439753	BC-SEC-USR	Generating SAP_ALL with a transport of authorization objects
*	439122	BC-SEC-USR	CUA: Assigning correct company addresses before distribution
610	436964	BC-SEC-USR	Upgrade: Generating users causes a short dump
610	433773	BC-SEC-USR	FSUSR_GET_TIMESTAMP module: remote capability
45B—610	433444	BC-SEC-USR	Performance increase when accessing profiles
46B—610	432061	BC-SEC-USR	Transaction SUIM: Return does not work
*	410424	BC-SEC-USR	Customizing to generate profile SAP_ALL
40B	409842	BC-SEC-USR	User parameter: double entries with SU3
46B—46D	392304	BC-SEC-USR	SUIM User Information System as area menu
46B—630	389702	BC-SEC-USR	Authorization fails in batch but not in dialog
46D	358122	BC-SEC-USR	Function description of transaction SE97
46A—46D	357690	BC-SEC-USR	SU21: No F4 help for authorization fields
46B	337383	BC-SEC-USR	Help texts in Transaction PFCG
46C	334426	BC-SEC-USR	Missing Customizing in address
31H—46D	325812	BC-SEC-USR	SUSR_SYNC_USER_TABLES: long runtime, terminations
46C	314843	BC-SEC-USR	Authorization object S_TABU_LIN
46A—46B	202083	BC-SEC-USR	Changed transaction selection in Profile Generator
46A—46B	199921	BC-SEC-USR	Missing authorizations after upgrade to 4.6A/B

Release	SAP Note	Application area	Title
46A—46C	191660	BC-SEC-USR	CC-ERROR: No authorization for client copy
31G—45B	171538	BC-SEC-USR	Structure AUTHC does not exist
40A—46A	161578	BC-SEC-USR	Termination when maintaining user data
40A—46A	160092	BC-SEC-USR	User address: House number not written to street field
40A—46B	153681	BC-SEC-USR	Migration of old user menu 3.1 to 4.x: How?
30F—40B	144008	BC-SEC-USR	Missing TA start authorization check in SU01
40A—45B	140191	BC-SEC-USR	SU03: Problems when maintaining field values
40B	138253	BC-SEC-USR	SU01: Copying users: activity groups
45A—46B	133932	BC-SEC-USR	SUIM: Activity group display without text
40A—45B	132037	BC-SEC-USR	SU01 decimal format not transferred from profile
45A	130296	BC-SEC-USR	Case-sensitive file name in authorization S_DATASET
31G—31I	124441	BC-SEC-USR	SU01 Dates and decimal format of copy reference
*	97911	BC-SEC-USR	Customer exit 001 & Office inbox: Security gap
40A	91885	BC-SEC-USR	Performance: reading user ID
*	76829	BC-SEC-USR	Problems with wildcards in user names
30F—31G	74999	BC-SEC-USR	SU05: Mode termination
*	28002	BC-SEC-USR	System messages of more than 3 lines
*	506008	BC-SEC-USR-ADM	SU10: Dialog box for messages 01 321 and 01 322
45A	129727	BC-SEC-USR-ADM	SCUL, SCUA: Raise_exception in child system
30A—31I	123245	BC-SEC-USR-ADM	SU01: Change fixed values despite missing authorization
31H—40B	101551	BC-SEC-USR-ADM	Information system: incorrect where-used list
46B—630	537001	BC-SEC-USR-KRN	USRBF2: User buffer is empty for some users

Release	SAP Note	Application area	Title
46B -620	506825	BC-SEC-USR-PFC	Incorrect authorization names after uploading roles
46B—620	452827	BC-SEC-USR-PFC	Missing authorization data for generated transactions
*	442906	BC-SEC-USR-PFC	PFUD: Buffer problems caused by changes to AGR_TIMED
45A—610	450176	BC-SRV-ADR	Correction report for the USCOMPANY table
46A—46D	323656	BC-SRV-ADR	BAPI_USER_CHANGE: Message AM 086
31I	307258	BC-SRV-ADR	In user maintenance phone number truncated
45B—46B	305553	BC-SRV-ADR	CC-ERROR: Data loss (addresses) after Support Package
40B—46D	302767	BC-SRV-ADR	Communication language user in USR03 structure
45A—46C	206839	BC-SRV-ADR	Company address in lowercase cannot be maintained
40A—40B	102783	BC-SRV-ADR	User masters: Shadow tables and client copy
40A—46D	360254	BC-SRV-GBT	SU01: Cannot change user after BAPI call
*	338177	BC-SRV-REP	Authorization check when executing programs

C   Bibliography

Quoted Literature

Federal Ministry of Finance (BMF) Unit IV D2: Draft of an ordinance involving framework conditions for electronic signatures and changes to other regulations—letter of Oct. 6, 2000

Grundsätze ordnungsmäßiger DV-gestützter Buchführungssysteme (GoBS)— AWV paper 09 546

Grundsätze ordnungsmäßiger DV-gestützter Buchführungssysteme (GoBS)— (BMF letter of Nov. 7, 1995—IV A 8 S-0316—52/95)

Heese, Klaus (WP StB Dipl.-Kfm.): IT-Systemprüfungen im Rahmen einer risiko- und prozessorientierten Prüfungsstrategie, PwC Deutsche Revision 4/2002

IDC: Western European Enterprise Information Portal Software Forecast and Analysis, 2002—2006, August 21, 2002

IDW Inspection Standard: The Internal Control System During the Final Inspection (IDW EPS 260)

IDW Opinion on Rendering of Accounts: Principles for proper accounting under use of information technology of September 24, 2002, Tz. 57 and 60

Information Systems Control, Volume 1/2001

Informationweek: Portal Gives Workers Cruise Control, November 19, 2001

InternetWeek.com: Portals: Beyond Enterprises, March 21, 2001

IT Management—Issue 03/99

PwC Deutsche Revision Aktiengesellschaft Wirtschaftsprüfungsgesellschaft (Publisher), Interne Revision—Eine moderne Dienstleistung, Frankfurt am Main, January 2000

RSA Laboratories: Frequently Asked Questions about Today's Cryptography, May 2000

SAP AG (1): SAP Portals—Delivering The Next Generation of Business Technology, 2002

SAP AG (2): SAP Security Guidelines, Volume II, Version 3.0, April 2001

SAP AG (3): SAP Enterprise Portal 5.0: Security, January 7, 2002

SAP AG (4): mySAP Enterprise Portals, 2002

SAP AG (5): Secure Network Communications and Secure Store & Forward Mechanisms with the SAP R/3 System

SAP AG (6): SAP TechEd Presentation, 2001

SAP Labs: Authorization Made Easy, Release 4.6, 2000

SecurInfo: Integrating SAP Application Security with the Enterprise, June 2002

Schiwek, Peter/Buchholz, Frank (SAP AG), AIS—Audit Information System, February 2002

Schneider, Guido/Zwerger, Florian: Sichere Unternehmensportale mit SAP, 2002

Watkins, Harko (PwC Wirtschaftsprüfungsgesellschaft): SAP R/3 Interrogation, October 1999

Referenced Web Sites

agens Consulting GmbH: *http://www.agens.de*

Arbeitskreis Revision für Deutschland: *http://www.sap-ag.de/germany/ aboutSAP/ revis/ais.asp*

CheckAud for SAP R/3 Systems: *http://www.CheckAud.de*

Parks Informatik GmbH: *http://www.parks-informatik.de*

SAPNet: *http://service.sap.com*
http://service.sap.com/AIS
http://sapnet.sap.com/securityguide
http://service.sap.com/technology

Securinfo: http://www.securinfo.com or
http://searchsap.techtarget.com/whitepaperPage/0,293857,sid21_ gci848943,00.html

realtime AG: *http://www.realtimegroup.de*

http://www.buyformetals.com

http://wp.netscape.com/directory/v4.0/faq.html

SAP Online Documentation

Wildensee, Christoph: *http://www.it-audit.de*

D   About the Authors

Sascha-Alexander Beyer has worked at IBM Business Consulting Services (formerly PwC Consulting[1]) since 2001, in the area of "Business and Information Security." His area of expertise is security, particularly application security. Based on a First Partner Shipment of the SAP Portal, he developed a complete security concept for the SAP Portal and implemented it at SAP's own Global Center of Expertise in Walldorf in early 2002.

Helge Hermann Fischer has years of international experience in security consulting (security management, cryptography, and Internet security) and has managed numerous projects for telecommunications companies and financial service providers. He has worked at IBM Business Consulting Services (formerly PwC Consulting[1]) since 2001 in the "Business and Information Security" area, and is certified as Lead Auditor under international security standard BS7799.

Gregory Guglielmetti has worked at IBM Business Consulting Services (formerly PwC Consulting[1]) since 2001, in the area of "Business and Information Security." During this time, he implemented security concepts for major corporations in the pharmaceuticals and foodstuffs industries in Germany, Spain, and Switzerland. His area of expertise is the technical implementation of SAP R/3 authorization concepts, and the development of methods and tools for auditing and quality assurance of authorization concepts in large SAP landscapes. He also has years of experience in software development.

Dr. Hendrik Hartje has worked at IBM Business Consulting Services (formerly PwC Consulting[1]) since 2001, in the area of "Business and Information Security." He has worked on numerous projects in the area of SAP R/3 security for major corporations in the machine tools and automotive sectors. His areas of expertise include the design and implementation of authorization concepts, support concepts, and administration concepts in the authorization area.

Matthias Hessler has worked at IBM Business Consulting Services (formerly PwC Consulting[1]) since 1999, in the area of "Business and Information Security." During this time, he developed and implemented security concepts for major corporations in heavy manufacturing and medical technology. His area of expertise is on project management for implementing authorization concepts in both standard SAP systems and component systems (such as the SAP Business Information Warehouse). He has years of experience in the areas of accounting and controlling.

Klaus Jäck has worked at IBM Business Consulting Services (formerly PwC Consulting[1]) since 1999, in the area of "Business and Information Security." He has worked as project manager for SAP security for various international implementation projects, major corporations in the high tech industry, consumer products, and heavy industry sectors, as well as medical technology and insurance companies. He has also developed authorization concepts for the SAP component systems Business Information Warehouse and Strategic Enterprise Management, as well as in shared service center environments.

Mirjana Kelderman-Matkic has worked at IBM Business Consulting Services (formerly PwC Consulting[1]) since 1998, in the area of "Business and Information Security." Her areas of expertise include managing and conducting projects for implementing SAP authorization concepts in the automotive and power-generation industries, as well as designing and implementing business process controls within the framework of SAP R/3 rollouts. She has years of experience with SAP, in review projects for SAP authorization concepts, and in SAP implementations in the Finan-

cials and Sales areas.

Uwe Probst has worked at IBM Business Consulting Services (formerly PwC Consulting[1]) since 1996, in the area of "Business and Information Security." His areas of expertise include managing and conducting projects for implementing SAP authorization concepts, enhancement of underlying methods, and the development of business process controls and risk management procedures within an enterprise. He also has years of experience in auditing systems and processes, as well as in SAP R/3 authorization concepts.

---

1   PwC Consulting
    Please note that IBM purchased the global management and IT service provider division of PricewaterhouseCoopers ("PwC Consulting") in October 2002. IBM Business Consulting Services is the new consulting unit at IBM, which was formed from some 30,000 employees of IBM Global Services and some 30,000 employees of PwC Consulting.

Index

Learn about the dos
and don'ts in SAP EP
5.0 and SAP EP 6.0

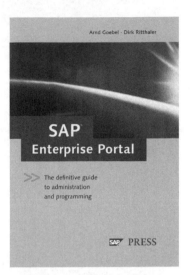

310 pp., US$ 59.95
ISBN 1-59229-018-3

SAP Enterprise Portal

www.sap-press.com

A. Goebel, D. Ritthaler

SAP Enterprise Portal

The definite guide to administration and
programming

This book is a complete overview for the installation,
operation and administration of a SAP-company
portal (EP 6.0). Learn all there is to know about
system requirements and the establishment of the
portal in the system landscape. Get a step-by-step
guide to the installation of a test system and discover
how to adapt the portal to the requirements of the
user and how to define roles.
The book focuses very much on content and
application integration. You learn how to program
Web-services and Portal-iViews, plus all there is to
know about Unifer, and by use of the SAP Business
Information Warehouse you get in-depth knowledge
on content-integration.

Unlock the full potential of your SAP systems!

220 pp., 2004, US$
ISBN 1-59229-026-4

SAP System Landscape Optimization

www.sap-press.com

A. Schneider-Neureither (Ed.)

SAP System Landscape Optimization

This reference book serves as an essential collection of insights, procedures, processes and tools that help you unlock the full potential of your SAP systems. First, hit the ground running with a detailed introduction to SAP NetWeaver and the mySAP Business Suite. Then, elevate your mastery of key concepts such as system architecture, security, Change and Transport Mana- gement, to name just a few. All of the practical advice and detailed information provided is with a clear focus on helping you guide your team to achieve a faster return on investment.

Keep flexible while ptimizing cost structures

270 pp., approx. US$
ISBN 1-59229-035-3, may 2005

Adaptive Hardware
Infrastructures for SAP
www.sap-press.com

M. Missbach

Adaptive Hardware Infrastructures for SAP

Constantly changing business processes pose a critical challenge for today's hardware. In order to conquer this challenge, companies must respond quickly and in a cost-effective manner, without risking the future safety of their infrastructure. This unique new book helps you to understand the most important factors for determining what hardware you'll need to support flexible software systems in the months and years ahead. Plus, discover the ins and outs of exactly how SAP systems support your business processes. In addition, you'll benefit from highly-detailed insights, essential for helping you calculate your true Total Cost of Ownership (TCO).